TRIUMPH OF THE CHALLENGED

Conversations with especially able people

Elspeth Waldie

Elspeth C. Waldie

For The Rowlands Family
with love & happy memories
19.7.02

PURPLE FIELD PRESS

Published by Purple Field Press
10 Hill View Terrace, Ilminster, Somerset TA19 9AL

ISBN 0 9542797 0 0

ACKNOWLEDGEMENTS
Photographs: Roger Varney, Tony Kendall and the author
Map: James Hayllar

Design, typesetting & production: Country Books:
Courtyard Cottage, Little Longstone, Bakewell, Derbyshire DE45 1NN
Tel/Fax: 01629 640670
e-mail: dickrichardson@country-books.co.uk

Dedicated in loving memory
to my parents
John and Thelma Waldie

CONTENTS

ACKNOWLEDGEMENTS

There can be few occupations which so increase the awareness of our indebtedness to others as that of author. This book could never have been written without the help and support of countless friends in both Bangladesh and England.

I am indebted, first and foremost, to all those named on the contents page who have given so generously of their time, and of themselves, in recounting their stories. I trust that the resultant book will act as a tribute to the tremendous courage and determination thus revealed.

My special thanks, too, to my many interpreters, travel companions and hosts; most notably – Alam, Chris, Daisy, Ekki, Feroz, Kabir, Katy, Kokhon, Mafuz, Mushfiqul, Nurpur, Patricia, Pia, Robert, Shanu, Tarique, Treslyn, the Benhams, the Hazlewoods, the Millichamps and the Wiesenfelds.

I would like, also, to express my gratitude to Valerie Taylor, and to CRP, for providing a base as well as the initial inspiration; and, in addition, thank the numerous other organisations who have given support and information: The Acid Survivors Foundation, ActionAid Bangladesh, The Christian Memorial Hospital at Malumghat, COOPI, Impact Bangladesh, InterLife Bangladesh, The Leprosy Mission, The Pirgacha Mission, and The Taize Community at Mymensingh.

Appreciation is due to the Dhaka Daily Star and the Bangladesh Observer for permitting reproduction of extracts from their columns.

Finally I would remember all my friends at home. Their encouragement, support and patience has known no bounds. My thanks, in particular, to Roger Varney and Tony Kendall for the photographs, to James Hayllar for the map, and to the four people who spent long hours in reading the early drafts: Joe Burlington, Ruth Hayter, Rita Millard, and my brother John Waldie.

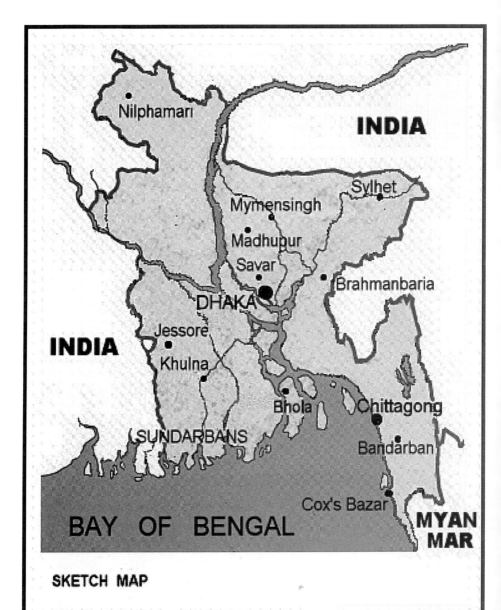

INDIA

Nilphamari

INDIA

Sylhet

Mymensingh

Madhupur

Savar

Brahmanbaria

DHAKA

Jessore

Khulna

Bhola

Chittagong

SUNDARBANS

Bandarban

Cox's Bazar

MYAN
MAR

BAY OF BENGAL

SKETCH MAP

BANGLADESH

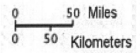

0   50 Miles

0   50   Kilometers

PROLOGUE

As soon as we started our descent the water became visible. For a full twenty-five minutes we lowered ourselves over a shining golden expanse; the whole lit magnificently by the afternoon sun, and broken curiously into neat squares and parallel lines. We dropped lower, and the nature of the boundaries became apparent. They were the tops of trees, their presence indicating the outline of submerged fields and roads.

I was flying into the worst floods Bangladesh had known for many years. A decade ago, in 1988, the water had reached a similar level but had receded after fifteen days. This time it had stayed.

The majority of my fellow passengers had wisely disembarked in Delhi. I was the only European woman arriving. Conspicuous, no doubt, but still surprised to be addressed by name even before I had reached Immigration. The welcome came from a smartly-attired Bangladeshi who stepped out of the crowd with the confidence of privilege. Introducing himself as a representative of the British High Commission, he led with speed and authority through Passport Control. But on delivering me to the sanctuary of his driver, brought our progress to an unexpected halt.

"Please forgive me if I desert you for a little while," his tone was measured, polite and matter of fact. "I must go back to the Departure Lounge. We are evacuating all High Commission women and children on the plane on which you have arrived." He left me to digest the uneasy feeling of someone going in totally the wrong direction.

Indeed, I had been in two minds about coming at this particular time, but the Centre For the Rehabilitation of the Paralysed (CRP), for which I was to work as a voluntary English teacher, seemed to have no hesitation in advising me to travel. Only after I had left home, did they realise that they could not meet me in Dhaka as promised. The road from the Centre was by then completely submerged.

Too late now to doubt the wisdom of my actions, I busied myself with formalities. One of my cases had been lost in transit and by the time this was duly reported my charming guide had returned. I soon found myself en route to staying with High Commission contacts in the capital.

Our vehicle ploughed through deep and filthy water extending thigh high into the deserted shells of roadside shops. To our right, on slightly higher ground, were hundreds of makeshift tents made out of the blue plastic sacking supplied by UNICEF. Pathetic and inadequate shelters such as these, I was told, were multiplying daily as more and more people were forced to flee from their homes.

We swerved round rickshaw wallahs valiantly pulling their gaily coloured contraptions through the chaos, and I was suddenly struck by the incongruity of the sky overhead. It was strangely, cruelly beautiful – grey, black and silver, shot with gold from the setting sun.

Nature, it seemed, was playing games with Bangladesh. Like a false lover, disguised in beauty, she dealt out death. Already disease had reached epidemic proportions. The so-called "Diarrhoea Hospital" in Dhaka was admitting patients at the rate of one a minute. The city was unable to get rid of its rubbish, and sewage was flowing along the roads and up through the pipes. Everyone was aware that worse might follow. There was still a great deal of water to come from China and Tibet, and exceptionally high tides in the Bay of Bengal could prevent it from travelling out to sea. A serious concern was the possible collapse of one of the main dams. The lives of twenty million people, about one sixth of the population, were seriously at risk.

Three days were to elapse before I could make the twenty kilometre journey to the CRP Centre at Savar. And I did so then in a manner rather different from the one I had visualised.

The instructions were to leave most of my luggage behind, but like many inexperienced travellers I found myself compelled to retain the "essentials", a bulging haversack as well as a small case. Fortunately the rickshaw wallah, a family retainer, was tolerant. With cargo and passenger balanced unsteadily one on top of the other he resignedly navigated potholes, and ploughed through the water. Dirty to the point of opacity it swirled around us, at times rising at least halfway up the wheels and completely submerging the chain.

Beth awaited me at the bus stop. A young and blond Australian, she had been working at CRP for some time and was well versed in the ways of the milling crowd.

"Ignore the stares," she advised authoritatively as we got on the bus. "And don't sit beside a man. It is considered impolite."

The third leg of our journey was achieved by boat. We stumbled aboard in the blistering sun and I looked with dismay at the wide gaps between the slats beneath my feet. The engine was a dubious, rusty looking affair which churned out black smoke and seemed to be in need of constant poking from an elderly man with a wooden stave. Fifty or sixty passengers sat precariously round the edge of the vessel.

I was later to learn, and perhaps not surprisingly, that this particular voyage had a tendency to be lethal. Only the day before, someone who had been balanced on the side of the boat had been thrown overboard when receding floods caused a sudden current to swing the vessel round. Others had died when a similar boat had capsized completely. Some of its passengers, struggling desperately to survive, had caught hold of a live electric cable lying unseen below the water.

Blissfully unaware of these facts, I sat in the stern and surveyed the strange aquatic landscape on which we moved. Once an area of paddy fields, it might now have looked like a vast lake had it not been for the many road signs incongruously rearing their heads above the water. I felt as if I had entered into the imaginary and totally crazy world of children's story books, and it came almost as a shock, on finally scrambling ashore up a slippery and near vertical bank, to perceive a smart, and perfectly normal, white mini bus. The driver from CRP had made it to our meeting point.

The Centre for the Rehabilitation of the Paralysed, known to all its friends as CRP, exists to provide treatment and rehabilitation services to paralysed people, and does so regardless of their ability to pay. By the time of my visit, the organisation had behind it nearly twenty years of pioneering activity and dramatic growth.

The British founder, Valerie Taylor, had first arrived in Bangladesh shortly before independence. She found herself then in a country where physiotherapy was virtually unknown, wheelchairs unavailable and superstition rife. In her work as a physiotherapist for VSO she was to become increasingly concerned about the lack of proper care for paraplegic patients. Many were dying unnecessarily, and those who survived were condemned to a life of permanent immobility, often with no other means of livelihood apart from begging.

For a person of Valerie's character there was only one response. She would have to set up an appropriate service herself. Acting against the advice of friends both in England and Dhaka, she gathered a small team of Bangladeshi staff and opened her first four-bedded unit in a disused hospital warehouse.

"We all told her it was crazy," one of Valerie's earliest supporters told me. "But she wouldn't listen."

This same friend was to watch amazed as the unit grew against all odds. Soon it had thirty-five beds, then more. But without permanent accommodation of its own, staff and patients were subject to constant upheavals. In 1981 they transferred to a rented house in Dhanmodi and, in 1986, acquired larger premises in Farmgate. Moving day on that occasion coincided with a general strike; but Valerie, as usual, was undaunted. Patients were instructed to hold tight to their possessions, then fifty beds pushed the two miles through Dhaka.

All involved now felt a permanent home essential to the effective continuation of their work. Land in Savar was purchased in April 1990, and a couple of months later the team moved to temporary premises on the new site. Once again they were back under a corrugated iron roof but this time it was different: work on a long-term, purpose-built facility had at last commenced.

Having read this much of the history and seen an early video, I was little prepared for what I found in 1998. CRP now comprised a one hundred-bed hospital with two modern operating theatres, and departments for pathology, X-ray, occupational therapy, physiotherapy and out-patients. Not only this, but there was also a mother-and-child unit, a half-way hostel where patients could adjust to the home environment, a number of workshop and training facilities, a special needs school and a training institute for student therapists.

No less of a surprise was the person of the founder. Somehow I had developed a completely erroneous mental picture of Valerie. Perhaps to me, it seemed inevitable that a woman who could overcome the sort of odds presented by Bangladesh and set up an organisation on the scale of CRP, must, of necessity, be large, domineering and aggressive.

Nothing could be further from the reality. The only two aspects of Valerie Taylor which can be described as "large" are her generosity and her smile. Indeed the gentle humility of her manner strikes everyone with whom she comes into contact.

A slender figure, with long hair tied Bangladeshi style at the nape of the neck, she is to be seen moving quickly, quietly and purposefully around the compound. Valerie mises nothing. No item, no person, is too small or insignificant for her attention. Often will she divert from her path to pick up a piece of litter or, more frequently, to converse with someone in need of encouragement.

Though teased for her talking, it is conversation with a purpose, a discourse strong in motivation and rich in experience. One of Valerie's greatest attributes, perhaps, is that she can size up other people, know what they do best and persuade them to do it for the Centre. In this, I suspect, lies the secret of CRP success. No one can refuse the quiet smiling lady upon whom her students have conferred the title "Mother Teresa Bangladesh."

If an ability to motivate others is one of Valerie's strengths, then a sheer dogged persistence must undoubtedly be another. On perceiving a need she will work at it relentlessly until an answer is found. Until late in the evening she is to be seen at her desk, swamped in paperwork and supported by a trustworthy thermos of tea, whilst churning out long missives of supplication. If the need is financial, she will write letter after letter. And should the potential donor indicate any possibility of giving he can, from then on, expect a daily telephone call until he has complied.

I listened to such calls with a mixture of admiration for Valerie, and pity for the person at the other end. My turn was to come. I too was to experience the tenacity of the Taylor approach.

Adverse social attitudes had long been perceived by Valerie as one of the most serious of all problems confronting disabled people in Bangladesh, and the size of the task of tackling it did not deter her.

With typical logic she concluded that the best medium for her message was the most popular one. CRP, she decided, must produce a full length feature film.

For my part I had come to CRP simply as an English teacher, and when Valerie asked me to write the script for a Bollywood-style movie, I was horrified. My instinctive reaction was first to laugh, a response which she ignored, and then to seriously protest my ineptitude. In carrying out the latter I failed abysmally. How can anyone look Valerie Taylor in the eye whilst uttering the words, "I can't"? The phrase is completely foreign to her, an expression which she herself has never used.

Thus it was that I agreed to return to Bangladesh for a further year. I did not regret it. Not only was CRP an interesting place to work, and the film world fascinating, but I gained immeasurably from those around me. Valerie was by no means the only person to make a lasting impression. My research for the film brought me into close contact with some of the most incredible people I have ever met. Here were dedicated members of staff carrying out difficult jobs and making an important contribution to the lives of others – despite having a severe disability of their own.

Their achievement was all the more amazing when thought about in context. In Bangladesh, people with disabilities are beset by problems of almost unimaginable magnitude. Medical help is limited and often disastrous. Everywhere, sometimes even amongst their own families, the disabled have to overcome fear, superstition and prejudice. At best, they are considered as economically worthless; at worst, as possessed of an evil spirit. If they want to disprove such theories, show their worth and earn a living, they have to do so in a hostile environment devoid of special facilities or easy access, and without any form of training or employment support.

Against such a background, the tendency of outsiders is to think that all disabled people in Bangladesh, if not dependant on family and friends, must of necessity become beggars. Unfortunately many are forced to do just that, and as such they constitute the more visible element of the disabled population: the sad, desperate and sometimes frightening people that we see along the streets of Dhaka and gathered

14

at the entrance to every hotel and railway station.

Not so those like Madhab and Mohua at CRP. Both had triumphed over the most daunting of hurdles and were committed to helping those less fortunate. Lives such as these, I thought, should be celebrated. And perhaps they were not alone. What about people with other disabilities, in varying circumstances and different parts of the country?

I was at the start of an inspiring journey.

CHAPTER ONE

GONOKBARI: A REFUGE FOR WOMEN − **MOHUA: ADMINISTRATIVE OFFICER** − THE QUESTION OF ACCESSIBILITY − SEVEN MODES OF TRANSPORT IN FIFTY-ONE HOURS.

It was Rajah's third birthday. Mohua was determined to go to Gonnokbari to celebrate, and it mattered little that no suitable CRP vehicle was available to take her. Undaunted, she asked to be lifted, wheelchair and all, on to the top of an open truck. There, seated on high, and gripping the back of the cab with an expression of cheerful resolution, she pronounced herself ready to depart.

We bounced forward and the wind tore at Mohua's hair releasing it from its careful coil and causing the strands to dance merrily round her head. She looked wilder than the Mohua I knew but somehow the general impression of dignity was actually enhanced.

It cannot have been an easy journey for her. The road was under-going massive repairs after the floods and we were constantly bumping and swerving. Sitting comfortably in the front, I felt concerned for my friend's safety although I doubt if any such thoughts passed through her own mind. Mohua was simply happy to be attending the party.

We stopped just once on the way, in order that the driver could buy, on Mohua's behalf, a very large ceramic tiger from a roadside stall. The two feet of heavy orange and white striped pottery was apparently intended as a birthday present for the three-year-old. I wondered whether he would actually be able to lift it.

Rajah had been born at CRP of a disabled mother and he was now to be found playing by her wheelchair in the friendly women's hostel a few miles down the road at Gonnokbari. His birthday was a good excuse for a party. We shared out the sweets that Mohua had brought and clapped and cheered as Rajah blew out the candles. This was a family celebration and a success story. A paralysed woman had not only borne a child but had also managed to keep him. It was a feat

16

which she would probably not have been able to achieve without the help of the Gonnokbari project.

The hostel looks ordinary enough from the main road. A low brick building constructed in an E shape with ever-optimistic rods poking through the roof as if to indicate that the planner intended adding a few more floors in years to come.

Indeed Gonnokbari is founded upon optimism and upon the conviction that society can and will be changed, that in due course, disabled women in Bangladesh will be able to enjoy the same rights as everybody else. At present they are beset alike by age-old superstition, cultural prejudice and unfair social custom.

Women who become paralysed often find themselves divorced as soon as the problem is recognised. In rural areas many still believe that the husband only has to say the words, "I divorce you" three times, and the deed is done. In reality, this type of "oral divorce" no longer carries legal validity, but sadly unaware of their rights, many of those concerned continue to accept the consequences. The disabled woman is cast out from the marital home, separated from her children and deprived of any means of subsistence.

In such circumstances the staff at the Centre for the Rehabilitation of the Paralysed found themselves with many female patients whom they were unable to send home. The solution was a special hostel, where destitute women could live for several years whilst gaining the skills necessary for independence.

Gonnokbari can house twenty residents and for each there is a separate and very individual plan. They all learn to look after themselves, and to develop at least three skills from any of which they can hope to earn a living in the future. Mohua has arranged training in a wide variety of income generating activities and is careful to choose for each resident, not just the things they are good at, but the things which they most enjoy doing. The next stage is to help with the marketing and, if necessary, provide a loan. In this way every resident has the opportunity to sell their products, pay their way whilst at Gonnokbari, and build up their own savings.

I visited the hostel many times and was always assured of a warm welcome. One July day, when the rain was drumming on the corrugated iron roof of the weaving shed, I found myself particularly mesmerised by the smile of Aysha as she carefully wound cotton thread onto a bobbin. The end result of her labours would be medical gauze for sale to CRP. Aysha had been divorced by her husband and separated from the four-year-old daughter whom she loved, but now at least, she had a secure future.

Across the courtyard in the main building, Lovely was sitting working at her easel: two cheeky black bunches of hair topping a face of deep concentration, eyes critical of the painting in front of her, cheeks aglow with the act of creation. Still only fourteen years old, Lovely had been a tetraplegic since the day when, working as a maid-servant, she fell from a roof whilst hanging out the washing. Paralysed from the neck down, but undaunted in spirit, she had learnt to paint with her mouth and had become the only student in Bangladesh to win a scholarship from the international Association of Mouth and Foot Painting Artists. Already her pictures of flowers and village life were good enough to sell as greetings cards and in due course Lovely hoped, not only to support herself, but also to help her impoverished family. I found in her the inspiration for the heroine of my film.

Discussing films and television is a favourite pastime at Gonnokbari. Sitting near Lovely that day, and gossiping about their favourite stars and programmes, were several other occupants of the hostel. For the most part, they were stitching moccasins for a local shoe company, but Kalpana, who had proved herself particularly good at sewing, was working on the Singer machine recently purchased with her own earnings.

Kalpana's husband had not actually divorced her, but he had taken another wife, separated Kalpana from her daughter and even appropriated the jewellery inherited from her mother. Such was the lady's determination however, and her aptitude for hard work, that her husband had now been forced to admit that, paralysed or not, his first wife was capable of earning her own way in society. It was a great triumph that he had started to allow their daughter to visit and that, despite several years of separation, a very good relationship was developing between teenage girl and disabled mother.

Rajah's mother, Hira, was more of a loner but she successfully ran a little *cha* shop situated at the far end of the Gonnakbari banana grove and fronting on to the village street. This, together with the younger residents' attendance at the village school, had ensured integration with the local community.

No one there had any doubt that it was Mohua who was largely responsible for the success of their project. I looked forward to finding out more about her.

Despite her hard work, Mohua was once described as someone who always looks as if she has just come out of a bandbox. Her beautiful saris are immaculate and her full, soft face carefully made up. Glossy black hair, parted in the middle and drawn gently back on either side, enhances a pale and lovely complexion. Her eyes are radiant and expressive, dark pools of thought which all of a sudden can spring to life and glisten with happiness.

She thinks of her life as a river. Her childhood provided a happy and bubbling start. Surrounded by a loving and educated family, Mohua enjoyed life to the full. Dancing was her greatest pleasure and she would gleefully try on her mother's prettiest saris and confidently perform on stage. Her brothers tell of a time when, dancing on the platform, she perceived the youngest of them fighting with another boy in the front row. "Don't beat my brother," she called out authoritatively without interrupting her performance, "I am coming." The incident displayed a fighting, protective spirit, every bit of which she was to need in the years ahead.

She was only twelve years old when tragedy hit. The river of Mohua's life entered a dark narrow gorge, isolated and lonely. It happened quite suddenly. She simply woke up one morning to find herself paralysed from the waist down by a virulent form of myelitis.

Society in Bangladesh makes it difficult for young girls to go out alone, so her female friends could not visit. Neither was it easy for her brothers to take her out. They lived in a first floor apartment, and, unable to get her down the stairs in a wheelchair, they had to resort to putting her over the balcony on ropes. Gradually it became more and more difficult for Mohua to face the outside world. She well remembers the time when one of her brothers first took her to see Valerie Taylor. So nervous and ashamed did she feel on that ocassion that she found it impossible to look up. All the way down the road Mohua saw nothing but the hem of her sari.

That visit, however, proved to be a turning point. At last Mohua's river escaped from the gorge and started to spread out. It was to become a shinning ribbon reaching out to countless other people. By the time of my arrival at CRP, she carried the modest title of Administrative Officer; but the more I got to know her and watched her at work, the more I wondered just how many duties this covered.

There was never time to talk during office hours. But one lovely June evening, when grey and black monsoon clouds moved slowly over a full moon, we sat together under a mango tree delighting in the gentle breeze which stirred the branches and caused dark shadows to dance around us. I was fascinated by the conversation. Despite the mosquitoes which descended on my feet and crawled up under my *salwar kameez* to attack the white skin beneath, we sat for a good three hours whilst Mohua talked about her life and work.

Thus it transpired that the job of Administrative Officer actually covered some fourteen substantial tasks as diverse as domestic supervision, liaising with the local elite, the development of women's groups and general fundraising.

When I asked Mohua how she managed to achieve so much, she smiled nervously and confessed somewhat reluctantly that in actual fact she had not taken any annual leave for about ten years. And what time did she finish work in the evening? "Honestly I don't know," she replied but then added hastily, "but I am enjoying it. It's OK and my colleagues are so kind and good to me. They believe it when I say that I am tired."

In the course of her work Mohua has travelled widely, and has visited Thailand, India, Pakistan, Nepal, Canada, Finland, Sweden and England. She has been Vice President of BDP, the organisation for Bangladesh Disabled Persons, and on many occasions was the first woman in the country to act as representative for all disabled people. Carrying out such roles with other NGOs sometimes produced a clash of loyalties. At first she had tried to do all her voluntary work on Fridays, the national day of rest, but increasingly she found herself expected to undertake voluntary duties during working hours. Finally she decided that, in fairness to CRP, she would have to cut down on extra activites. Not however, before she had done some valuable work amongst disabled tribal people in remote rural areas where, she said, some of the villagers had never even seen a shoe.

Getting around in a country like Bangladesh inevitably poses a major problem to someone in a wheelchair and it sounded as if Mohua had been considerably imaginative when it came to unconventional modes of transport.

She remembered a time when a male friend used to push her from house to office but she had thought, "This is not good. A man pushing me in the hot sun." So she asked him if she could hold on to the back of his bicycle instead. Succeeding in this, her thoughts had turned to speed. If a bicycle, why not a motorbike? "I managed it by holding on to the carrier at the back," she said. "It was faster than someone pushing me, but not too fast."

Access to buildings is also a massive problem. Mohua was able to think of only three places which have ramps for wheelchairs and conceded that all had been put there as a result of lobbying by herself and others at CRP. "But," she added, speaking cheerfully and in a manner which showed she intended to keep the conversation positive, "We have many kind friends who help us."

This was probably true, but at another point in the conversation Mohua showed very clearly that she liked to do things independently.

A cheerful man with untidy wavy hair had joined us under the mango tree and started talking to Mohua in Bangla. She turned to me, ever thoughtful to ensure that I was included, "This is the engineer. I have asked him to help me. At the moment I have to be lifted into the CRP vehicle but I would like to be more independent, to be able to get in by myself." She smiled. "He is suggesting a ramp which could be folded up inside the vehicle and let down so that I can push myself up unaided."

I asked Mohua what other things she had found particularly helpful in the past. Her reply was instantaneous. "Taking trouble with one's clothes and appearance. That does not mean wearing expensive things but just trying to look nice. It gives you a good feeling about yourself and you find that other people respect you more. For example, they don't crowd so close or ask so many questions."

I understood well what Mohua meant. The Bangladeshi people display an insatiable curiosity about anyone who is different. As a foreigner, and white, I was subjected to invasive stares wherever I went. I got used to it and also recognised that in choosing to visit that country I had laid myself open to their natural inquisitiveness. I doubt if I could have felt the same if they were staring at me because I was disabled.

The insensitivity of others can be very hurtful. Mohua told me sadly of instances when people talked about her as if she could not understand. There was also one terrible occasion when a government minister had so little respect that he lifted her sari and stared at her legs, a part of the anatomy which Bangladesh custom requires women to keep covered at all times.

She did not, however, ponder on these points for long. In no time at all Mohua had changed the subject and was telling me funny stories about a delightful old Christian brother who supported the Centre.

By now we had been joined by Madhab, the tetraplegic counsellor at CRP, someone else for whom I had already developed a special admiration. Together they recounted amusing stories of the past and laughed the evening away. Then Mohua demanded a free ride and caught hold of the chair pushed by Madhab's carer. Still chuckling, they moved off in tandem and disappeared into the darkness.

Mohua had highlighted the difficulty of getting round Bangladesh in a wheelchair, but I knew I lacked insight into the problems of which she spoke. So together with two young English volunteers, Katy and Chris, I set out one weekend with a small haversack, and no plans other than to travel for two and a half days using as many different forms of transport as possible. Everywhere we went we would imagine that we were accompanying a disabled person and, in so doing, attempt to visualize the difficulties involved.

We planned to start by taking one of the Rocket group of former paddle steamers that ply the Ganges delta. The full trip from Dhaka to Khulna would take more than twenty-four hours, and we were advised that we would be glad of first class cabins which apparently were not expensive. Chris accordingly made two excursions into Dhaka in order to acquire the necessary tickets, but both proved unsuccessful. All first class cabins had already been taken, and advance booking for second or deck class was not permitted.

Thus, straight after lunch on a Wednesday afternoon, the three of us climbed onto a rickshaw and set off without any very clear idea of what we were going to do. I had already seen how wheelchair users travel on this particular form of transport. Two rickshaws have to be employed and the wheelchair is put in one, while its user goes in the other. But to reach one's destination is another matter. On this particular afternoon the little town of Savar was so packed with traffic, that had we wanted to go all the way to the bus stop we would have had to wait a long time, and possibly miss several buses, before getting through. Being able bodied though, we were able to get off and walk.

The Premium bus from Savar to Dhaka is one of the delux modes of transport. Seats are guaranteed by the purchase of a ticket, and on entering the passenger finds himself greeted, almost stunned, by the icy cold air produced by the air conditioning system. On this vehicle, if on nothing else, it should be possible for a disabled person to travel in comfort. The doorway, however, is narrow, and the bus has very little spare space inside. For the wheelchair user it would be absolutely essential to have both a folding chair and a strong helper.

We arrived at Motijheel in Dhaka and decided to go first to the offices of the Bangladesh Inland Waterways Transport Company in the hope that, maybe – just maybe, a cabin had become vacant.

The BIWTC reservations room was very small, and crammed to the walls by a row of large chairs and an enormous desk behind which sat the officer in charge, a tired elderly man in white punjabi. He recognised Chris from the previous day, and indicated that we should sit down. This was not easy. We had to literally squeeze past his desk in order to take our seats in a row before him. I felt hopeful. The old man waited until we were seated and then inquired about our well being. Only after completion of all the formalities did he tell us once again that no first class cabins were available; though we might, he added, get a second class one if we hurried down to the port right away.

Hurrying to Sadarghat proved impossible. The first *baby taxi* driver refused to go. The second raised his eyes to the heavens, lifted his arms and uttered the fearful words, "Jam, jam."

Eventually we persuaded him to take us as far as he could and then let us get out and walk. Within a few minutes we had entered what Katy and I thought was the "jam" but Chris laughed at our naivete. "This is nothing," he assured us. From his experience the day before, he knew that there was much worse to come.

In some ways we were probably lucky. A big maroon Mitsibishi flying the Bangladesh flag nosed its way up beside us followed by a heavily manned police vehicle. The Mayor of Dhaka was attempting to move through his city. We kept close beside this entourage and were able to make reasonable progress through a tightly packed crowd created by rickshaws, pedestrians and an incredibly patient pair of ponies pulling a cartload of passengers.

A new problem arose when finally choosing to disembark. We could not get rid of our vehicle. Unable to go anywhere else, the driver decided to keep going at a snail's pace beside us and was thus able to embark on a protracted and unwelcome argument about the fare.

Walking this bit was quite hair raising enough. Much of the time we were balancing our way along a narrow stone ledge running down the middle of the road. *Baby taxis*, rickshaws and cars wove their way around us and displayed a disconcerting habit of changing direction without warning. This was possibly the only part of our journey during which I might have felt happier in a wheelchair.

Once at the port terminal we worked our way slowly through the crowd towards the river and aimed for The Rocket. She was clearly visible towering over the lesser craft around her, and after weaving our way past a maze of bread stalls and fruit sellers we found the shabby blue ticket booth belonging to BIWTC.

I was taking my place in the queue when a man, carrying an apparently unnecessary umbrella over his head, suddenly appeared out of the crowd and offered to help us. He proved to be the person responsible for tickets and, in answer to my request, immediately informed us that he did not have any second class cabins available. Then added sadly and almost inaudibly, "It is a pity you didn't want first class. Those I could have provided."

The struggle to get there had been worth it. A guide was allocated to us and in no time at all we were making our way on to the boat. The PS Lepcha was built in 1938 and converted to diesel in 1983. A large notice in English proudly informed us that she had a length of 190 feet, a breadth of 25 feet, a loaded draft of 5 feet 6 inches and a cargo capacity of 79 tons. Her passenger capacity apparently amounted to 16 in first class, 12 in second class, and 574 during the day in third class, but only 374 at night. What they did with the extra passengers when darkness descended was not at all clear.

Most people looked intent on staying. In the deck and intermediate class each family had staked claim to their patch by spreading out a towel or other cloth and walling themselves in with pineapples and general supplies. Many looked as if they had already settled down for the night, and at that stage it was not perhaps a particularly profitable area for the many vendors stepping over and around the recumbent bodies.

First class accommodation was upstairs and surprisingly well equipped. We found a central dining area flanked by clean, comfortable cabins and an exclusive viewing deck located in the front of the vessel.

Most of our companions were well-off Bangladeshis but there was one other British couple. A large cheerful builder who had nursed a life long ambition to go down the Ganges delta. His wife was clearly resigned to following her spouse to the ends of the earth. There were, she said, quite a few more similar dreams yet to be accomplished.

With several loud hoots announcing her supremacy of the inland waterways, the PS Lepcha moved out into midstream at 6.05 p.m.

only five minutes behind schedule. A multitude of small craft plied their way back and forth across a river made beautiful by the evening light. With our stern to the sunset we proceeded slowly downstream past factories, brick works and shipyards full of rusty vessels. A single porpoise curved out of the water and then disappeared. The boats and boatmen behind us were transformed to silhouettes.

The sun was almost down, and on attempting to go through the dining room in order to reach the bathroom I found my way blocked by Muslims at prayer. Mats had been laid on the floor and the majority of first class passengers had turned towards Mecca. I went back to the evening sky. They were right, it was a time to think of higher things.

By 7.30 p.m. it was dark. But for the white spray thrown up by our prow, the murky green waters had turned to black. The Lepcha forged her way forward on the golden path provided by her headlights. Brightly lit ports appeared, claimed their passengers, embarked others and were gone. My pleasure in watching had to struggle with exhaustion and eventually lost. Bed was the only option.

I awoke at 6 a.m. to a very different scene. Bustle, activity and concrete buildings seemed gone forever. We were in a narrow part of the river fringed on either side by palms and rich green foliage. Fishermen in slim barrel topped boats were working quietly away in the morninglight. Simple homesteads slipped noiselessly past, and children, appearing from the small thatched houses, waved from the bank.

I stood alone on the viewing deck, drinking in the unsullied beauty and tranquillity of my surroundings. There was a magic in the air and I longed to catch hold of it, somehow to trap it and store it for ever in the depth of my being. But time moved on, and with it a change of scene and interest.

We stopped at many different landing stages and at each were greeted by a crowd of heavily laden passengers and vendors. Loading and unloading of cargo could take anything up to an hour and allowed plenty of time to observe life in the other boats moored around us. Most of the larger vessels had a wide outer ledge useful, no doubt, for a variety of purposes, but not least for morning ablutions. Undisturbed by the proximity of our vantage point, a number of male passengers could be seen hauling buckets of murky water out of the river and scrubbing themselves assiduously. Each then put on a fresh *lungi*, removed the soaking one from underneath and washed the discarded garment in the same dubious-looking water as he had used upon himself. All in all it was a thorough process; but gazing down at the debris floating past, I could not help wondering whether those involved would actually be cleaner at the end of it. Just round the corner from their activity I could see a young boy outside the kitchen quarters preparing freshly killed duck and chicken. Blood from the corpses dripped over the edge of the boat and joined the rest of the filth around us.

Up on our own first class deck we had been joined by an anxious little man whom I mentally dubbed as the "Ear Doctor". A small black box hung from one shoulder and he willingly displayed its contents: a wax covered instrument for looking inside the ears, a lethal looking metal spike for poking them, and various small bottles of lotions and potions. Would I like my ears cleaned, he enquired pleadingly. My answer surprised even myself by the speed of delivery. "*Lagbe na*," I said firmly. And sure though I was of the Bangla for "not needing", I moved quickly away.

At one stop I managed to purchase a green coconut by shouting down to a vendor on the quayside. His friend, who had climbed right up the side of the boat to join me, now negotiated a price, and in no time at all I was drinking the cool refreshing liquid.

I was really enjoying this trip but sadly reflected that it would be extremely difficult for someone in a wheelchair. The gangplank in Dhaka was wide enough for a chair to get across, but after that they would have had nowhere to park unless a helper was prepared to carry them up the stairs and over the little ledges in every doorway.

With this in view, we decided to take a look at accommodation and facilities on the lower deck.

Leaving our own verandah after lunch and walking back through the dining room we were mildly surprised to see that one of the stewards had already placed a pillow on the dining table and stretched himself out. The others were sitting in a circle on the floor eating their meal.

The upper deck is for "Inters" passengers who pay about a hundred *taka* more than the deck class. In the former, everybody has their own space and can settle down reasonably comfortably amongst their possessions. Some were now sitting round playing cards or listening to a broadcast sermon while others were enjoying something from the small snack bar situated at the far end of their domain.

The lower deck is dominated by the enormous diesel engines and consequently is very hot and unbearably noisy. Here we found men, women and children sitting on hard benches or lying on the floor amongst sacks, motorbikes and hens. For passengers on this level it must be a suffocating, deafening and comfortless journey; and for the wheelchair user there is no alternative. I doubt though whether many attempt it, for although boarding the ship seemed possible, it would be a great deal more difficult to disembark. At most landing stages the gangway is but a single plank bridging a wide strip of water, and at one of our stops this led only to an island. The far stream of the river had to be crossed by balancing on a bamboo pole.

Despite the season it was a perfect afternoon. The water sparkled in the sunshine under a clear sky dotted only by the most innocent puffs of white cloud. On such occasions it is sometimes difficult to believe in the proximity of monsoon storms, but here the evidence was all around us. The river had obviously risen considerably. People and cattle walked along the narrow causeways edging former fields. Palm trees appeared to have been planted in the depths, and banana leaf fences, rising directly out of the shallows, provided scant protection for the houses behind. Yet further downstream the tiny homesteads became almost totally marooned, accessible only by the most narrow of raised pathways.

The stewards' after lunch nap permitted an influx of curious second and third class passengers onto our hitherto exclusive deck. With them came an increase in interest and activity.

A cheerful woman in black *burkha*, the all-enveloping garb of Muslim women, sat down beside me and smiled broadly, displaying, as she did so, a row of bright *betel* stained teeth. It was the invitation to enter into a language-limited but friendly conversation. Her name was Nyama. She had five children, three of them sons, and on this occasion was travelling to Khulna to stay with a daughter and visit some of the grandchildren. And she was interested in what I was doing, what I thought of Bangladesh, and what I ate. Nyama, it seemed, had an idea that foreigners consume strange things, and was probably well satisfied when I told her that I did not eat meat, a denial which she clearly considered the height of folly. She then opened her canvas bag and showed me her clothes before bringing out the inevitable black plastic bag of *pan*. My heart sank as I knew already how little I liked this particular treat. Kindly she selected a particularly large leaf for me, smeared on some lime and filled it with betel. I thanked her, and, much to her disappointment, nibbled cautiously at one corner instead of putting the whole thing in my mouth as custom demands. Anxious to get rid of the rest, I then offered pieces to the English builder and his wife but unfortunately they were unwilling to oblige. I was still standing holding the folded leaf and wondering what to do next when a crew member appeared and evicted the kind donor from our deck.

The mooring at Mongla was the most hazardous we experienced. Strong winds and tides made it particularly difficult for our captain to pull alongside, and we were all advised to stand back as the frayed cable went taut and the vessel strained like a frightened puppy on the lead for the first time. We bumped another boat hard and caused an angry exchange between the two bridges but otherwise came to no harm. This was our most sizeable port, an industrial jungle poised on the edge of the wild and beautiful forests of the Sundarbans.

The second evening on the first class deck of the Lepcha was an experience to remember. The river had lost its glitter and turned to dark grey-blue, the trees lining the banks reduced to a fringed silhouette. The sky was fantastic: purple clouds, a flush of pink, a magic strip of pale green and, higher still, wisps of gold and apricot floating beside a silver slither of moon. We gave the dining room a miss and sat outside eating bread and marmite and feeling inordinately happy.

Twenty-seven hours after leaving Dhaka, we landed at Khulna and were pounced upon by a number of eager rickshaw wallahs. We were very tired, and finding an affordable hotel in a dark, unknown town was not so easy. The first one we tried had vacant accommodation on the fifth floor only, and the higher we climbed the greater the smell emanating from the lavatories. The rooms were minute and claustrophobic, the bedding wriggling with insects. In comparison, the second hotel seemed relatively bearable. The bedrooms were larger and more airy, and although the sink was blocked and filthy, the staff did at least fetch clean sheets. For sixty *taka* a night (about seventy pence) we could hardly complain and we were too tired to explore further. It was some concern, though, that we had not been able to find any available rooms on the ground floor. I do not know where we could have taken a wheelchair companion. Lifts were non-existent

Next morning we left the hotel at seven-thirty, and took a rickshaw to the station. A notice at the ticket office advertised an "English course basic grammar with", so perhaps it was fortunate that we did not have to carry out any complex transactions. Instead we bought second class tickets to Jessore and went straight for the train.

Four vertical steps led up the side of each carriage to the doorway, and it would have been very difficult to lift a disabled person on board. For ourselves, however, the second class accommodation proved quite adequate. As it was Friday there were relatively few people travelling, and we had a reasonable amount of space. The two hard bench-like seats each had room enough for five passengers, and there were only six of us in all. Moreover, two of our number disappeared very fast when a couple of hefty ticket collectors entered the compartment. Actually, despite their looks, these officers were not particularly effective. I do not think they even saw the fellow on the luggage rack, and the two who scuttled away could not have gone far. Both reappeared very quickly.

A rail journey in Bangladesh provides much to watch inside the train as well as out. We were visited by white coated stewards offering a variety of fried savouries, a *cha* boy with water bottles in a bucket plus a large thermos of boiling liquid, other youngsters with sweets and nuts, and a number of armed soldiers who walked back and forth along the corridor as if on the look out for trouble. Outside, bright green paddy, banana groves and coconut palms, sheets of shining water reflecting the sky, and smiling waving villagers all slipped past.

On getting out at Jessore, I inspected the entrance to the guard's van. This would have been wide enough for a wheelchair, and the platform here was somewhat higher, reducing the number of steps from four to two. Perhaps it is possible for a disabled person to travel by train in Bangladesh; but only if they choose their stations carefully.

A rickshaw took us to the bus station and we were lucky in getting an almost immediate connection.

Despite the shattered windscreen, our rusty old bus had pretensions of grandeur. Magnificence it had, though restricted to the ceiling. The floral lampshades and variety of coloured carpets fixed above our heads was quite amazing; but the accommodation for our nether regions painfully cramped. We had three numbered seats in a space most of us would deem appropriate for only two. Anyone who was disabled would have found it extremely uncomfortable. Even for us, the three and a half hour journey demanded a certain modicum of endurance.

Getting onto the bus would have been possible for a disabled person if they had a carer at hand. Boarding the ferry at Aricha would have been almost out of the question.

I had imagined a large drive-on ferry that would take our vehicle. But instead we were asked to gather up all our luggage, get off the bus and clamber aboard a small rickety boat. Once there, you had no choice but to go either up or down, both options necessitating the negotiation of a very narrow flight of stairs.

Quite impossible for the disabled, I thought; but maybe I was wrong. During the journey, I spied an elderly beggar with a paralysed leg who was working his way round the boat. By manoeuvring his way between the levels on hands and knees, he showed that it could be done – at least by those with three good limbs.

The crossing took about one hour, and finding the correct bus on the other side without a guide might not have been easy. We were grateful to a kind, podgy little man, with maroon striped shirt, dark sun glasses and brilliant betel lips, who took us under his wing.

31

Uninvited, but appreciated, he led us proudly along behind an entourage consisting of anxious wife and heavily laden porter. The latter had been employed to carry their luggage in a huge yellow sack on top of his head.

We had another one and a quarter hours to go on the second bus. Apart from a shattered windscreen, this vehicle had little resemblance to the first. No carpeting or decorative lampshades this time; but, as if in compensation, brightly coloured tinsel hung round the front window, and Bengali tunes blared from the loud speakers. Though persistent and jangling in nature, the music suceeded in adding a note of triumph to that last leg of our journey.

Fifty-one hours after leaving CRP we were back. We had completed a large circle round a substantial portion of southern Bangladesh and employed seven different modes of transport. We had also become horribly aware of how difficult it would have been for a disabled person to do likewise.

CHAPTER TWO

THE MARTYRS' MEMORIAL – SALIM: PRESS OFFICER – THROUGH
MUD AND WATER: CRP OUTREACH – ANIL: ENGINEER – ZAKARIA:
TRANSLATOR – HORITOSH: FISHMONGER

News programmes on Bangladesh television start with a picture of
Jatiya Shaheed Smriti Sandha, the National Martyrs' Memorial, a
symbol of pride and unity with which all the people of the country can
identify. It is situated at Savar, not so very far from CRP, and on more
than one occasion provided me with a pleasant afternoon's outing.

Set well back from the noise and dangers of the "four-accidents-a-
day" Aricha Highway, the monument stands alone and at peace in
beautifully manicured grounds. Reverence prevails around this
memorial to the millions who died in the Liberation War.
Successfully, it attains a dignity and distance from the squabbles and
struggles of everyday life.

I experienced the feeling of release as soon as I passed through the
gates. Safely behind me now, were the crazy overloaded buses and
bargaining vendors. No longer did I need to struggle against the
crowd. Here were only a few students wandering in the gardens, and
a small barefoot child proffering garlands of sweet smelling flowers.
So real was the atmosphere of retreat, that colourful birds,
abandoning shy behaviour, flitted conspicuously from one lovely
shrub to another. Here the waters of the lake lay pure and undisturbed.

I walked in further, and found the grassy platforms which provide
a calm green mantle of peace for the unknown but deeply honoured
occupants of the mass graves beneath. They lie at the foot of the
monument, a striking structure some fifty metres in height and
consisting of seven isosceles triangles representing the seven stages of
the fight for independence.

Removing my shoes as custom required, I winced briefly as the
thin soles of western feet came into direct contact with sun-struck
brick. Of necessity I hastened up the shallow steps and over the paved

outer area into the shadow of the monument walls. Towering above me were the solid grey triangles: dramatic, enduring, of sufficient size to impress upon the visitor the insignificance of man, and each pointing relentlessly up towards the soft blue of eternity. It is here, wandering quietly between them, that you can best appreciate the beauty and simplicity of this incredible piece of architecture. Nevertheless, the extent of geometric skill may only become apparent later. Wander in the grounds and take a path right round the memorial and from each new viewpoint you will gain a totally different impression of shape and structure.

Though seldom mentioned, there is also something else to be noted about the National Monument. It is one of the very few places in Bangladesh providing ramp access for those who are disabled.

CRP's Accessibility Programme was started in 1993, and one of the people responsible for its success is Salim Nazrul, then Publications Officer and himself a wheelchair user. The aim of the programme is to create an accessible environment for disabled people in Bangladesh and to increase awareness of their needs.

"For someone like myself," Salim told me forcibly, "if there is no access, then education and everything else is useless."

We were sitting in the Centre's dining room, sharing coke and crisps and talking about his work. The Accessibility Programme. Salim explained, targets local government offices at *thana* (the area under each police station) and district level. Already it has supplied a specially written Accessibility Manual and regular Accessibility Newsletters. The former highlights the physical barriers encountered by people with disabilities and provides detailed suggestions as to how these can be overcome. The Newsletter gives updated information and includes articles by architects and engineers.

I asked Salim if he thought their programme was making progress. His answer was immediate and emphatic. "Absolutely. The Local Government Engineering Department has now bought 560 copies of our manual and distributed it to all their offices. This is our greatest achievement because we are not talking about another NGO (non-governmental organisation), we are talking about the Government."

"Also," he continued enthusiastically, "I wrote an article last year which really did have an effect. I sent it, together with a letter, to three of our leading newspapers. The purpose was to point out that there was no disabled access for visitors to our National Monument, and by December the Works Ministry had responded by erecting ramps."

Though justifiably proud of this particular success, it had not caused Salim to relax his efforts. A quiet man of intense fervour and conviction, he was now working to get a ramp at Shaheed Minar, the memorial inside Dhaka University.

Naively I told him about the two days Katy, Chris and I had spent looking at the accessibility of public transport. He looked at me sadly, almost uncomprehendingly.

"But without me, this experience, you cannot even begin to understand." He paused, then added, "I am not a man. I am an animal." The simple, passionate words gave me a jolt and I can still see the deep, dark eyes with which Salim seemed to search the distance in his effort to explain what he meant.

"Perhaps you do not know. Every two months I go home to Chittagong by public transport. I am going soon so I am mentally prepared, for I know the curiosity with which people will look at me."

"I have to take a taxi from here to the bus station at Gabtali, and there the young boy, my helping hand, will lift me onto the bus, fold up my chair and put it beside my seat. We prepare for a very long journey, eight hours if there is not too much traffic, ten to twelve if there is a jam. A problem for me this, because after three hours I have to pass urine and somehow I must maintain privacy." Here Salim gathered up some surrounding magazines and newspapers to show how he would create a screen. Such a procedure might seem obvious to us in the West but here it struck me as an indication of his exceptional politeness and sensitivity for I was now well used to the sight of men relieving themselves in public without any inhibitions whatsoever.

"In Chittagong," he went on, "I get another taxi to my home, and sometimes while I am there, I go to the beach because years back it used to be something that I did every week. But now, if I go there, people will look at me with curiosity. Many people go to the beach to enjoy the seaside. Now they enjoy me as well and sometimes they take pictures."

"If I had been born like this it would be one kind of experience but it was not so. For twenty-eight years I was going everywhere and doing everything. Now when people look at me I find it very terrible."

Salim had been a successful journalist before his accident. For eight years he was the Chittagong Sports and Culture Correspondent for *Ittefaq*, one of Bangladesh's most renowned newspapers.

Then, one rainy June evening in 1993, he was returning home in a baby taxi when it was overturned by a truck. He suffered severe spinal injuries and spent three months in Chittagong Medical Hospital until his brother, a doctor, got him transferred to CRP. There, whilst still a bed patient, he produced a hand written article which was published in the newspaper and led to him joining the publications department at the Centre.

As well as heading the Accessibility Programme and taking responsibility for CRP's own publications, Salim was editor of "The Commitment", the newsletter of a network of disability groups established to disseminate information. Since 1994 he had also been engaged in road safety campaigns, a cause understandably very close to his heart. "I have attended every campaign and every rally since we started. We meet in public places, put up banners and distribute leaflets and newsletters," he said. "I speak loudly. My message is clear. Stop! No more accidents."

Our conversation went on to range over various other subjects. An issue on which Salim spoke with particular passion was that of marriage.

"No one," he said, using his thin sensitive hands to emphasis the point. "No one is interested in marrying his son or daughter to a disabled person."

He went sadly on to explain some of the difficulties. "Our community is not aware about these things. They think marriage is just about the birth of a child, but it is a lifelong relationship, and psychologically it is very important. Perhaps sexual things are important for the first ten to fifteen years after marriage, but older people need a partner. This is particularly true for those who are disabled because they always feel alone. They need a husband or a wife with whom to share everything. Someone to motivate and encourage them."

For a brief moment Salim stopped, rested his chin on his hands, and contemplated the significance of his own words.

"Every day, every moment I learn something more. No one wants to marry even the brother or sister of a disabled person. They think also that a disabled woman will produce a disabled child. They do not know that she can be like Hira at Gonokbari who has a beautiful little boy. About 90 per cent of disabled women in this country are unmarried."

Salim spoke in a rush of intense feeling and then, quite suddenly, stopped and said he was tired. I was not surprised. He had poured himself into every word.

I bade him goodnight and walked slowly back to my room thinking over our conversation. I still felt shattered that someone so sincere, sensitive and intelligent should have felt that the only way to explain his treatment was with the words, "I am not a man. I am an animal."

"Our challenge," he had added later, "is to get people to understand that we are not different. We are part of your community, part of your family. I am also your brother. I am also your son."

Happily, only a few days later, I was able to bring Salim a message that confirmed my own high opinion of him.

I had taken a few days off to join a party of Bangladeshi friends exploring the Sundarbans, the largest littoral mangrove forest in the world and a most beautiful place in which to relax.

We spent our days cruising down ripple dimpled rivers hedged in on either side by the soft and varied greens of the jungle. Brilliant kingfishers darted across our path and a majestic White Bellied Sea Eagle surveyed us from lofty heights. By taking a low country boat we were able to explore the narrow creeks, and bending low under overhanging branches, ferns and vines, catch glimpses of the beautiful Spotted Deer, the yellow patterned Water Monitor, and even, on one rare occasion, a Royal Bengal Tiger.

After such an excursion I was leaning on the rail of the boat one evening, idly gazing at the stars, when quite unexpectedly, I was joined by a small academic looking man with pointed eyebrows and gold rimmed spectacles. He had heard, he said, that I worked at CRP. Did I, by any chance, know Salim Nazrul? He went on to explain that he was sub-editor of the *Daily Prothom Alo* and had seen and included various articles submitted by my friend. He did not know whether or not Salim was disabled, what mattered was the quality of his work. Pallab Mohaiman was impressed. He wanted to meet the writer and visit CRP. His words were few, but the praise considerable.

"Our challenge is to get people to understand that we are not different. We are part of your community ...." Sooner or later every CRP patient has to face that challenge. And happily the hospital does not desert them. I soon had the opportunity of going out with the CRP Outreach Team, a social worker, physiotherapist and accompanying students, who regularly go to check on the progress of former patients and to provide help as necessary.

It was a very wet morning. The path down to the first patient's house was a slippery mess. We slid about in the pouring rain and I hung unashamedly on to the arm of one of my students. The ex-patient here was a young lad called Kamrul, who had been a college student when he was involved in a traffic accident in 1998. He was in CRP for just two months and was now miraculously back at his studies and even enjoying running, swimming and cycling. A handsome smiling boy, in an orange and maroon *lungi* and white tee shirt which somewhat ironically advertised watersports, he hurried his dripping visitors into the shelter of a verandah.

Our physiotherapist enquired as to progress and then led Kamrul aside to show him some additional exercises. This completed the work side of our visit; we were free to enjoy the customary Bangladesh hospitality.

Proceedings were headed by Kamrul's uncle. Politely he invited us into the house, and we found ourselves in a room dominated by three main possessions, a double bed, a motorbike and a television. Here other members of the family entertained us with Sprite and biscuits while the uncle did the talking. He was a man obviously given to considerable thinking and capable of adopting attitudes somewhat outside those of traditional Bengali philosophy.

I had come to dread the oft repeated question as to whether I am married, for my answer inevitably met with an unhappy mixture of incredulity, concern and pity. Once, on recovering from the shock, one of my students ran off to pick me some flowers as a gesture of sympathy. It was with surprise and relief, therefore, that I found that Kamrul's uncle showed genuine approval of my single state. "That is good," he said, when I murmured apologetically that many people in England choose to remain unmarried. "In our country there are too many people and many problems."

Few could argue with the veracity of his statement. With a population of over 120 million in an area of approximately 143 thousand square kilometres (roughly equivalent to the combined size of England and Wales) Bangladesh is, with the exception of a few of the city states, the most densely populated country in the world. For the visitor this is not just a fact that remains in the head but a very real experience. Though initially overwhelmed by the crowding of people, one gradually becomes accustomed to it. On first returning to England and going out to shop in the small rural town in which I live, I found myself wondering what was happening – where had everyone gone, why was the town so deserted? It seemed strange, too, to be living all alone in my house and to visit so many of my friends who did likewise.

In the domestic situation in Bangladesh I have little doubt that numbers bring an atmosphere of community and support which many of us here lack, but on the larger scale, density of population is a very real problem. Land per person is becoming scarcer and scarcer and poverty increasing as a result. The outlook is bleak. In about thirty to forty years' time the country is expected to have a population of between 230 and 280 million.

It is a problem of which the people are now well aware and most families do want to have fewer children. Government family planning schemes seem to have been quite successful in their publicity, although horrendously ineffective and blundering when it comes to delivering the goods. In one village I was told that a government team had visited ten years ago, had told people about contraceptive techniques and promised to return with the pills but had never done so. Similar stories are reported by the sociologists, Hartman and Boyce, in their book, "A Quiet Violence". They spent several years in rural Bangladesh, and record making considerable efforts to get family planning workers to deliver the contraceptive supplies for which local women were pleading. Yet, despite it all, statistics point to a certain degree of success. Fertility rates have declined dramatically from 6.2 births per woman in 1980–85, to 3.4 in 1990–95. No other country has seen such a large reduction in its fertility rate over the same period; and Kamrul's uncle was typical of many of his compatriots in telling me, with some pride, that he had only two children and did not intend having any more.

Our efforts to find our second patient were, for me, something of a nightmare. People with phobias about heights, I quickly decided, should not try to travel round Bangladesh during the wet season. The first bamboo bridge was not too bad, but the second was much higher and steeper and a great deal wobblier. And having stifled a panic attack in the middle of this, I came to a complete halt before the third, for it was comprised of nothing more than one thin pole hung horizontally above the water. "Not me," I said firmly to my companions. "I will wait for you here."

The students would have none of it. "Come, come," they said. "What is wrong? This is our country. This is what Bangladesh is like."

Neither of us appeared willing to give in, and I do not know how the matter would have ended if it had not been for the return of the advance party with the news that our patient was not at home. I was well and truly humbled. A disabled person, apparently, went daily over a bridge which I felt incapable of crossing. Such feelings, however, were of little help in dealing with my immediate problem. I still had to get back over the first two bridges.

The patient whom we had been seeking was discovered in a shop in the bazaar; and the other English visitor and I were both asked to stay in the vehicle. The shopkeeper was of the opinion that the crowds drawn by two foreigners would be bad for his business. A point of view which, for me, merely provided unwelcome time to contemplate the possible conditions which might surround our next destination.

Thankfully there turned out to be just too much water. Too much, at least, for bamboo bridges. We had to take a boat, and in this I felt a great deal safer, even though it lay so low in the water that we sat level with the surface.

The patient we met on landing, was an older man who had been in government service prior to the accident in which he fell from a tree. He too seemed to have made an amazing recovery, and wished to discuss with our social worker the possibility of joining a CRP training course in poultry rearing or horticulture. We sat on his pleasant verandah, overlooking trees and water, and then went inside to partake of a tempting selection of fresh fruit.

Our next two stops involved visits to the offices of BIWTC (the Bangladesh Inland Waterways Transport Company) in order to request permission to organise a road safety campaign on some of their car ferries. What better place could there be in which to find a large captive audience of drivers?

The fourth patient had been in CRP some nine years ago after suffering a sudden onset of paralysis in the lower limbs. We found him in the small pharmacy he had opened opposite a health complex. Though still weak in the right leg, his problems now, he said, were largely financial. Anyone, apparently, can sell medicines in Bangladesh. Qualifications are not necessary, but you do need capital, and in this his little shop was seriously lacking. Looking round I saw that the shelves were extremely bare, the few drugs carefully displayed, each at a considerable distance from the next. To my western eye it looked like the final stages of a closing down sale. But the Bangladeshi temperament is not so easily discouraged. All he needed, the erstwhile patient was telling our social worker, was a certificate from CRP confirming his disability. He could then apply for a loan from another NGO and everything would be alright.

Our last call was to someone for whom the team did not have a file. This man had once been a patient at CRP but he was now, they

41

said, "just a friend". Our visit was to be purely social.

We drove into the pleasant grounds of one of the many centres of the NGO, Gonoshasthaya Kendra (People's Health Centre) and found Anil Bowmick, their Chief Engineer at his home. He was lying on a bed, a telephone by his right ear and a pile of papers to his left.

Some fourteen years ago, whilst still an engineering student, he had dived into a pond, hit his head, and become a permanent tetraplegic with just a little movement in one shoulder. After some time in a government hospital he went to CRP and there met Valerie and another English woman who together inspired him to return to his studies. "You can do it," they said. "You can finish your course and set an example for all disabled people."

Thus motivated, he went back to Rajshahi University, got his degree and met his wife, a botanist who later went on to take a Master's degree in Education. They now have two children. As he spoke Anil looked proudly across at his partner. Having served us all tea, she stood smiling in the doorway; a happy understanding radiated between them.

"I don't like the term 'Disabled People'," he was saying. "Everyone has some disability; you do as well as me. But no one is completely disabled. It is better to refer to us as 'people with some disability'."

The main problem, he felt, was a lack of credibility. "It is just that people here do not think that people with disabilities can do anything."

By way of explanation, Anil told me that when he had applied for his current job, only one person on the Board had wanted to appoint him. Yet now he was the Chief Engineer responsible for thirteen Gonoshasthaya Kendra Centres dotted about the country and four more under construction. He currently had eight engineers working under him.

At this point, Anil's wife interrupted the conversation in order to complain teasingly about her husband's tendency to work "all hours". The only way she could stop him, she said, was to quarrel. They looked across at each other and laughed.

I surveyed the man prostrate on the bed before me. He had a

mischievous face framed by curly hair and a wayward beard. It was really quite difficult to believe that he was actually paralysed and not just lying there for fun.

"I enjoy things," Anil said as we got up to go. His head motioned towards the television. "I watch TV and videos, gossip with my children and make quarrels with my wife."

The first European settlers to establish themselves in this particular corner of the Indian sub-continent were the Portuguese. They arrived as early as the fifteenth century and although most were ousted by Bengali opposition in 1633, their bloodline remains to this day. Descendants of these early traders display their identity not by looks, for indeed they are as dark as any of their neighbours, but rather by name and faithful adherence to the Christian tradition.

One such is Robert Gonzalves. A husband of one of our nurses, and a former worker for the Christian organisation World Vision, he has good English and proved a helpful guide and interpreter. It was he who suggested that I should meet Zakaria Chowdury, and went to some effort on my behalf in order to discover in which part of Dhaka the former patient was now living.

We took a rickshaw and, on turning off the Mirpur Road, entered almost instantly into a totally different environment. Here were trees, grass and cows. But the large black crows encircling great mounds of rubbish were still distinctly those of Dhaka. By the roadside, men crouched mending mattresses, and a group of women, sitting atop a pile of rubble under a cluster of black umbrellas, were laboriously hammering the bricks around them into small pieces.

Herein lies one of the many anomalies of Bangladesh. On journeying between towns the traveller will pass endless kilns puffing black smoke into the air in the process of preparing the thousands of regular rectangular bricks neatly piled up in the vicinity. Should he then enter the city, he will find large numbers of poverty stricken labourers working long hours every day in order to reduce identical bricks to a pile of rubble. The reason for this is the country's almost complete lack of stone. Great rivers dominate the whole area and have formed the plains around them from a fine rich top soil washed down from the Himalayas. The only place with any quantity of rock is a quarry in the far north west. For whatever purposes the rest of us would use small stones, Bangladesh has to employ fragments of brick.

The rickshaw came to a halt under a noticeboard interestingly advertising "The Elegant Builders" and I was a little disappointed that Robert led the way to a totally unrelated door at the back of adjacent premises.

Zakaria Chowdhury was expecting us. A small man with a striking mass of wavy hair, an enormous black and grey beard and a long sensitive face, he led us into a room piled high with magazines and newspapers. Then, after a few preliminaries, he sat down opposite me and started to fiddle with a Biro, thoughtfully threading it back and forth through a key ring as he recounted his experiences.

In 1986 he had been a Deputy Secretary of the Parliament Secretariat and had been responsible for work related to the Public Accounts Committee. Then, one February evening, instead of taking the official transport he took a rickshaw from the National Assembly towards Newmarket. Near Ashad Gate, a bus knocked into the back of the rickshaw and very nearly killed him. He was rushed to the Suhrawardi Hospital and given a transfusion of eight pints of blood. It was forty-eight hours before the doctors decided that survival was possible.

Zakaria returned to his home in Sylhet nearly nine months later. There had been some serious mistakes in treatment, he was still more or less bedridden, and very depressed. As the months passed he got worse, and another two weeks in a Dhaka hospital did nothing for him. In 1991, still seriously ill, Zakaria retired from government service and drew his pension benefits in order to go to Bankok for treatment. There they recommended a course of physiotherapy, but he could not afford as much as was needed and remained unable to walk.

Fortunately, as I had guessed from the newspapers all around him, Zakaria liked reading. One day nearly nine years after the accident, he was lying on his bed looking at a magazine when he saw an article about CRP. Here at last was an organisation which offered proper treatment and rehabilitation at a price he could afford. Zakaria's sister immediately went down to see Valerie Taylor, and in December 1994 he was admitted to the Centre.

CRP appreciated the eagerness and determination of their new patient. They started afresh with a course of both physiotherapy and occupational therapy. Zakaria laughed now as he remembered that he had felt rather annoyed when he, an former government official, was given a pair of scissors and asked to carry out the menial task of cutting cloth. Later, however, he was to help the Western staff with interpreting, and found various other worthwhile activities such as advising and encouraging other patients and working in the library. At last he was starting to make real progress.

After two or three months Zakaria was able to walk on two elbow crutches and was capable of going to the bathroom without help. Mentally he felt quite different. He was ready to look for a job.

Friends in Dhaka helped him to find Gono Shahajjo Sangstha (GSS), a Bangladesh NGO working in the fields of education and agriculture. Here Zakaria got a job as translator working on reports, journals and other material. He was now able to get back into a house of his own and, anxious to help others as well, he relocated a family from the slums to look after him.

In the past, GSS, the fourth largest NGO in the country, had done some excellent work, but by the time of my visit to Zakaria it was in grave trouble. Serious allegations had been brought against the Executive Director with regard to the misuse of funds, and the Bangladesh Government had decided on temporary closure of the whole organisation pending a High Court hearing. Six thousand employees, including Zakaria, had to wait patiently at home until things could be sorted out.

My host changed the subject, for it clearly worried him and he preferred to talk about CRP. Smile lines, ever evident around his eyes, seemed to take over his whole face whenever he mentioned the Centre and especially when he spoke of Valerie Taylor.

"She inspired not only me, but many other persons," he said. "Her way of life and her thinking. She is a great asset to our country. Everybody has got a great deal to learn from her." He was proud, he

45

added, to have been present in 1998 when she was made an honorary citizen of Bangladesh.

Zakarai was still threading the Biro back and forth through the key ring and this activity seemed to intensify with the sincerity of his feelings.

"After treatment at CRP, I was a fresh and changed person. I was rehabilitated, no longer a burden to my family. Now I can help others. All credit should go to CRP, particularly for their counselling methods. Madhab and Mohua are living examples of how disabled persons can become an asset to society."

I asked Zakaria what he felt were the main problems confronting disabled people in Bangladesh. He answered without hesitation that it was the lack of medical and welfare services. "Treatment and rehabilitation are limited to a very few organisations like CRP. They should be spread around and made available." In Government hospitals, he explained, medical treatment is carried out without any thought to rehabilitation, or as to how a disabled person can be accommodated in society and his abilities used. Financial difficulties also present enormous problems for many people.

"It is not so bad for those like myself," Zakaria pointed out. "I am, shall we say, middle class. I have a chance of treatment, but for others there is very little hope of getting the help needed."

Jobs, he went on to explain, are also a problem. "Bangladesh lags seriously behind India where 10 per cent of posts are reserved for disabled people. This country agrees with the principle but in practice does nothing."

Zakaria went back to his favourite topic. "CRP activities should be published," he said. "If I had known about it earlier, I could have gone straight there instead of wasting time and money on Bankok."

"The point is, this can happen to anybody. In hospitals there should be motivating activities and counselling. They should be saying, "You are not finished, you can still do things."

The smile flashed across his face again. "I don't consider myself now as a disabled person. I only need one stick and I can walk very short distances without any assistance at all."

To prove his point, Zakaria left his stick behind and accompanied us to the gate.

❖   ❖   ❖

All the disabled people I had met so far, had been spinal injury patients and had benefited from the help of CRP. What of the many others? I needed to explore further; but how was I to find the people I was looking for?

I arranged to meet one of my students in the cafe of *Aarong*. Situated on the top floor of a rather up-market shop, it provides a particularly pleasant meeting place. In comfort we could gaze out at wet roads, colourful rickshaws and sombre parliament buildings.

Daisy, who could often look really ravishing, was on this occasion wearing a simple grey *salwar kameez* and white *orna*, and appeared every inch the serious minded student. She was a fourth year physiotherapist with a passion for her studies and a mission to help wherever she was most needed. Pouring a liberal helping of sauce over her *chopoti*, she shook her head firmly.

"Not achieving – trying." Her voice was uncompromising. "The disabled here do not have the opportunity to achieve."

"But surely you agree that Mohua is an achiever?"

"Yes, but CRP is not Bangladesh. In Bangladesh the parents of the disabled are negligent."

"You mean the parents do not understand how to help?"

"That's right, the parents are negligent and the disabled cannot achieve. They try."

"So you know of no disabled person outside CRP whom you would describe as an achiever?"

"No – or maybe I know one, but the majority are beggars."

They were grim words, and it occurred to me for the first time, that my intention to celebrate the successful lives of disabled people might, outside the context of CRP, be just so much wishful thinking.

But I disliked this word 'achievement' that had crept into our conversation. What, after all, does it mean? Does it not depend upon the context? If the odds are stacked against you then surely success in even the simplest things in life can be ranked in the order of achievement?

A few days later Daisy took me to see the only disabled person

47

who had come to her mind as being other than a beggar.

It had rained heavily all afternoon and our feet sank into the thick and filthy mud surrounding Savar market. Our senses were assailed by the combination of lurid smells, wet colours and the pitiful sight of doomed hens.

We turned down a narrow, brick surfaced alley and aimed for the depths of the market. The smells got stronger, and Daisy stopped in front of a stall selling dried fish. A smiling young man, with curly hair and a trace of moustache, was perched more or less on top of the stall amongst a pile of paper. Flies collected on his wares which were displayed in open-topped plastic bags all around him. His customers, mostly male, peered at the many varieties of emaciated fish and scooped up handfuls of the smaller ones in order to inspect them more closely.

This stall, Daisy had explained, was normally manned by someone with cerebral palsy, a disabled person who without the support of any organisation was earning his place in the community as opposed to begging. Achievement in Bangladesh is frequently measured in purely economic terms and success of this sort is sufficiently rare to have attracted both Daisy's interest, and her admiration.

She addressed herself now to the smiling character sitting amongst the fish and enquired as to the whereabouts of the usual stallholder. He was not here today, we were told, but would be back tomorrow. Our informant was apparently the elder brother, and he saw no objection to the inclusion of a member of his family in my book.

It is rare, in Bangladesh, to do anything on the day on which you plan to do it. Content with the information gleaned, we squelched back through the mud, bought a couple of mangoes and headed for home.

It was a slow journey. Our rickshaw was trying to get away from the market by taking the wrong side of the road, and we became wedged between a double line of vehicles: trucks carrying huge mournful white cattle from India, buses topped by people, and rickshaws loaded with green bananas. It was a relief when at last we got clear of it all.

Thick blue-grey clouds rose from the horizon like fluffy mountain

Paddy fields
Elspeth Waldie

Preparing a meal
Elspeth Waldie

Fishing Boats
Tony Kendall

Roadside stalls
Roger Varney

Baby taxis, rickshaws and pedestrians
Roger Varney

Savar
Elspeth Waldie

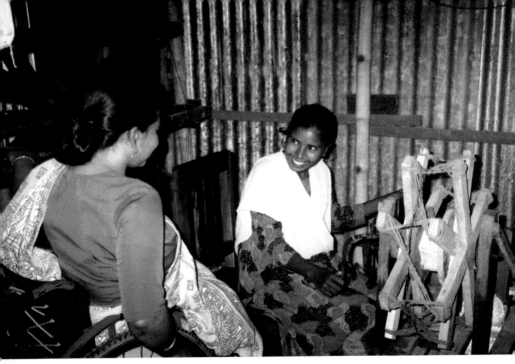

Work and conversation at Gonokbari
Elspeth Waldie

Coconut seller
Elspeth Waldie

peaks, and together with the gentle shades of apricot above them, were reflected in the vast puddles beneath.

The next day we returned as agreed, and found several members of the family awaiting us. Horitosh Rajbonshi turned out to be a young man of twenty years who suffered, not from cerebral palsy, but from the effect of a very serious road accident. Now, with clean blue shirt and carefully combed hair, he looked as if he had prepared specially for our visit; and when an older cousin and a married sister with a baby on her hip appeared eagerly out of the crowd, I realised regretfully that they probably hoped for some form of financial help.

Daisy's friend Mithu led the way into the main building and up the stairs to a relatively quiet corner and then arranged for a small boy to bring six cups of tea.

But Horitosh could not indulge. With two rods in his head, swallowing was extremely difficult and speaking impossible. He merely motioned politely for someone else to take his cup, and then studied us with intelligent eyes whilst listening mournfully to the account of his own tragedy.

When still a schoolboy, Horitosh had been returning home from the Funfair one evening, when the rickshaw carrying him had collided with a bus. The injuries to his head were severe, and he was taken to Dhaka Medical College Hospital. But such were the medical fees that by the end of one month his family had run out of money. No longer able to pay for his bed, they had no option but to take their son home. He was still unconscious.

It was another five months before Horitosh came round, and his memory was permanently impaired. The family, however, did not give up. With their help, and through his own effort, the lad regained many of his abilities, and for the last two years had been helping on the family fish stall. It was success, both sister and cousin insisted, which was due largely to Horitosh's own determination. Help from outside had been minimal. At one point the family did take him to CRP, but the Centre's doctors could do little without a CT scan or MRI. Neither were available at the Centre and the cost elsewhere was prohibitive. In the absence of a free health service, lack of finance had been a constant problem for them. The main concern now was what would happen to Horitosh when his mother died. He still needed a great deal of care, especially as his memory was apt to fail and could even cause him to forget the way home.

Yet by serving in the fish stall, taking the money and managing to give small change, Horitosh was making his own contribution. Daisy was right. He and his family were greatly to be admired.

Darkness had descended when the two students and I piled into a rickshaw for the return journey to CRP, and the traffic was as bad as on our previous visit. Again we were hemmed in an all sides; and this time the feeble rickshaw lights were blurred by the dirt and dust suspended in the air around us. I peered anxiously forward; my thoughts returning to the young man who had travelled so unsuspectingly from Funfair to disaster.

CHAPTER THREE

TAIZE COMMUNITY — RIVER GYPSIES AND SWEEPERS —
WEDDING BY THE RAILWAY LINE — KLEOPA: CARPENTER — ATTACK
BY ACID — NOMITA: TEACHER — EXPLORING THE FILM WORLD —
MAJIBUR: FILM EDITOR

Blaring its horn, our bus hurtled northward at an alarming pace. The
many and wonderful greens of Bangladesh flashed past the window,
and in less than two and a half hours, Katy and I were in Mymensingh.

We had come to visit the Taize Community which, nestling
peacefully amongst a group of trees beside the Brahmaputra river, lies
about three kilometres from the town centre. Here some six or seven
whitewashed buildings, surrounded by pretty gardens of variegated
foliage, cluster round a tiny chapel built in the days of the British Raj.
An atmosphere of tranquillity pervades the scene and seems to reach
out to the visitor even before he has dismounted from his rickshaw or
put his hand to the metal gate.

Brother Guillaume met us at the top of the drive and instantly led
us to a small open-sided sitting room where he plied us with coffee
and words of welcome. Throughout our stay this tall and gentle monk
from Belgium, radiating a special peace and happiness, looked after
our every need. He arranged for us to visit the various projects,
personally brought towel and sheets to the little guest cottage, and
gently advised us of the times of prayer.

Worship took place three times a day and combined the beauty of
a male voice choir with the power of silent contemplation. Attendance
is optional but is, I suspect, enjoyed by people of all faiths and none.

Simplicity, trust, compassion, these are the keynotes of the Taize
philosophy, and the rules by which Brother Guillaume and his
colleagues conduct their lives. In many ways theirs is a very spiritual
existence. Fitting, therefore, that one of the stories of particular
inspiration which I brought away from the Community was not one of
physical achievement, or of material and economic success —

standards by which it is only too easy to pass judgement in a small country – but one of personality and of inner wealth. It is the story of someone who enriched the lives of others not by doing, but simply by being.

Babul became paralysed after diving into a pond and hitting his head. He was then only a boy of some fifteen or sixteen years, and he was to spend the next fifteen years in a wheelchair until a second accident, this time involving a baby taxi, abruptly ended his life.

With difficulty, Babul learnt to paint, and produced Bangadeshi scenes in the bold, colourful style of rickshaw art. The Taize brothers often bought his paintings, but it is not so much for these, that they remember him as for his character.

"It is my experience," said Brother Guillaume, "that many poor people, and many disabled people, return to us far more than we can ever give to them. Babul was one of these."

When Brother Guillaume had first arrived in Dhaka from Chittagong, he had not found it easy to settle. He missed the countryside and the companionship of previous friends. But then, on a visit to one of Valerie's early hospitals in the capital, he had been met by the smile of Babul and immediately felt his spirits lifted.

Babul was always smiling, and this despite severe paralysis. He drew friends to him like a magnet and strengthened and enriched the lives of each and every one. Brother Guillaume's eyes filled with tears as he talked of his deceased friend. The worthy brother must have worked amongst many people in similar situations but no other seemed to have made quite the same impression.

Sitting on the verandah of the little guest cottage at Taize and gazing out at the trees and birds, I reflected on how often we rush round madly in an effort to succeed, or to to make an impact. Babul had probably achieved a much greater result than most of us, but he had done it quietly and with very little movement at all.

It would be wrong to suggest, however, that the Taize Community attaches little importance to the act of doing. On the contrary, their many projects bear witness to a firm belief in practical action.

Towards the end of our first afternoon in Mymensingh, as the sun cast long shadows over the road, we set off to visit one of the several poor communities for whom the Brothers have established schools. Taking the path beside the Brahmaputra, we reached an area inhabited by the river gypsies. Brother Guillaume, walking ahead, was now immediately joined by a bunch of eager children who, by seizing his hands and clustering tightly around him, lent my host the rear-view appearance of a scholarly Pied Piper.

The gypsies' school was a small circular building which had previously housed a water treatment plant, and which must now be a contender for the title of "smallest educational premises in the country". It's services, nevertheless, are available to over thirty pupils at a time. For these children, being crowded close together is, after all, nothing out of the ordinary; a fact I came quickly to realise on a visit to one of their homes.

To enter, we bent low under a makeshift roof cobbled together from bits of corrugated iron, bamboo matting and the inevitable blue plastic sheeting. The interior, though spotlessly clean and tidy, could not have been more than eight feet square. Nevertheless we were soon joined by four or five other adults and some eight to ten children who, eager to express their welcome, squeezed happily into every available gap.

River gypsies comprise one of the many different ethnic groups in Bangladesh, a country with at least eighty distinct languages in everyday use. But for us, on this occasion, communication was not a problem. Music, the gypsies seemed to say, is universal. Each sang his favourite song, and the first ten minutes was thoroughly enjoyable. But then came the moment when they indicated that it was our turn. Too nervous to sing solo, Katy and I considered a duet, only to discover that, with several decades between us, we I could not agree on a single item about which we both felt confident. We ended up presenting an extremely chaotic version of Frere Jacques; and it says a great deal for the politeness of our hosts that their smiles remained undiminished.

When we emerged from the house everybody wanted their photograph taken. The sun was setting, and the sky, behind magnificent rain trees and gentle palms, had turned a glorious shade of rose. This, together with the corrugated iron and blue plastic of the homesteads, provided a backdrop for the many smiling faces jostling to get into every frame. We promised to send the pictures, and by the time we left, both Katy and I, as well as Brother Guillaume, had acquired appendages of several happy children.

Next day we had an opportunity to visit another group with whom the Brothers work. People who do the sweeping and cleaning, Brother Guillaume had explained, are traditionally considered to belong to the lowest caste in Hindu society. And they tend to live in communities which, since Muslims do not eat pork, can often be recognised by the presence of pigs on the outskirts. Sure enough, on reaching their vicinity we found a group of these animals wallowing in the filth and mud of an open sewer. It was not an attractive approach, but once we got inside the area we could not but be struck by the cleanliness of our surroundings. The appearance was that of a village complete in itself, although the community apparently comprised four distinct groups of people. According to Brother Guillaume, they all got on well together but there was never any question of inter-marriage. For myself, I could not detect the difference between them. We were treated with equal warmth and enthusiasm wherever we went.

The last of the external projects we visited was the school for children who live and sleep on the station and adjacent railway line.

Anyone who has travelled by train in Bangladesh will have become aware of the hundreds of beggars, including the very young and the very old, who are to be found at every station. I remember so well the first time I saw them. It had been nearly six months earlier when I was awaiting the departure of the train from Sylhet. Viewing my surroundings from the comfort of a first class compartment, I had been horrified by the number of beggars, mostly maimed and old, who lay on the bare platform. Many had pulled their ragged clothing right up over their heads so that they looked like corpses. Around them, apparently unnoticing, stepped passengers, vendors and railway staff. There too was a mad man with naked torso, and head almost completely wrapped in black plastic sacking. He was walking along the platform emitting a prayer-like drone. Not far off, a small girl, looking no more than six or seven years old, struggled to carry a baby. As I watched she tried to readjust her grip, but so little difference was there in size between her and her burden, that she almost dropped it.

Such impressions stick in the mind, and when Brother Guillaume mentioned a project amongst the railway children I was immediately interested. There was, too, an additional reason for our visit. We had been invited to a wedding. It was the marriage of a daughter of one of the many families the Brothers had been helping, but a family who were slightly better off than most. They traded in rubbish collected off the streets by others in their community and, as a result of this business, they did actually have a roof over their heads.

At the entrance to the little alley where their house is situated, we found the wedding gate, two small adjacent banana trees decorated with coloured crepe paper. We had arrived at the time given for the start of festivities and the whole family was assembled and eager to welcome us, although the bride herself still looked extremely unbride-like. Her hands had been hennaed, but her *salwar kameez* was badly torn, and she was standing unconcernedly picking her nose and rubbing a mattery eye. She was only thirteen or fourteen years old, but did not know which. The family had decided to marry her off, Brother Guillaume told us, because she had started to show a more than proper interest in the opposite sex.

With time to spare we wandered down to see the school set up by the Taize Community. Of reasonable size, this had four classrooms decorated with posters, pictures and numerous photographs of a picnic organised by the Brothers. Most of the children attending this school slept rough, but one little boy took pride in leading us to the single room inhabited by his family of five. The father was a porter in the market, and earned less than five hundred *taka* a month (about six pounds) on which to keep them all.

Back at the wedding house we found the celebrations in full swing. The bridegroom, wearing a gold-coloured paper turban, was sitting outside the wedding gate covering his face, as tradition demanded, in order to show his official shyness. A table with water and *pan* had been placed in front of him, and the age-old bargaining between his party and that of the bride's family had begun. A bridegroom must always pay for his entrance through the wedding gate, and the price is not easily settled. It is a playful argument much enjoyed by all concerned.

The bride, head now covered, looked suitably sad and frightened. Whether she really felt thus was impossible to tell. In Bangladesh, it is as mandatory for a bride to look miserable as it is for her western counterpart to look happy. For better or worse, this one was now closeted with close female relatives who attended to the last details of her make up. Thick glossy lipstick was being heavily applied. We wished her well and permitted ourselves to be led away to a feast of homemade *mishti*, the very sweet treat enjoyed on all such occasions.

In addition to their work amongst the various communities outside, the Taize Brothers run their own special project for disabled people. The Community Centre, as it is called, is attended by a therapist, and incorporates various income generating schemes such as carpet weaving.

Near the church they also have a wood workshop which produces the most lovely carvings. It was here that I met Kleopa, an exceptionally skilled carver who is both deaf and dumb.

Kleopa is of the Garo race and comes from the far north of Bangladesh on the borders of India. His family are devout Christians and two of his brothers are priests. Kleopa's greatest pleasure before coming to the Taize community had been the creation, for his own church, of large statues made of mud. This talent, when transferred at the Brothers' suggestion to wood, has resulted in some of the most beautiful nativity sets I have ever seen.

When I met him, Kleopa was hard at work, seated on a low stool and bent almost double over the carving of a small figurine which he held with one foot whilst chiselling away carefully at some minute detail of the character's clothing. He greeted us with a wonderful open-mouthed smile which stretched right across his face and engulfed eyes, nose and mouth in one big beam of happiness. It was not difficult to believe Brother Guillaume who had been telling me that Kleopa is considered a great strength to the whole of the Community. The woodcarver, I was told, "is always in a good mood."

In fact, only once had Kleopa given any indication of being unhappy. It was when marriage was on his mind. The Muslim culture of Bangladesh leads most people to think that if you are not married you are nothing. Affected by this attitude, Kleopa had come to the conclusion that there are two groups of people: those who can hear, speak and marry; and others like himself who cannot and who are thus second class citizens. Somehow these concerns were conveyed to the Brothers who, full of sympathy for their young friend, decided to talk to Kleopa's family and suggest an arranged marriage. This is something that is neither common nor easy amongst the Garo people, but eventually it was achieved. Kleopa now lives in a house, just a short walk from the community, where he has both a wife and a baby.

That wonderful smile suffused his face again when he "talked" about the child. Showing us the size of the infant with his hands, he then pointed proudly at his own upper lip to indicate a moustache. The baby is a boy: the father, a very happy man.

Kleopa, Brother Guillaume, the very air at Taize seemed tinged with serenity. But Bangladesh is a land of sharp contrasts, with few grey areas in which the emotions can be permitted to rest. The traveller who wishes to truly get to know the country will find him or herself transported quickly, and with little warning, from happiness to horror.

It was a bright and glorious morning. The sun shone down on the grand white portals of Dhaka Medical College Hospital as Ekki and I entered.

He had warned me to "be prepared" but at first I was anaesthetised by a feeling of normality. The long arched corridors were not dissimilar to those of older hospitals at home, and they were filled with a bustle of purposeful activity which was somehow reassuring.

Then Ekki lifted one of the white sheet curtains which acted as a door; we entered the strangled agony of the burns unit.

I doubt whether anything could have prepared me for the scene before my eyes. On nearly every bed lay the victim of one of the most horrendous and atrocious of all the crimes in our modern world – attack by acid. Here were young and once beautiful women, now mutilated beyond all recognition. Acid causes skin tissue to melt and the results of throwing it directly at someone's face are catastrophic. Before us now, were mouths and eyes pulled down into ghastly shapes, and nothing but holes where once were delicate ears and noses. Everywhere, angry red scar tissue covered necks, chests and shoulders. Arms and hands lay destroyed and immobile.

Ekki is a physiotherapist working for Cooperazione Internazionale (COOPI), an Italian organisation set up to help the victims of this terrible crime. One of the worst aspects of his job is that he actually has to inflict more pain on those who have already suffered so much. There is no alternative. Badly burnt joints such as shoulders, elbows, wrists and fingers will contract if not exercised. Ekki tried to work gently, but his efforts were met by the most terrible screams and my attempt to murmur soothing words seemed as stupid as it was ineffectual.

Most of these girls were very young, perhaps only thirteen or fourteen, and ironically the only reason for the attack had been their beauty. Someone had seen them and fancied them. They, or their parents, in receipt of a undesirable marriage proposal had turned it down, and the suitor, infuriated because he could not have the woman he wanted, had taken an action which ensured that she would marry no one else.

For me that morning, the most difficult thing to cope with was not the sight of so much mutilation, but the knowledge that it had been intentionally inflicted. Never before had I experienced such a brutal confrontation with the ugly capabilities of human nature.

In one corner of the ward there was even a three-month-old baby, her face destroyed, her future gone. She was the victim of a land dispute and had been lying in bed, asleep beside her mother, when the aggressor threw acid at them both through a window.

One of the most alarming facts about acid attack in Bangladesh, is that it is on the increase. Exact figures are impossible to obtain, but in 1996 there were forty-seven "reported" incidents, the following year one hundred and thirty, and in 1998, over two hundred. No one doubts that the actual number of cases is considerably higher.

On 1 September 1999, shortly after my visit to the hospital, The Daily Star published figures produced by Odhiker, a coalition for human rights. They had studied ninety-nine incidents reported in the first part of the year, and in two thirds of cases analysed the reasons for attack These were given as three due to arguments about dowry, twenty-three for rejecting marriage, seven for rejecting "indecent proposals", twenty for family feuds, seven for turning down love proposals, two for seeking justice after rape, one for refusing to give toll and three out of "frenzy of rapists after the act".

With this crime on the increase, men are also starting to become victims. On one of the men's wards, Ekki treated a patient who had been blinded by acid and who suffered terrible agony whenever my friend attempted to move him. This man had owned a shop and decided to sack one particularly bad worker. The boy in question had returned and attacked his former employer with devastating effect.

The acid used is either nitric or sulphuric. Both are frighteningly easy to obtain. They are used for car batteries, jewellery making, cleaning and much else, and one litre can be purchased for as little as fifty *taka* (about sixty-five pence).

Acid violence has always been a capital offence but no one has ever hung for it. Few of the attackers are brought to justice. The silence of the victim's family may be due to fear, poverty or bribery; and corruption in the police service is said to be a contributory factor. COOPI showed me their files containing large numbers of case histories; very few ended with a conviction.

The law needs to be strengthened, and organisations such as the Acid Survivors Foundation do valuable work in providing legal representation for the victims. Opinions, however, vary as to the best deterrent. Ekki told me that many of his friends advocate capital punishment, but, despite the terrible cases which confront him every day, he is still against it. Often the aggressors are boys of only thirteen or fourteen years old and, Ekki suggests, not properly aware of what they are doing. COOPI believes education to be the only real answer, but it is a very long term policy; and there is also a fear that the increase in the crime may be due, in part, to copycat attacks resulting from the increase in publicity.

I emerged from Dhaka Medical College Hospital that morning and blinked in the sunshine, too deeply moved to speak.

"Well?" Ekki was asking a question, awaiting my reaction. But I had no words with which to answer him.

Back in the offices of COOPI, Mr Naseem Khan, the Administration Manager, was hospitable and affable, but I remained stunned. Kindly he served us tea and shooed out an over friendly kitten of which one of his other guests seemed to have an inordinate fear. He was doubtful, however, when I eventually managed to ask him whether it might be possible for me to meet a survivor. Did he know of anyone who had suffered an acid attack but was now back in the community, perhaps even doing a job? Mr Khan shook his head sadly. Apart from Beni, who worked for a related organisation, and who probably suffered from over exposure to journalists, he could think of no one. On top of everything else, he explained, victims are faced with social isolation, and undergo enormous damage to their self-esteem and to their confidence as well as to their economic position. Return to normal life is practically impossible.

A few weeks later, however, Mr Khan did arrange an introduction to someone who has achieved the near impossible: one whose life can lend hope to all who suffer like her.

Nomita has been described by Dr John Morrison, the Executive Director of the Acid Survivors Foundation, as one of "the worst case we have come across."

She was just twelve years old, and a schoolgirl living in Dhaka, when her father became involved in a serious family feud. Chased from his village, he fled to the capital to join his daughter, but there his enemies caught up with him. They lay in wait with acid with the intention of throwing it at their opponent, but on seeing Nomita, decided that an attack on the girl would bring greater distress to her father than an attack on him directly. Thus, without scruple, they threw acid at a totally innocent child on her way to school. Her face was completely destroyed, and she was blinded for life.

Nomita, however, is someone of incredible courage and determination. In due course she returned to school, went on to get a degree, took the chance of going to Spain for plastic surgery and eventually became a teacher at the Baptist Sangha School for Blind Girls.

All this information I gained from John Morrison. I was determined on meeting Nomita not to mention the past at all, but to concentrate on her work and achievements now.

It was helpful, therefore, that the CRP student, Daisy, was genuinely keen to see the school. Her little niece had gone blind, and Daisy had been wondering whether the Baptist organisation might provide the answer. In acting as my interpreter, she was thus able to convey to Nomita a real interest in the questions I wanted to ask.

The approach to the school was depressing. We had to leave our rickshaw on the main road and walk down a rubbish strewn side street to reach the main entrance. Inside of the gate was little better. The walls in reception were in desperate need of a new coat of whitewash, paint was peeling off the furniture, and the photographs on the notice board were faded and curling. The fan was motionless and the air stifling. Passing staff seemed unwilling to smile. The whole contrived to bring about an atmosphere of suffocation to which Nomita's arrival brought welcome relief.

She appeared through the doorway, carefully dressed in a mauve and white *salwar kameez* and white *orna*; her sandals, decorated in gold paint, complemented by a gold chain around her neck. A long fringe and large dark glasses hid her face.

Not surprisingly, Nomita seemed to greet us rather guardedly, and it was sometime before we could get her to relax. When she did so, it was to reveal a lovely tinkling laugh which, in view of her history, I found amazing.

She told us that her degree was in Philosophy, Political Science and Sociology and that here she taught the primary children. She had between four and fifteen children in each class and, with the exception of the smallest ones, they studied in Braille. They were able to sit for the Secondary School Certificate, but there was little hope of employment.

"To be blind," Nomita said, "is a big problem. But it is no good just saying that. You have to solve the problem." This was the spirit in which she herself had operated. It is undoubtedly her own determination and courage that has got her to where she is today, although she generously gives much of the credit to her family whom she says have helped her a great deal. The family, to her, is very important.

"The majority of blind people in this country come from poor communities. Rural people do not know the value of vitamins, and also they have very many accidents at work. Most of the children here are very poor. But the families do care. They take the children home for the holidays."

Of the organisation for which she worked, Nomita talked with considerable pride. "It is the only school for blind girls in Bangladesh." Then added firmly, "All blind children should be able to study. I have read that there are ten *lakh* (one million) blind children in this country, probably more, who don't go to school." She felt strongly that the Government needed to spend more on education for the blind and also on providing job opportunities.

I asked Nomita if she had any advice she would like to pass on to others without sight. For a moment she went quiet, and when she spoke her voice was gentle, but the words revealed an enormous determination and courage.

"Blind people have to fight in order to live because they are born as human beings, and if they try for a good future, one day they might gain one."

At the beginning, she said, she didn't know how to study but she tried to do so for the sake of her parents. "I tried for my future." she added. "So Allah gave me the result."

As our discussion came to an end, we asked if we could see the school. For a moment Nomita looked worried and her concern conveyed itself to us. What could be the problem? Surely it was a fairly straightforward request? Then came the explanation.

"The girls' rooms, I think they are not so tidy."

We all laughed, perhaps at relief at finding so much in common. "Neither are ours back home," we assured her.

We wandered through a gate into an attractive garden and at once our surroundings seemed more cheerful. Nomita, too, had grown less serious and the tinkling laugh became more frequent.

We looked in the workshop and inspected the stools and rugs which the pupils had made; then poked our noses into some dormitories. It was Thursday afternoon, the first day of the weekend, and the girls were lying on the beds, doing each other's hair and generally messing around. They teased each other and giggled like any other schoolgirls the world over. Daisy was delighted and resolved to do everything she could to enable her sad introverted niece to join them.

Nomita then led us into her own room and laughingly displayed a stuffed toy which she had brought back from Spain when she went there for treatment. This whole trip had been organised by a charity. Six victims of acid attack had benefited from the excellent plastic surgery available in Europe, and the plan now was for the surgeon to come to Bangladesh and transmit his skills to the doctors in Dhaka. It had been a life-changing experience for Nomita and she delighted in her chief memento, an enormous white chimpanzee-like animal wearing a blue and white striped T-shirt. Then, conscious of the duties of hospitality, she showed us some pictures whilst her friend prepared an orange drink. Sitting together on the bed, I felt the atmosphere at last become truly relaxed.

For a little while, Nomita herself had caused us to forget. But outside the atrocities continued. An article I later clipped from the Bangladesh Observer of 23 September 1999, is sadly typical of many.

ACID BURNT HOUSEWIFE SEEKS JUSTICE

MANIKGANJ September 16 – Shahida Akter (21), wife of a day labourer Amzad Ali of village Beguntu under Singair thana of the district demanded justice to the higher concerned authority.

According to the allegation four miscreants led by Mojer Ali of the same village kidnapped Shahida when she came out of the house to respond to nature's call. They took her to the nearby jungle and attempted to rape her there. At that time some people of the village rushed to the spot to rescue her. The miscreants fled away throwing acid on Shahida. Her chest and belly were seriously burnt. She was admitted to the Singair Health Complex in a critical condition and after one year she was released from the Health Complex recently.

A case was filed with the Singair police station in this

connection. But no police action has so far found in last one year. At present, the criminals are threatening to kill the housewife. The helpless Shahida has taken shelter in house of her elder brother.

For those such as the victims of acid attack, life must be well-nigh intolerable. For a large number of others in Bangladesh, though existence be bearable, it is short, tough and practically devoid of hope. Many people feel the need for escape.

The nation's obsession with cinema will quickly become apparent to even the most casual observers in her capital. In garish colours the heroes and heroines of the big screen stare out from amongst the flowers and birds painted gaily on every vehicle. From poverty, sickness and despair, they signal a temporary liberation, for the rickshaw wallah and the garment worker, a few hours of relief from the drudgery of everyday life.

To understand this need for escape was, for me, very important. I was now committed to writing a full length drama featuring a disabled woman as the heroine. My aim must be to get the audience to identify with her, to share her struggles and triumphs and, hopefully thereby, to increase public understanding of the issues involved. But I had to remember that what people really wanted from the big screen, was relief and entertainment.

The local cinema was therefore high on my list of priorities. It was important, not just to see Bangladesh films on video, but also to study audience reaction.

I asked Feroz, a local student and long time volunteer at the Centre, to accompany me on my first expedition. He laughed a little dubiously when I made the suggestion, adding that he had not been to the pictures himself for a long time. The cinema, in Bangladesh, he explained a trifle contemptuously, had been abandoned by the middle classes and was frequented only by the poor and less educated.

Feroz did not think that I would enjoy the show, and even appeared to consider certain aspects of the experience to be unsuitable. Before

I knew what was happening, he had whisked me past the enormous crowd waiting outside the locked doors of the picture house, introduced me to the management and secured priviledged seats in the balcony. I had not wanted such treatment but it seemed to ease Feroz's worries even if certain doubts remained.

"I don't know this film," he advised in a low voice. "But I'll be able to tell you the story. They are all the same. Boy meets girl. Her parents object. The hero proves himself, and after an appropriate number of song and dance routines and several big fights, the dilemma is resolved."

The film being shown that afternoon was called "The Victory of Love", and I had to admit that, in terms of plot, it matched Feroz's description exactly. But, judging from the behaviour of the audience, it also contained a generous dose of humour, and there was certainly some good imagery and symbolism. For me, the most surprising aspect, given the strict Muslim culture in which we found ourselves, was the extent of the love scenes: nothing exciting in western terms, but a proximity of man to woman which would normally be considered quite unacceptable. With this too came an unexpected frequency of short skirts and bare shoulders, and a tendency of the same to dominate the screen. At the time I could not think how such shots had got past the censor. Only later did I learn the full extent of the lubricating power of money.

Apparently, daring scenes constitute a relatively new development, and one with which the intellectuals in the country are less than happy. Previously films had been much more restrained and after the War of Independence they usually carried a serious social message. The implication for Feroz was that things were "not what they used to be", especially after he had noted that we were the only people in the auditorium to stand for the national anthem.

There is an alternative cinema in Bangladesh, one that produces beautiful, thought provoking and low budget art films. But it does so at enormous economic risk. In an article entitled "Problems of a Bengal Film Maker" by Satysjit Ray I found a warning from the Master himself.

"Films must have the adornment of the latest favourite star team,

65

the usual concomitant of songs and dances and must not be below two and a half hours in length." A film which dares to disregard this last "may never see the light of day".

CRP was lucky in its timing. We found that there were now a few of the top directors interested in creating something in between the art film and that which was purely commercial. A production that was worthwhile as well as popular. It was a gamble because the distributors had to be persuaded to buy, but people such as Abdullah Al Mamun, the Director General of the Institute of Mass Communications, and Humayan Ahmed, best selling writer, were of the opinion that the public was ready for change

Abdullah Al Mamun finally became the director of our film and was a great help and inspiration. But my first glimpse into the Bangladeshi film world came at the invitation of Humayan Ahmed. He had shown an interest in my script and was anxious to ensure that I had a first-hand knowledge of village life.

"You must go and stay in a village," he said. "Live with a family, sleep there, observe them twenty-four hours a day. Experience the life. I will arrange it."

Several weeks passed, and then came the message that everything was fixed and his vehicle would pick me up. It could not have arrived at a worse time. In the interim I had been quite ill and to my diary I confided, "I am not feeling as brave as I should. I have an upset stomach and terrible heat rash, and the thought of village food and water, no fans and no easy loo, fills me with dread."

But Valerie Taylor was unrelenting. "It is for the film," she said. "You must go. Just fill your haversack with loo paper and don't worry about it."

It seemed a long drive. We turned off the main road on to a rough track and made our way through poverty stricken villages and over uncertain bridges. Mr Ahmed's choice of location appeared to be particularly remote.

Then, all of a sudden, a uniformed guard jumped out as if from nowhere, and saluted us. We turned through an opening in a wire fence and drew up under a large tree. There before us, was a table elegantly laid with coffee cups, saucers and even teaspoons. We had arrived, not at a village homestead, but at Humayan Ahmed's country estate; and the unsuspecting "guest of honour" descended from the vehicle wearing a very old *salwar kameez* and clutching a haversack full of toilet rolls.

At a sumptious lunch I was informed that I was to spend my daylight hours in a near-by village, but to live in one of Humayan Ahmed guest cottages, and at night to attend the shooting of his latest film. The first afternoon was "free" to wander around as I pleased

The estate comprised forest, field and lake and was laid out with attractive little bamboo houses plus a swimming pool, riding stables and a library stocked with a goodly collection of antiques, books and pictures. It was here that Humayan Ahmed went on retreat, or gathered around him the leading actors, actresses, cameramen and producers of the day. He was a perfectionist, had time only for the best, and expected from everyone their total commitment.

While the leading actress reclined in the heat of the day, fanned and fussed over by a doting mother as well as an ayah, Humyan Ahmed held endless briefings with production staff and technicians.

The shoot itself took place at night. As the sun went down behind the trees, a team of buffalo arrived to take the generator, camera crane and lights down to the village. The actresses roused themselves, the make-up studio set to work, and Humayan Ahmed dissappeared temporarily into his own small house.

At about 9 p.m. on my first evening, I accompanied the leading actor and actresses on the short dark walk through the forest to the village. The set had been established on the verandah of one of the local houses. Detailed arguments about the all important arrangements of lights were still in progress. I was told that about sixty people were working on this particular film and, at my estimation, at least thirty of them must have been in the small village compound that night. There was also a host of local onlookers, men to the fore, women peeping from behind the buildings, and children and dogs playing in front of the cameras until forcibly removed. At last, with a shout from Humayan Ahmed, came the event for which they had all been waiting.

"In the Name of God," he cried; and with that the shoot commenced.

67

Work was serious and hard. Make-up had to be constantly perfected, glycerene put in the eyes to fake tears, lens changed, distances measured, light adjusted and readjusted, actors briefed repeatedly. Sometimes a shot was deemed satisfactory first time; but, more often than not, it had to be done over and over again. Something as small as a moth flying across the light could call for another retake.

These men were real artists and the shots planned with such care would be beautiful: the shadow of a musical instrument on a mud wall, gentle lamp light seeping through the slats of a window, the branch of a tree against a star-studded sky.

The work went on without a break for about three and a half hours. At one in the morning a brief halt was called for a meal, but only half an hour later the activity recommenced. The unit's labours were to go on until dawn commenced to creep acrosss the sky and thus to interfere with the lighting.

Long intensive hours for all of the thirty-five to forty days required for the shoot, and this was only the beginning. Cutting, editing, dubbing, music and sound effects was still to come, and would doubtless take much longer. I subsequently made several visits to studios to see this side of film making, and still later, became directly involved myself. On each occasion I caught something of the lure and glamour of the cinema world, but at the same time became increasingly aware of the hard work and commitment required of everybody concerned. In some ways it is a luxurious life but in others it is extremely tough, not an easy profession by any stretch of the imagination. Hence my particular admiration for a man named Majibur.

The cameraman, Mahfuz, had called him "a magician"; and the studio in Bankok awarded him the title of "wizard." He had won the National Award for film editing five times, and yet had been disabled from birth.

Majibur Rahman Dulu lives close to the centre of Dhaka, and our mutual friend, Mahfuz, offered to take me round there. It was a short but amusing journey. Our *baby taxi* got stuck in the alleyway, jammed tightly beside an on-coming rickshaw which had tried to squeeze past us. Our driver seemed unperturbed. He dismounted from his vehicle, and with the same sort of nonchalance he might have applied to removing a few bricks from his path, lifted the fully loaded rickshaw out of the way. The two elderly lady passengers contained therein, let out a muted cry of protest but otherwise all went well.

We climbed the stone staircase to Majibur's apartment and he came smilingly forward to greet us. A smooth-shaven jovial man in his early forties, he walked with a rolling movement which looked both difficult and painful but he did not use any form of aid.

At birth, Majibur told us, his mother had noticed nothing unusual. But when he started to learn to walk it became obvious that something was wrong. By the age of seven, his foot was badly turned over and his parents took him to Dhaka Medical College Hospital. The doctors there explained that the problem was due to "a shortage of tissue" and recommended an operation, but Majibur's mother was too frightened to let him have it.

"I was the only son and very dear to my parents." Majibur explained. "My mother said, 'He can walk, that is enough for me'."

Some benefit was obtained from massage, and after this Majibur did his best to live a normal life. He was determined neither to receive help nor let his disability get in the way of his ambitions. And he was lucky. He always had friends who inspired him and everybody seemed to want to help. He remembers one person who followed him all the way home in order to offer herbal medicines, and an old man who, after watching him everyday from a window, invited Majibur into his house and put him on a course of homoeopathy. Majibur tended not to believe in these sort of treatments but his mother usually insisted on trying. Majibur smiled now as he recounted the story of the herbal medicine. "When mother says something you cannot say 'no'."

Help was also offered by one of the film directors who, when they were both working in Bangkok, took Majibur to the British Red Cross. Again, however Majibur found himself unable to take the treatment advocated. The doctors there wanted him to have a six-month course of therapy, but by now he had a wife and two sons to support and he simply felt unable to take the necessary time off work.

Here, my friend Mahfuz, who was acting as interpreter, added his own explanation.

"For people in our profession," he explained, "it is unthinkable to miss a schedule. If we do so, the producer could face a one million dollar loss." Such an event could presumably have led to the end of Majibur's career.

As we pondered this point, Majibur's wife, Suraya, came in with a tray laden with food. She had a pretty, twinkling face and was dressed in a striking dark purple-blue *salwar kameez* and black *orna*. They had married when they were both very young and Majibur sees her as the greatest of his helpmates. Again Mahfuz elaborated, "When he is happy, I know she is happy. When he is sad, I know she is sad."

As I listened, I viewed with some trepidation the enormous mid-morning snack which had been put before me. How was I, a vegetarian, to choose between the sausage rolls and the hot dogs?

The answer was taken out of my hands. "Come on, eat up." Mahfuz said, placing a large dollop of chilli sauce on my plate. "You have got to eat everything."

I dutifully took one of the hot dogs and tried to bury the taste of meat in the sauce. It was a grave mistake! My mouth felt as if it had filled with fire. I was very glad that someone else was due to do all the talking.

Majibur started out in the film world when he was just fifteen years old. He really wanted to be a cameraman but physically that was impossible. He would not have been able to move the heavy cameras or to work on a crane. Instead he took a two year apprenticeship with his uncle who was already a well known film editor. From there he moved up the ladder of assistant and chief assistant until, in 1975, he edited his first movie.

Majibur smiled broadly at the memory. The film had been called Noyan-moni (Eye and Eyeball) and took the form of a romantic love story coupled with a large dose of village politics.

Nine years later came his first great success, Give Me Food, which premiered in 1984 and brought him the highest award in the country, the coveted National Award. From here, there seemed to be no stopping him. He went on to win the same prize four more times, and also to win the Film Producers Award, The Critics Award and The University Award. Mahfuz indicated the handsome brass sculptures

70

which had been presented on each occasion. They were arranged on two shelves taking pride of place in the centre of the room, and had been among the first possessions to catch my eye when we entered.

I asked Majibur which, of all the great films he had been involved in, was his favourite. He stroked his chin thoughtfully but did not hesitate for long.

"The first one," he said with a smile of certainty.

"Was that because it was your first?"

"No," he didn't think so. Noyan-moni had had a good message. It was about an elderly village leader who thought he could take any beautiful girl he fancied, regardless of age. Through this film, Majibur explained, the village people had come to know that such behaviour was not good and need not be accepted.

So far, Majibur had been telling me about the facts of his life, but now he moved on to talking more about the effects. Working in the film industry could be tough. Sometimes he and his colleagues worked for three or four days and nights without stopping. He remembers one time when he had come home after such a stint and his wife laughed at him when he got undressed to go to the bathroom. He had been sitting so long on the same chair that its mark was imprinted on his back!

Sometimes, he admitted, he does feel frustrated. But he never tells anyone, not even his wife. He just talks to the pillow; or perhaps to the dog.

Here he called Snowy into the room. The little canine had long white hair, a pointed nose and small sharp eyes that viewed me suspiciously. He jumped up on to Majibur's knee, simultaneously wagging his tail for his master and growling at the intruder.

With so many successes to his credit, I wondered whether Majibur still had any unfulfilled ambitions.

"Yes," he said. "I would like to be a producer." He had, apparently, had several opportunities to direct a film, but what he really wanted, was to make one himself. This would mean raising considerable finance but some people had already expressed themselves willing to back him. He smiled, and I had the feeling that in this, as well as in everything else, the Magician might succeed.

As I got up to leave, he invited me to go through to the back to view his courtyard-like balcony, the source he said, of much of his happiness.

I went through somewhat hesitantly, for Snowy, who was now being held in the back room, was furious at the increased intrusion. The balcony, though, was a pleasure. I describe it as courtyard-like because it had a concrete floor and high walls around which were arranged a profusion of pot plants. On the far side, the crest of a heavily laden coconut palm provided a pleasant backdrop and simultaneously obscured the outside world.

Majibur reached up and picked a cluster of deep pink florets from one of the shrubs he had grown. It was the only flower at that moment in bloom in his garden; and with typical Bangladeshi hospitality, he presented it to me.

CHAPTER FOUR

LOST IN DHAKA — **ABU TALEB: GOVERNMENT OFFICER** — LEPROSY: TOO EARLY TO DECLARE VICTORY — NORTH TO NILPHAMARI — **ROBI: RICKSHAW MECHANIC** — **SHOMBARI AND ANJEARA: VILLAGE TAILORS**

I was sure we had come to the right place. The whole of the front of the building was covered with the huge puce faces of film stars.

"Go to the Shamoly Cinema Hall," my friends at CRP had advised. "And then go into any shop and show them this note in Bangla. Everybody will know where Abu Taleb lives. His place is easy to find."

My *baby taxi* driver did as I asked and took the note into a shop beside the cinema. They looked at it with puzzled expressions and then started to argue about the whereabouts of the Roads and Highways Department, the complex in which Abu lived.

The driver returned to the vehicle looking far from confident.

"Alright?" I inquired.

"Alright."

We started up the road beside the cinema, and asked a second group of people who gave much the same response as the first; although, after considerable discussion, they decided that we were probably aiming in the right direction. Alas, they were wrong. Many potholes later, we came to a pharmacy and were directed back whence we came.

Seven times we repeated our enquiry. *Punjabi*-clad shop keepers, we tried, security guards erect in khaki, and even a cluster of blue-shirted policemen leaning idly on their guns. Between them they sent us back and forth and round about for a good forty minutes. One of the most unnerving aspects of this sort of exercise is that when the driver is told to turn round and go back the other way, he does exactly that, without making any attempt to cross over! Thus I found myself constantly tearing up the wrong side of the road in the face of all oncoming traffic.

It was time to take charge, I decided. And with more mime than language, attempted to tell the driver that I would like to go back to a telephone shop recently spotted on one of the side roads. But my efforts were useless. As we continued along the main thoroughfare, it became increasingly apparent that the communication lines between us simply had to be improved. We stopped at another group of people and I asked whether any of them spoke English, an inquiry which was greeted with a lovely smile by one eager to try out his skills. My desire to go to the telephone shop was now confidently converted into Bangla.

"Alright?" I asked my driver for about the fifth time.

"Alright."

With a splutter, the engine bounced into action and we roared up the road – straight past the required turning. Impatience grabbed hold of me. In self-surprising manner, I tapped the driver smartly on the shoulder and delivered firm instructions to turn back.

For once he did as he was asked, and although he did not look happy, I managed to get him to stop in the right place. Now at last we could ask directions from the one person who was sure to know. Wondering why a moment ago it had all seemed so difficult, I motioned for the driver to follow, and walked happily into the shop. It never occurred to me that the poor man might not wish to enter. With enormous reluctance he got out of his vehicle, advanced half way across the pavement and then came to a stop.

"Please come in." My polite request was augmented by the shop-keeper to an insistent, "Come in. Come in. Come in."

Hesitantly the driver opened the heavy glass door, looked round uncertainly and then withdrew. I left him to the merciless encouragement of the shopkeeper and dialled the number. Abu himself answered; and after explaining our situation, I held out the receiver. The driver sidled cautiously up to the equipment and lifted the handpiece with the tips of his fingers as if it was red hot. Terrified, he held the receiver about a foot away from his head whilst making every pretence of listening. He gave the nasal sounding "yes" at intervals and finally, *"Tik ache"*, those now ominous-sounding little words which should mean "alright." Then, very carefully, he returned

74

the receiver to its cradle. Had he heard the directions? I shall never know. On getting back into the vehicle we careered off up the road and shot straight past the gate which I later learnt belonged to Abu.

My sanity was saved by the tenth group of people. They actually knew the man we were seeking, and one of them was even prepared to get on board the *baby taxi* in order to act as navigator. And so at last, we reached our destination – a building we had passed many times before.

Abu was sitting in his wheelchair on the porch, obviously on the look out for his visitors. A handsome man, probably in his mid-forties, he welcomed us with a smile and indicated that we should enter the main room. This was surprisingly large, and having little furniture, felt unusually spacious. The few chairs were low and comfortable and an interrupted game of patience on the computer screen added to the general atmosphere of relaxation.

Not so my host. He was very much on his guard. Clearly he felt cautious about the interview, even though I came as a friend of Valerie Taylor, the person to whom, he later told me, he owed his life.

He asked many questions about my proposed book, but then quite suddenly plunged into action.

"We need to make a barrier free environment," he said "India is much better. Here everywhere there are steps. Look at the market, always steps. Sometimes they have lifts, but they have no ramps so you cannot get to the lifts. And public transport is totally out of reach for the crippled. Friends in the UK say it is no problem there."

Abu Taleb is a Fellow of the Institute of Engineers and an executive engineer with the Government Department of Roads and Highways. He knew his subject; and he went on to explain that Bangladesh does have a Building Code, carefully written to ensure access for all, but that in practice the rules are not followed.

I was shortly to learn the sad irony that this man, who had devoted his working life to the improvement of roads, was himself the victim of a traffic accident. The paralysis, from which he suffered from the waist down, was the result of a car crash.

"After my accident," Abu explained. "I could find no hope. How was I to get around? How to move? To Valerie Taylor I owe my life.

I have the courage now to move anywhere."

Whilst Abu Taleb was still a patient at her small hospital in Dhaka, Valerie had got him going back to his office part-time. And after four months he was able to resume his previous position. But although Valerie had encouraged him, and rebuilt his confidence, it was in this case actually the Government who made his return possible.

"They were very kind," Abu told me, "very helpful. They widened the doorways, and provided a ramp into the office. And though I am in a wheelchair, I try to do – not only try to do, but actually do – all my jobs."

This was clearly no false claim. Little more than a year after the accident, Abu got promotion to Executive Engineer.

As we talked, Mrs Taleb entered the room with a tray of food. The culinary aspect of my research interviews was becoming increasingly interesting. I was now offered *chola*, a small spiced bean mixed with *muri* or fried rice, a tasty snack traditionally eaten at the end of the Ramadan fast.

It was certainly a filling dish. I ate slowly as Abu described his work. And having satisfied herself that I was well supplied, Mrs Taleb settled on the floor beside us in order to continue work on a new back for her husband's wheelchair.

His first job after promotion was administrative. He dealt with the transfers and posting of staff, liaised with the Ministry, and scrutinised papers relating to complaints. Then four or five years later, he moved to the Road Research Laboratory where he still works.

What, I asked, had been the greatest problem he had encountered since becoming disabled?

"Presently, no problem. The people who are with me, my colleagues, pick me up when it is necessary to go upstairs. I appreciate all my colleagues, and bosses also. My driver has been with me since July 1984. They are all invaluable to me because, without their help, I cannot go."

Did he think things were improving generally for the disabled in Bangladesh?

"I cannot comment," came as the immediate reaction. And for a moment I wondered to what extent all Abu's answers might be drowned in caution. But his next words rung with conviction. "Some things have improved. Awareness for example – at least once a year there is a Disability Day covered by the TV and in the newspapers. It is about attitude; and now, if I go anywhere with only one companion, somebody else always offers to help. Wherever you seek assistance there are people ready to give it."

As he talked I realised an enormous variation in attitude between the rural poor of Bangladesh and the urban educated of whom Abu spoke.

I had already read about this with regard to mental retardation. In a research paper of the Asian Journal of Psychology and Education, Dr Sultana Zaman records that 85 per cent of the rural general public were found to consider mental retardation "a curse from God", whereas only 7.5 per cent of the urban general public were of the same belief.

What Abu Taleb was saying now, when compared with what I had heard elsewhere, indicated that a similar gap in attitude applied to physical disability. I had been appalled, when listening to people from the villages, by the degree of fear and superstition surrounding the disabled. But the experience of Abu amongst his colleagues in Dhaka had been quite different. And as he pointed out, his very existence at the Department of Highways was proof of a congenial environment – "If there was superstition, I could not work."

It is a difference which exists, not only between the urban and the rural, but also between the educated and the uneducated. "There is some (superstition) maybe," Abu conceded later, "at the bottom level, among the lower classes. Some of the illiterate poorer classes may believe in evil winds."

Regarding the plight of disabled women, Abu agreed that they had less privilege, but added that he believed this to be true of women in his society generally.

Was there anything, I wondered, that could be done about road safety in Bangladesh?

"In my department," Abu replied "there is a Road Safety Division who try to increase safety on the roads. But what can you do? Is there anything they can do? I assume they try to eliminate the problems, but if a driver drives at high speed nothing can be done."

"Bangladesh roads," he added with pride, "are much better than those in India, much wider, much smoother." As I listened, I made a mental note to be extraordinarily careful about travelling on the Indian highways!

For my final question I asked Abu if there were any big changes he would like to see with regard to the condition of disabled people in Bangladesh.

"Big changes?" He thought about it for a moment before answering. "I would like to see disabled people able to work anywhere. Private organisations will find disabled people are most sincere. It is not easy to get another job. They do not want to risk loosing the one they have."

Somehow the talk of work led to his computer.

"Computer is a great subject for me, but at this age I cannot learn which finger should hit each key. But now I do have a good speed. In my office I type many of my own letters in Bangla as well as in English."

We went on to talk about the importance of hobbies and relaxation, and laughed together about his card game. Then his daughter came in and displayed her good English. Abu has two children, one in Class 10 and one in Class 12, and both will go on to higher education. They were a bright and cheerful family who gave all the appearance of having conquered the worst trials of the disabled. When they invited me to lunch I wished I could stay.

Superstition and fear – the words were to come up repeatedly during my travels around Bangladesh, but with few diseases or disabilities are these two responses so undeniably connected as they are to leprosy. In many countries of the world, little has changed since the early days of the Old Testament when the author of Leviticus gave instructions as to how sufferers should be treated.

"And the leper in whom the plague is, his clothes shall be rent, and his head bare, and he shall put a covering upon his upper lip, and shall cry, 'Unclean, unclean'. All the days wherein the plague shall be in him he shall be defiled; he is unclean: he shall dwell alone; without the camp shall his habitation be."

Two years ago, Bangladesh was placed third from the top in a world league table recording the incidence of leprosy. Now it is almost thirtieth.

"But," says Dr Jonathan Quimpo of the Leprosy Mission, "It is too early to declare victory." He points to the inaccuracy of all statistics relating to the disease and explains that nobody really knows how many cases there are.

Most of the figures available are based on clinical symptoms, skin patches and signs of paralysis, but the incubation period averages eight years and can be anything up to thirty. Then there is the problem as to when you consider a patient cured. Modern multi drug therapy (MDT) is very effective but it takes a long time for the body to reject the bacteria which cause the disease. MDT is usually given for three years in the belief that the body will continue the rejecting process. Sometimes, however, this does not happen, and patients suffer a relapse after about seven years.

Yet another complicating factor, as far as the statistics are concerned, is the fear experienced by sufferers. Many are simply too frightened to go to a doctor; and as a result, a significant proportion of all cases remain unrecorded. Thus it could be said that the number of registered patients is, in reality, no more than a measure of medical activity.

"The logical conclusion from trusting such figures," Dr Quimpo added jokingly, "is that if you close all clinics you eliminate leprosy."

The fear and stigma which prevent sufferers going to a doctor are in themselves the cause of some of the most intractable problems relating to the disease. Fear, I was told, is due not so much to the initial symptoms as to the disability which may result. Leprosy attacks the peripheral nervous system and can bring about a selective paralysis. One set of muscles may become paralysed whilst the others not, a dysfunction likely to result in foot drop and clawing of hands. Paralysis can also affect the eye, causing it to dry up and make the sufferer blind. At the same time loss of normal skin flexibility invariably leads to a dryness and cracking whereby the skin looses its protective layer and becomes vulnerable to infection and ulcers. Such secondary infection often necessitates amputation and it is this, rather than the leprosy bacteria itself, which is the most usual cause of digit loss. Only occasionally, and in very severe cases which have never been treated, are bones actually absorbed into the body.

Happily, there is now a dramatic reduction in the number of patients suffering such serious long term effects. Much can be done to prevent disability. Surgical correction, removal of dry skin, appropriate exercises, together with protection of eyes and desensitised limbs, all such methods can be applied effectively. For patients without disability, there need not be too much of a problem in getting back into the community. But for those who are disabled, the situation is very different. It was in order to find out how these people fared, that a friend and I took a plane up north to visit the Leprosy Mission Hospital at Nilphamari.

We left Dhaka in brilliant sunshine but landed in Saidpur amongst a mass of black clouds. For some reason too an unexpected and total silence descended upon the passengers even before we to came to a halt. It seemed we had dropped into a eerily dark and muffled world.

Leaving the airport we found ourselves surrounded by acres of brilliant paddy stretched remorselessly under a glowering sky. In brightness the earth pulled at the heavens. And when the rain came it did so in thick unrelenting sheets, instantly obscuring fields, houses and people.

At the Leprosy Mission we were welcomed by Juan, wife of the Project Director, and next day she took us on her own self-styled "Grand Tour",

The hospital is attractively laid out round the four sides of a square central garden. Juan led us first to the women's ward and here we heard some very sad stories. One woman had been married at the age of ten but her husband left her a few years later when she contracted leprosy and developed an ulcer. Worse still, he had taken their baby daughter; and the child, being not yet weaned, had died of hunger. The poor woman wept as she related the details. I watched her wiping her eyes with the edge of her sari, and I could think of little to say.

Another had lost her entire family in the War of Independence; and now, severely paralysed as a result of leprosy, was left all alone in the world. She could not work, for her fingers were permanently clawed up, and her feet deformed. She had virtually no toes. Begging provided her only means of survival.

Leaving this ward, we came to an open area where a group of male patients were sitting with their feet in bowls of water. This is a regular treatment, after which the dry hard skin on the foot is scraped or cut away to prevent it from cracking and developing ulcers.

Walking past the kitchens and the laundry, where the bed sheets are boiled in enormous cauldrons, we came to the Self-Care Centre. Here patients can learn to look after themselves in a village setting and so prepare for returning home.

Next came the Physiotherapy Department where we met the Disability Prevention Officer and learnt about surgical correction, remedial exercises and hot wax therapy, all of which can be used to reduce the long term effects of the disease. Finally to the shoe department to look at protective footwear, and to the Training Unit which runs courses in woodwork, tailoring, household electricity and rickshaw maintenance. The work here looked impressive, but to understand its real value it would be necessary to visit the local community.

That afternoon the weather was gorgeous. The paddy looked radiant under a perfect white and azure sky. The floods had receded, but there was still enough water for ducks to swim contently amongst the rice plants. And everywhere cows lay peacefully sleeping along the edge of tree-lined roads. It was an idyllic rural setting which once again belied the suffering and struggle faced by many who lived there.

We came to a village bazaar and Alam, the accompanying field officer, pointed out a closed bicycle maintenance shop. It was owned by Robi Kanto, the ex-patient whose home we were en route to visit. A few minutes later we got out of the vehicle and started to walk across the fields.

Helpful villagers appeared almost immediately, and then led us in single file along the narrow raised path to Robi's bamboo bari. One of our guides, darting ahead, carried news of the visit, and we got a brief glimpse of our man scuttling across the compound into his house. A pair of trousers pursued him in the hand of a neighbour, and within a few minutes Robi re-emerged, dressed and ready to greet us.

He was a tiny man with a wrinkled face, grey hair and stubble beard. Round his neck hung a double row of beads and he wore very thick glasses through which he peered up at us with a slightly bemused expression.

We wandered round the house to the shade of some trees and somebody brought out a wooden bench on which I could sit beside our host.

The villagers gathered round with typical unabashed curiosity to see what would happen next. The men, with a row of young boys lined up in front of them, stood closest to the action, whilst much further back, and a little out of the way, stood a cluster of women in their colourful saris. They were all quite silent and very serious, lending the whole occasion an air of importance and even *gravitas*. Alam, declining to sit, became the Master of Ceremonies. He was a kindly and relaxed translator and I was grateful to him, for I had no idea which questions Robi would be happy to answer before so large and attentive an audience.

Asked his age, Robi himself thought that he was probably now around eighty, although the facts of his life and the information available from the Leprosy Mission, led me to estimate that he was more likely to be in his mid-fifties. It seemed certain, however, that his leprosy became manifest when he was about forty and working as a farmer with a small amount of land in another village. He remembered the onset as a generalised experience of pain and the appearance of skin patches all over his body.

Robi went first to a government doctor for treatment and then to the Mission. By this time, his left foot was anaesthetised and he had an ulcer; but he was careful not to tell anyone that he had contracted leprosy. When his wife eventually found out, she divorced him, his sister deserted, and the community condemned him to isolation. The disease was surrounded by fear and superstition, and Robi himself believed that someone had put a spell on him. Up to a point, I suspect, he still believed this at the time of our visit.

The Leprosy Mission put Robi on multi drug therapy for three years, and at the end of the treatment his test proved negative. Special shoes to protect his feet were also provided, as was health education with regard to hand and foot care, and finally, a training in cycle and rickshaw maintenance. All this helped a great deal, but the real challenge had to be faced by Robi, and Robi alone. He had to return to a frightened and antagonistic community and within this environment to set about earning a living.

He decided to go to a new village in order to start afresh. But it was not as simple as that. Once again he had to confront the fact that his neighbours felt unable to accept him. The villagers standing around Robi that sunny afternoon several years later, agreed that they had been genuinely terrified of catching the disease. But now, they said, things were different. They remembered the slide show put on by the Mission and a drama done by the leprosy patients themselves. A Leprosy Control Officer had also made regular visits to their homes. Now they were no longer afraid, and anyway, "Robi was a good cycle mechanic."

It had been difficult at first, Robi explained. No one would visit his shop but then, gradually, a few people came and then more and more. Now he had customers from other villages as well.

His business was successful, but, he added sadly, he still had personal problems. He had no one to cook for him or wash his clothes. He had to do everything for himself, a really terrible situation for any man in Bangladesh, and it was getting more and more difficult now that his sight had become impaired as well.

Robi had, in fact, been cooking when we arrived, but he laughed a little nervously when I asked if I could see how he managed. Rather doubtfully, he led us to the little bamboo hut which served as his kitchen. The "stove" was a round hollow in the mud floor into which dry sticks were fed through a scooped out channel.

Leprosy had desensitised Robi's hands, and he had been taught by the Mission to be very careful when lifting hot metal pots; but I sensed that he was not, perhaps, as conscientious about the rules as he should be. He had to run over to the house in order to find the two tatty pieces of cloth which acted as oven gloves, and when reminded that he should be using a much larger and thicker piece of material, he expressed himself frightened that it might catch fire.

The most encouraging thing about his situation now, was the way the other villagers stood round in order to assist and advise. Robi was very much part of their community. As we turned our backs and said our farewells, the whole "audience" burst into a wild and excited chorus of chatter.

Later we drove south to visit Anjeara and her husband Shombari.

After leaving Nilphamari, the road gradually degenerated. At one point the ruts and mud became so deep that it looked unlikely that we could proceed any further.

"We need a landrover." the driver said despondently, as both he and Alam got out to weigh up the possibilities of getting through. Somehow we managed it, but we then had to take the car onto such a narrow causeway, that one could imagine even the slightest wobble on the steering wheel taking us off the edge and into the paddy. But our driver's concentration was good, and we got safely to some outlying houses before taking the final leg of our journey on foot.

Once again we were met by villagers happy to lead the way.

Anjeara was combing her hair when we arrived at her *bari*. She stuck the bright green plastic comb on the back of her head and came smilingly out to greet us. Having contracted leprosy when she was only eight years old, she now had one artificial leg.

On walking into her compound, the first thing I noticed was the cradle. Wooden and crate-like, indeed it might have had a former life as a crate, it hung splendidly on a jute rope from the ceiling of the open-sided kitchen, and was so placed that Anjeara could rock the baby and see to the cooking at the same time. She had three children, a boy of eight, a girl of three and the baby of three months. This last was gathered up into her arms whilst the rest of the villagers organised proceedings.

Anjeara and I were both ordered to sit down. I was given a bench and Anjeara provided with a low stool in front of me. She sat Madonna-like cradling the infant against her breast, and for the first time I took in the full beauty of her face: oval shape, high cheek bones, smooth complexion and gentle smile.

It was now many years since the initial onset of the disease. There had been one recent relapse, but after a second course of treatment, Anjeara was once again pronounced recovered.

When she had first become ill as a child, her mother also had leprosy and her family were isolated. But Anjeara was sent to boarding school at The Leprosy Mission and thus escaped the threat of loneliness. She completed five years of education, and at the age of fourteen, married another leprosy patient at the Centre. Such arrangements are quite common, for marriage into a family without leprosy is almost impossible.

Anjeara's husband had by now entered the compound and taken his seat beside Alam. He was a tailor, and as if to advertise his profession, wore a particularly smart green and white floral shirt.

Shombari had done his tailoring course at the Mission and then come back into his own village to set up his business. It could not have been easy. The small muscles in his hands were weak and wasted, and his feet were very deformed, but he and Anjeara had made a successful working partnership. Shombari did the cutting and worked the treadle machine and Anjeara did the sewing by hand.

At this point, the interview was interrupted and Alam explained to me that the young couple had a problem which they wished to discuss. In order to give them his full attention, he would not, for a little while, stop to translate. The point in question was solely concerned with Shombari's own business arrangements, but nevertheless, all the neighbours took part in the deliberations. Shortly the matter was resolved. Everyone had agreed that Shombari needed a permanent stall in the market and Alam had offered to talk to the local Chairman.

Most of the neighbours in this village, I was told, had been helpful and supportive from the very beginning. Even so, at first it was only those who knew Shombari well who were actually prepared to buy the things he made. Business had gradually improved, but before the harvest no one here had any money to spare. At a good time of year Shombari could earn fifty *taka* a day (about sixty-five pence) but at the moment, because of the season, it was only ten to fifteen *taka* (about twenty pence). Determined not to be beaten, Shombari had developed a sideline dealing in hens. He went round the houses buying the chickens off the other villagers and then took the birds to market.

There was much laughter as Alam teased Anjeara that, if she did not pay the nominal two hundred *taka* for her new prothesis soon, he would retaliate by cutting off her head. Then more laughter when the villagers apparently told Alam that he looked like a film star. On looking again at my guide, I could not but agree with them. Alam had wavy hair and long-lashed laughing eyes which would certainly look good on screen.

Turning the conversation back to more serious matters, I asked if Shombari and Anjeara had any message for other leprosy patients. Shombari was quick with a reply, "If you see any early signs of leprosy take treatment at once." He and Anjeara, he said, had already found two people with the disease. They had sent them for treatment quickly, and both were now fine.

At my request, Shombari then went to fetch some of his work, a selection of children's clothes including a pretty little dress with ruffled yoke, front panel in a different material, and edging of lace. Something like this, he said, he could make in about half an hour.

Before leaving, I asked what had been the greatest problem they had had to encounter. Again the answer came without hesitation.

"Stigma. When people say you have leprosy, and particularly if you have deformities, they will not buy from you. And they will put others off as well."

CHAPTER FIVE

LIPY: TRAINER – JOURNEY TO BHOLA ISLAND – JOYNAL: TRAINEE
– THE HINDU PUJA – HOSSAIN: VILLAGE SHOPKEEPER

The moment we stepped into their apartment the electricity failed, and we were plunged into darkness. "Welcome to our new home!" The words were accompanied by laughter, as the girls searched for candles.

Nupur was an outstanding student, one whom you would notice both for her intelligence and for her eloquence, especially on the subject of women's rights. To the outsider, the severe limp, resulting from an attack of polio when she was one year old, seemed unimportant, but for Nupur it had led to a major struggle. In this, she said, she had been greatly helped by her friendship with other disabled women. They had been able to understand and support her in a way that nobody else, not even her loving family, were able to do. Key amongst these friends was Lipy, with whom Nupur now shared a flat. And it was in order to meet her, that Feroz and I had been invited to dinner.

As it happened, I could see very little of Lipy as we said "Hello". In the dark, it was just possible to make out a tiny figure in a low wheelchair, a small oval face, and sparkling eyes cleverly complimented by dangling white earrings.

It was a pleasant and spacious flat, and they said, reasonably priced, although they had had some difficulty persuading the landlord to let it to two disabled women. A sitting room led off the main reception area and was comfortably furnished with cane chairs, a desk for Nurpur's studies, and a couple of large and handsome pot plants. In pride of place were two very blond Cindy-type dolls, erstwhile childhood toys of Lipy's, but now claimed with considerable delight by Nurpur.

Dinner, to my western way of thinking, seemed upside down. We had black coffee and cake as a starter while Lipy was talking, and then moved on to *dal*, vegetables and *rooti*.

Lipy was one of five children born to a "typical middle class family" in Baraishal. "I arrived very early in the morning. My mother said I couldn't wait. One of my aunties went to get a nurse, but when they returned I was out."

The family noticed a little bump on Lipy's back but they did not think it a problem. Her father, who was a social welfare officer, had very little time, and not until the bump grew, did they realise that they needed help.

"At eight months I was standing up, but at nine months I was falling down; and the local doctor did not know what to do." A family friend raised the money to take Lipy to Dhaka, but the specialist there professed himself frighted to operate. More money was provided, and this time Lipy was taken to Karachi to see a world famous neurosurgeon, a dedicated man who berated her father for delaying treatment so long.

"I don't know why I'm always lucky." Lipy said somewhat surprisingly at this juncture in the story. The great doctor, she explained, had just completed a thirteen-hour stint of brain surgery when he saw her, but rather than wait any longer, he gave himself just three hours break before embarking on an eight hour operation on Lipy.

He found that the little girl now had two layers of tumour. "I've saved her life," he told the family, "But she will always be disabled." This was something Lipy's father was just not prepared to believe. Determinedly, he went on trying to find a cure.

They were, Lipy reiterated, "a typical Bengali family". Their reaction to her plight was to look after her, take great care of her in every way, but never to realise that she needed to learn anything. "What will she do with a certificate?" they said. "She will never get a job." By the time she was twenty-five, Lipy had still not been to school or received any formal education.

"I remember my mother telling people how lucky she was to have me because she thought I would never leave her." Lipy recalled laughingly. "But I was the first to go."

She learnt to read and write by imitating her brothers and sisters. Her elder brother also started to provide a little teaching and occasionally organised general knowledge competitions, for which he even awarded prizes.

By the time she reached her twenties, Lipy had spent her entire life virtually hidden from the outside world. One friend of the family, was actually surprised when he learned of her existence. Mr Hoq worked with her aunt and thought he knew all the relations.

"But I liked to hide myself." Lipy explained. "I hated patronage."

This new acquaintance was the founder of an organisation called Social Assistance and Rehabilitation for the Physically Vulnerable (SARPV) and he now sought Lipy out and provided a challenge. By use of a few subtle questions, Mr Hoq made it clear that, since Lipy herself was assured of a secure future, she should consider her responsibilities to other disabled people.

"But how am going to help?" Lipy asked.

"If you come to my organisation, you will see how you can help." came the unequivocal reply. " My 'yes' ", Lipy told me now, "was not a very loud one, but my mother pushed."

The first few days at SARPV seemed quite boring; but then Lipy had the idea of starting a school for the street children. These youngsters, she explained, had to earn their living by doing something like selling peanuts or collecting papers, so it was not possible for them to go to school during normal hours. Lipy collected together a few of them and provided non-formal education at a time of day when they could attend.

While thus employed, she met someone else who was to make a major impact on her life. The Red Cross worker, Julian Francis, pushed Lipy forward and recommended that she be given more responsibility. In no time at all she found herself President of SARPV.

"Absolutely nuts!" was her comment to me now. "I went there in January, and by June, I was President. Can you imagine?"

She had never seen a computer before and did not know how to write English. "I got a twenty-four page notebook and went to my younger sister. It took about seven days (to learn how to write)."

Soon she was doing all sorts of things, helping the street children get prescriptions, looking after the general administration and attending discussion groups.

It was at this point that she met Douglas, her current boss. He came to Bangladesh from Indonesia to evaluate one of the workshops for Community Based Rehabilitation (CBR) workers and she had a "big argument" with him about women's rights. It was a discussion which convinced Douglas that he had found someone of tremendous determination and eloquence. He invited Lipy to the workshop he was organising in Indonesia and, in doing so, used words that made it sound easy: "It will be very good if you come and talk about the things you have just said."

"Why not?" Lipy thought, although she confessed to me now, "I didn't know I had to present a paper." But anyway, she went, and in telling the story, emphasised with pride that she travelled alone, "All by myself."

After her return, Douglas and his wife Laura continued to talk to Lipy about their ideas for a project which would integrate disability and development. They needed trainers, and they wanted her. Finally they won; Lipy agreed to join them. She had liked SARPV, but felt a certain lack of fulfilment, and the future offered a challenge.

Douglas proved to be a particularly good guide. "I am not very patient or organised" Lipy confided, "Douglas made me see what I should be doing, and Laura showed me how."

In November 1996 the new project became a separate organisation under the title CDD (Centre for Disability and Development). The purpose was to provide training for CBR workers, and by the time of my visit, CDD was proud to have 112 partners, all of which sent trainees to the Centre. In just three years, Lipy and her colleagues had trained more than one thousand workers and reached over seven thousand disabled people.

"That is the reason I really love this job." Lipy told me, her eyes shining. "It is helping us to reach so many, and the beauty of it is, I can see the result."

As well as being a trainer, she is now the Assistant Coordinator in the Training Department, and as such, has additional responsibility for resources and materials, plus the opportunity to travel out to the villages.

"When I go to do the follow up, I see people I have trained; and they are helping so many disabled people. When I see this with my own eyes, it is really good."

At this point, our conversation was interrupted by a call from Nurpur, and we all moved through to the other room for the *dal* and vegetables. As is frequently the custom in Bangladesh, we ate more or less in silence while everyone appreciated the good food. Our conversation then turned to the thorny and oft-repeated subject of social awareness.

"The biggest problem is other people's attitudes." Lipy commented. "I am glad I have the opportunity to work in this area."

"At the beginning I tried to shock people by going to fairs and other public places. I wanted them to realise that we existed. Nurpur and I, and a couple of other disabled friends, went to a book fair, and people asked, 'What are those disabled people doing here? They should be in hospital.' "

Lipy was silent for a moment while Nurpur embellished the story. Then she added, more thoughtfully, "But now I am trying to think about why these attitudes have developed. I have realised that, as disabled people are kept behind the scenes, the rest of society is not used to seeing them. So it is fear. So in many ways it is up to disabled people. They have to learn that they are not objects. They must over-come their fears and integrate. Both the able-bodied and the disabled have to change their attitudes. It is a two-way process. If people don't know about you, they will be afraid. There is a real lack of information about disability, and CDD is trying to fill the gap. There are lots of superstitions etcetera and these have to be replaced by scientific knowledge."

There was a pause while I scribbled away in my notebook. Throughout our conversation, vivacity and strength of character had exuded from every pore of the diminutive figure in front of me. Firoz, who had only known Lipy slightly before, had been quietly listening, obviously fascinated, all evening. Now he addressed me tentatively but with a note of urgency "Do you know what time it is?"

I did not. The evening had fairly galloped away and it was time to leave. But Lipy had left her impression – that of a tiny lady of enormous stature.

$$\text{\Large ❖ \quad ❖ \quad ❖}$$

For the Puja Holiday, I found myself embarking upon a trip with an element of mystery. I had decided that I would like to visit the island of Bhola, and for five days had been attempting to make telephone contact with InterLife, a Swedish development organisation working in that area.

Telephone lines from Savar to Dhaka are constantly engaged, and getting through at all is a real headache. In this case, doing so when the right person was available seemed almost impossible. I had tried on Friday and Saturday, then made very brief contact with Ms Henderson, the Coordinator, on Sunday morning and been told to ring her back again later in the day.

As instructed, I rung just after 3 p.m. The line was engaged. I stayed by the telephone attempting the call every two or three minutes and eventually got through at 3.45 p.m. Ms Henderson, I was told, had just left. It was suggested that I wait ten minutes and then ring her home number. I did so, but it was busy. I tried again, and again, and at long last made contact with someone in the house. Ms Henderson had gone out. I was advised to ring back after 6 p.m. When the time came, there was no reply.

At 8pm I walked out to the little telephone shop outside the gate, for what, I had decided, would be my very last attempt. Whatever the outcome, I would leave for Bhola next day.

The young boy at the counter welcomed me cheerily; we felt as if we were getting to know each other quite well. He tried the number and immediately got through. But, so surprised and excited was he at this, that in handing me the receiver, he pulled it right out of its socket!

But the fact was that Ms Henderson was at home; and eventually a conversation of sorts was achieved. The problem this time, was that someone at the telephone exchange seemed to be even better at cutting me off than the boy in the shop. After every two or three minutes the line went dead and I had to start again. The result was the piecemeal collection of limited information. Yes, we could visit the project on Bhola. Redial: someone would be at the office to meet us on the twentieth. Redial: they would have a car and they would take us somewhere. Where was it they would they take us? For what purpose? The line had died finally and irrevocably.

But it was not all so difficult. Nupur, I discovered, had family on Bhola and she was delighted with an invitation to act as travelling companion and interpreter. She could also help with arrangements. At her suggestion, we left CRP early in the afternoon in order to avoid the holiday crowds, and went first to her parents' home in Dhaka. Here I received a warm but confusing welcome. I could not sort out who was who from amongst father, uncle, brothers and brothers-in-law.

The mother herself would have been obvious even if there had been twenty women on the premises. She was a lovely, gentle and caring lady who busied herself in the kitchen for the whole of my two hour stay, first plying me with delicious food, then making and packing an enormous supply for the overnight trip.

We were accompanied to the port by one of Nupur's brothers, a dazzlingly handsome national "black belt". Once again the road to Sadarghat was heavily congested, and we had doubts about catching the boat. But we made it just in time. Black Belt saw us into the security of our own cabin and, before departing, gave the crew strict instructions about looking after us during the journey.

Left to our own devices, the sense of adventure mounted. Nupur seemed as excited about the trip as I was. Young women in Bangladesh do not often have the opportunity to do much travelling without the supervision of their family, and in the light of this, the first person we talked to came as quite a surprise. The two of us had taken a walk along the deck and, on returning, found a lone woman sitting out in the gangway. She had been too late to secure a cabin, and with typical generosity, Nupur invited her to share ours. Momentarily I wondered how exactly we were going to cope, but I had temporarily forgotten that it is common custom, in Bangladesh, to sleep two or three to a bed.

Anjou was a newly-wed geography graduate going back to her native Bhola in order to attend an interview. This she was doing, she said, just to keep her parents happy. She had absolutely no intention

93

of taking the job and was therefore thoroughly relaxed about it. So saying, she curled herself up on Nupur's bed and went fast asleep.

The launch left on time at 8 p.m. and Nupur and I stayed up long enough to watch an enormous cargo of rice being loaded into the hold at our first stop. Additional entertainment was unintentionally provided here by a little group on the quay. One of the men had dropped his shoe into the water. It was a cheap plastic sandal, and in England, would have been considered lost in a murky river deep enough to support a vessel such as ours. Not so in Bangladesh – the depths were probed with long poles, and eventually a boy lowered himself to the river surface by hanging onto a quayside chain. A few impressive acrobats later, the missing shoe was secured.

We tucked into mother's food, including delicious *bapa pitta*, and lay down early. Sleep was elusive but it did not matter. I was content to feel the gentle movement of the vessel and to listen to the sounds of a night on board: hindi music, the rattling and shuddering of the ship's bodywork, someone hawking, the murmur of voices and, underlying it all, the gentle hum of the engine and swish of water. Quite soon, it seemed, I heard the morning call to prayer.

Dawn was beautiful. The sun, trying unsuccessfully to break through the clouds, graced them with rare patches and borders of gold. The surrounding paddy and palm trees appeared gentle in the morning light. Out on the water, occasional flashes of lightening broke dramatically over a myriad of tiny fishing boats.

We no longer had ports or even landing stages, just high muddy banks into which the vessel pushed its nose, and onto which the crew threw a narrow plank for the use of those embarking and disembarking. I was somewhat relieved, when we arrived at Bhola, to find that we had something a little more substantial along which to walk.

Anjou and the friend who met her, gave us a lift in their *baby taxi*, and for this we were particularly grateful. The clouds which had so delighted me at dawn were now emptying themselves heavily upon everything below.

Nupur had been unable to tell her relatives that we were coming. Nevertheless they gave us an incredibly enthusiastic welcome. The sudden, unexpected appearance of a cousin in search of beds for the night, for both herself and a totally unknown foreigner, did not appear to throw them in the least. I was the only one to be confused, this time by the numerous females of the tribe: aunts, cousins, cousins-in-law and all their daughters. Once again I could not sort them out.

After washing and eating, Nupur and I set off to find the offices of InterLife, and to continue the dialogue so unhelpfully interrupted by Bangladesh Telephone. Perhaps, now, we would discover where they planned to take us.

It was as promised, two people were waiting and they had a car. After the usual formalities, we were able to set off for a visit to the home of Abul Kasem, one of their clients.

We found it to be a wooden house on stilts. The family had previously lived in a different area and had lost their home three times when the river broke its banks. Abul Kasem, a religious man with mullah-like beard, was dressed in white *punjabi* and red and white headdress. He greeted us with half closed eyes and provided a reception which was, at the same time, both politely cautious and overwhelmingly hospitable. His second son, Joynal, had been born with two club feet, and Abul clearly felt very indebted to InterLife for the help they had given him.

Joynal was now seventeen and had started to learn tailoring from his father whilst at the same time continuing his studies at the local *madrasa*. The *madrasas* are religious schools at which the children study the Koran as well as learning Bangla, Arabic, Urdu, English and mathematics. Both boys and girls can attend but they sit separately and must be appropriately dressed, the girls by wearing the all-covering *burkha* and the boys, the white *punjabi* and *topi*. This indeed was how Joynal was clad when we made our visit. He sat down beside us on the big double bed which filled the front room, and smilingly dangled his legs to show off the success of the surgery already completed on his right foot. The left was still drastically twisted, but the other was now straight, with a neat surgical scar. All being well, a second operation in a few months time would result in two good feet.

At school, Joynal told us, some of the boys were very helpful, but others teased him and called him "bad names". Sometimes also, the adults in the community gave him the title of "Langra", an unfortunate term for cripple, and they had dubbed the house with a shortened and even worse version,"Lango's House". Most of the time, Abul Kasem said, he had tried to keep his son inside, so that people did not see him. Many were frightened because they thought the deformity might be contagious and that their own children might catch it

It was a superstitious community. Joynal's parents had taken him to a local healer and been given a variety of reasons for his club feet. The healers could not be specific as to the exact cause but they suggested that maybe it was due to "evil winds", or perhaps bad things that his parents had done, or possibly to the fact that, whilst pregnant, Joynal's mother had prayed with her leg bent during the lunar eclipse.

For treatment, the healers recommended such cures as drinking water, or taking medicine, while the Koran was recited. Occasionally they had arranged a meeting at which a group of healers had called on the spirits, and at which a chicken or goat had been sacrificed. The parents believed in such things. They had taken their son to different healers and had gone more then ten times in all; but it had been very expensive and had not led to a cure.

Fortunately, one of Abul's friends had eventually told him about InterLife, and in due course, the organisation had arranged for Joynal go up to Dhaka and receive surgery.

All these things were told to us by Joynal and his father. In such a strict household the women were not permitted to come through to the front room in order to talk to visitors. So, after a little while, we asked if we could join Joynal's mother out at the back.

The poor lady was really startled when we went through. Very quickly, she drew her pale green sari right over her head so that I could not see her eyes at all, only the long gold ring hanging from her nose. Even so, she turned her head well away and held her sari firmly in position with one hand whilst, at the same time, expressing her welcome by grasping my arm tightly with the other.

Thus she led me to sit down on one of the many beds in the back room and, after a good deal of persuasion, settled rather hesitantly beside me.

It was she, Joynal's mother said, who had told the healers about praying with her leg bent at the lunar eclipse; and even now, she seemed quite certain that this was the cause of her son's problem. She had worried about the boy from the time he was born. What would happen to him.? What could he do? How would he study? She had been frightened to let him go out, she said, and confessed to having favoured him.

Someone now helped our conversation by handing Joynal's mother a very cracked pair of sunglasses. She put these on, and obviously felt her face sufficiently hidden to permit the pushing back of her sari.

When the family had taken advice from healers, she explained, the cost had sometimes been prohibitive, but she had still felt sure that these were the people who could cure her son. After all, it was Allah who had caused the disability, and therefore those who served Him must be the most likely people to be able to remove it. Only gradually, as the healers asked for more and more money, did she realise that her hopes were not being fulfilled.

We got up and went back with her to join the other women in the kitchen and, to our horror, found them in process of preparing an enormous meal. The InterLife staff, now four in number, had apparently said that they would accept Abul Kasem's invitation to lunch, and the house chicken i.e. the very best one, had been killed in my honour. No one, apparently, had heard Nupur explaining that I was a vegetarian.

A number of female neighbours had come round to help with the sudden load of work, and their children crowded the open doorway in order to stare at us

The fowl was already plucked and portioned and the rice put on to boil. Now several women were squatting on the mud floor hard at work. One was squeezing out coconut milk for the fish; another rolling onions into a smooth paste, and a third preparing the *dal*, whilst a fourth, selected, ground and mixed the spices.

The meal was obviously going to take a long time to prepare and we were provided with a pleasant opportunity for further female conversation.

One woman wanted to share her worries about her small son. She placed the unhappy child in Nupur's arms and explained that, although he was now about two years old, he was still not talking and seemed inordinately thin in the lower part of his body. She had taken him to a local healer who had said that the boy had an evil wind and that he should eat eight different sorts of thorn. But the overall treatment had proved so expensive that the mother had been unable to pursue it.

Later, back in the home of Nupur's family, I discovered that one of the older aunts had actually been a healer herself. I had the opportunity, then, to find out what was meant by an "evil wind".

Apparently, according to the Muslim religion, there existed before man, a number of different spirits, some of whom did the will of Allah and some of whom did not. These latter were little pleased by the creation of human beings and immediately set about causing trouble. In consequence they are considered to be the source of much of the world's suffering. "Wind" in this context, thus appears to be another name for "spirit". The healer believes that the reciting of the Koran can chase these evil spirits away; and certainly there have been times when this has appeared to be the case, although my informant conceded that non-believers would put such occurrences down to coincidence.

Joynal's family were certainly not amongst those who perceive such cures to be accidental. They were a very religious people and their belief affected every aspect of life. The women explained, for example, why they were totally opposed to family planning. Children, they said, were sent by Allah and it was not for humans to decide whether to have them or not. Such ideas were like a "red rag to a bull" as far as Nupur was concerned. A deeply concerned, modern and somewhat outspoken young lady, she immediately launched into the attack.

"Birth," she said, "is a source of power, like water, of which the Koran says you should take only as much as you can carry." I sensed that Joynal's mother was none too happy with this response!

The meal was finally ready, and Nupur and I sat with the men on the big double bed in the front room in order to be waited on by the

98

Head of the Household and his son-in-law. The women remained out of sight at the back. We ate quickly and almost in silence and then departed immediately as appears to be the custom. The food had taken about two hours of hard work to prepare, but in less than thirty minutes it was all gone.

Later that day, I was able to learn a little about the Hindu religion. It was the final day of the Puja Festival, and neighbours of Nupur's family invited us to see the statue of the goddess Durga who, according to tradition, comes down to Bangladesh from the Himalayas every year. She has, they say, the power of ten men and has killed Oshure, the bad man or devil who brings hate and violence.

Her statue was life-size and magnificent: Durga, with all ten arms outstretched, mounted upon a lion. Beside her, with a gaping wound in his chest, stood the dark-skinned Oshure; and gathered round were four of her children: Ganesh, the elephant god of business, Shorashati, goddess of education and culture, Laxmi, goddess of wealth and Kartic, much admired for both looks and bravery. All the statues were dressed in beautiful clothes; and Nupur muttered darkly about the obvious expense of saris and jewellery, all of which were shortly to be destroyed.

The Hindu women were performing puja, feeding the deities, fanning them and offering gifts. A Brahman priest, who at other times of the year worked as a pharmacist, was also in attendance. Rather hesitantly I asked if I could take a photograph and was quite surprised by the enthusiasm this invoked. Police appeared to hustle the children out of my way, candles were lit and everything made ready for the picture.

This was the ninth day. At midnight the goddess and all her children were to be taken to the pond and reverentially cast into the water in order to mark the end of the festivities. But before that, there would be plenty of time for music and dancing.

Puja is the most important festival of the Hindu year, and a very happy one, a time for families, for present giving, and for special food. We took *mishti* in one of the houses near the image of Durga, and were greeted by several generations, all of them dressed in the most lovely new clothes. Nupur, of course, knew what she was doing, but it was an act which shocked her brother-in-law when later he heard about it. We had eaten in the house of Hindus, something, he believed, no good Muslim should ever do. The ensuing argument between him and Nurpur was good tempered, but lengthy and heated, and provided entertainment for everybody else present.

"So if you came to England, would you refuse to eat in my home because I am a Christian?" I was unable to resist adding to the flames, and received the ungracious reply which I deserved..

"If there is no alternative, one sometimes has to do undesirable things."

Next morning we took a small boat across the river in order to visit a young lad I had read about in the InterLife newspaper.

We found Hossain sitting amongst the blue tins and red-topped jars of biscuits and spices in his shop. A slender figure with tight curly hair and a slightly worried expression, he came through to the adjacent room to sit with us on the rush matting covering his bed.

Hossain had been born deformed, with shortened arms, and hands arising from each elbow joint. He was now eighteen, the second of a family of six. He had gone to school, he said, and studied up until the sixth grade, at which point he had had to leave because his parents could no longer afford the fees.

We asked whether he had ever approached the local healer; and here the assembled villagers, pressing closely round the door and shop front, interrupted our conversation. They held the same beliefs as Joynal's mother, but had responded differently.

"No," they said. "It would have been unwise to spend money in this way because Hossain was born with his disability, it was sent by Allah".

Hossain, for his part, explained that he had been to a healer and had been told that his deformity was due to the fact that his mother had broken a stick for the fire at the time of the lunar eclipse, a time when pregnant women should do nothing. For himself he did not actually believe this, but thought it more likely that his problems had been caused by a very strong drug that a doctor had given his mother in order to cure a fever.

Between us, we worked out that Hossain must have been between twelve and fourteen when he left school, and we asked him what he did then.

He had received, he said, a loan of about two thousand *taka* (approximately twenty-six pounds) from his father, and with this had started a shop. Nupur immediately expressed surprise. Hossain's father was a poor agricultural labourer. How had the boy managed to persuade such a man to part with a sizeable sum like that?

Not a flicker of a smile crossed Hossain's worried face, but he explained that he had started trading in a very small way on his own, and, by proving what he could do, had gradually won his father's trust.

Helped by the parental loan, and later by a more sizeable one from InterLife, Hossain had gradually built the shop up and up. Now, as we could see, it was a big four *chala* (or four roof) shop with a good supply of stock. Certainly it was impressive. We had seen one or two other very small shops on the long rickshaw ride from the river, but none of them contained nearly so much merchandise. Even from a distance, Hossain's shop looked better. It was freshly painted and built of new corrugated iron.

Now, Hossain explained, again in a tone more serious than proud, he was able to give his family about 1,200 *taka* each month, and his younger brothers and sisters were all going to school as a result of his help. He was also paying back the loan from InterLife and even making a small saving. In all, he was passing the organisation 120 *taka* a week, 100 as part repayment of the loan and another 20 to go into the savings account kept on his behalf. His ambition was to have a big shop in Bhola, or near the river; but he did not wish to leave his friends in the village so would aim to keep this one as well.

Earlier, we had asked whether he experienced any social problems because of his disability and once again his neighbours interrupted, eager now to tell us how much they loved him.

"Did you ever have any thought that perhaps Allah did not like Hossain?" Nupur asked the assembled company. "Or that maybe you should keep your own children away from him in case they became disabled as well?"

"No," several voices answered in unison. "We love him very much and always try to help him." There seemed little doubt that this was true. Even now one of them was serving customers while Hossain answered our questions.

There was also support from his family. Although Hossain slept at the shop, he always went home for his meals, and his younger brother looked after the business for him whenever necessary.

Hossain explained that he liked to go to Bhola himself in order to buy stock, although he usually took someone to help him. He had developed a good relationship with all the traders and clearly thought that this was important.

InterLife were able to confirm the young man's skill in working with others. They had discovered him running his shop and had subsequently asked him to become a Group Leader for their credit programme. As such, he was responsible for weekly meetings of about twenty members. Health and business problems were discussed, and Hossain also acted as cashier, collecting in repayments on the loans which InterLife made available to everyone in the group.

We asked whether there were any other disabled people amongst the members. "No," he said, although one man did have a child with a problem.

And what was the main piece of advice he would give to anyone who was disabled?

"I would point to my own life," Hossain answered without hesitation. "And tell them that if I can do it, so can they."

We asked about marriage. The villagers smiled. Some families were apparently already interested in marrying their daughters to Hossain. He was successful and reasonably well off, and this they now considered far more important than his disability. Hossain, how-ever, shook his head. There is a law in Bangladesh, he explained, that a man should not marry before he was twenty-one. This surprised me, for I knew of many younger men in wedlock, but nevertheless it was Hossain's belief, and he had, he said, no intention of breaking the law. Anyway, he added, he wanted to improve his business first. Then, if he found someone good, he would marry them.

Nupur threw out a question about dowries, the trouble-causing payment many bridegrooms in Bangladesh demand. Hossain was adamant in his reply. He would not ask for a dowry. They were bad.

Unbeknown to me at the time, for I was not able to understand what was said, Nupur, who was feeling provocative, then pressed him further. She apparently suggested that Hossain might be able to get as much as twenty thousand *taka* as dowry, a sum which would go a long way if invested in his business. Hossain's resolve did not waver. He could, he said, earn all that he needed by his own effort.

Before I left, I asked Hossain whether he thought I had covered everything important, or whether there was anything else he would like to have written about him. He replied in the negative at first, but then, after everyone else had started talking, added quietly in an aside, "I want to spread the idea of working as a team. It is helping very much."

With only half a day left on Bhola, it was now only right that Nupur should have time to visit other branches of her family; and she seemed to have an unlimited supply of them. We went to two more households and at every stop were plied with food and drink. It came to the point when I felt quite incapable of eating any more. And that was before we returned to the aunts' house, where they were anxiously waiting to provide us with lunch!

Still the job of meeting friends and relatives and answering questions about myself was not ended. In the afternoon the house seemed to fill with neighbouring women and children who gathered round to watch whatever I was doing, be it writing, combing my hair, or just sitting silently wondering how to escape.

I decided that the best thing to do, was to take advantage of the apparently acceptable habit of going to lie down for an afternoon sleep. Still I felt the presence of people. Opening one eye, I saw them all grouped around the bed. I shut the eye again hastily and remained as if sleeping for a few more minutes, but then could bear it no longer. I got up and made for the lavatory. The procession followed – but stopped at the door.

I was, I discovered, the first western visitor to this household, and they seemed to have an insatiable curiosity regarding me. I must confess, I was becoming more and more curious about them. What must their lives be like? Nupur's cousin and aunts were sufficiently well-off to have a young girl working in the house, but despite time on their hands, they were not permitted to go out unaccompanied. During the two or three days I was there, they did not leave the home at all. The older two, one of whom may only have been about the same age as myself, seemed to spend the whole day just sitting around intermittently eating, talking, sleeping and praying. Nupur said she would hate to live such a life. And certainly it was quite impossible to imagine her doing so.

CHAPTER SIX

CHRISTIAN DISCIPLESHIP CENTRE (CDC)
GRADUATION & DEDICATION CEREMONY 1999

Dear Friends
Greetings in Jesus Wonderful Name! We are happy to invite you to our Christian Discipleship Centre's Graduation and Dedication Ceremony for the nineteenth Batch of students which will be held:
on : December 10th 1999 (Friday)
at : 4.00 P.M.
at : C.D.C.
Badekalameswar
Board Bazar, Gazipur
Your Presence will be a great encouragement to us.

Yours in the Master's Service
   Rev. Biswanath A. Chowdhuri
      Director

It was this invitation, shared by Valerie one cool December afternoon, that led to my first meeting with Biswanath Chowdhuri.

He was clad in an immaculately pressed short-sleeved cotton suit, and sat upright and gracious on the platform. If I had not already been told that this was the grandson of a former Maharaja of Mymensingh, I might still have described the wheelchair bound Director of CDC as "regal".

The ceremony was opened by the harmonium and drums accompanying a loud and cheerful rendering in Bangla. I fell prey to a sudden pang of homesickness; and it was a couple of minutes before

105

I recognised the cause of my distress as the slightly estranged notes of Once in Royal David's City.

The presentation of certificates was preceded by a service of worship; prayers were led by one resounding voice whereupon the whole congregation broke into loud and voluble intercession. I do not know whether or not this might rightly be described as "speaking in tongues", but it was certainly a most amazing noise which could well be likened to a great wind rushing through the room and tossing voices in all directions. The final dedication involved the new graduates kneeling to receive the blessing of their elders, who laid hands upon the students' heads before starting to pray in the same manner as before. It was a process which reduced several of the female students to tears; and caused one to fall upon the ground and seem unable to rise.

Perhaps I should not have been surprised. Bangladesh had already impressed itself upon me as a country where religion is important, and where all creeds practise publicly and proudly. No one feels the need to speak quietly about the spiritual aspect of life. It is recognised as being as essential as eating, and at times even more so. The previous day, being the first of Ramadan, our entire working schedule had been adjusted to meet the requirements of the Koran. The morning call to prayer now summoned the faithful to a day of fasting. The midday break was cut to a minimum, and work stopped at half past four in the afternoon Almost to the instant, the shops outside the hospital gate came alive with hungry customers milling round the displays of *muri* and other specially prepared delicacies. *Iftar*, the evening meal which followed, and with which the fast is broken, was particularly good.

Christianity certainly has to be a little more cautious. CDC is authorised to "teach theology to Christians" but not to evangelise. Biswanath Chowdhuri had found it necessary to overcome many obstacles in the twenty years since his organisation was born. He would, I thought, be an interesting man with whom to talk; and a telephone call a few days after the graduation ceremony secured an invitation to lunch at his home in Dhaka.

It was a comfortable rented house in Gulshan, the westernised up-market area inhabited by many of my expatriate friends. A small door in the metal gate led into an external parking area, the home of four husky-type dogs who set up a ferocious barking as soon as they saw me. I skirted round the outside of their domain and gratefully reached the open door and warm welcome provided by Biswanath's wife, Vijaya.

The large comfortable living room made clear that the couple's earthly priorities centred on people. Peeling orange walls were bedecked with heavily framed family photographs, and paintings which they proudly pointed out as the work of their second daughter, Sumita, now standing beside her mother in greeting.

Biswanath wheeled himself in, greeted me graciously and entered easily into conversation.

It was true, he said, that he was descended from the Maharajas of Mymensingh. Indeed his family had started their rule more than two hundred years ago. His grandfather had probably been the last to hold the title for he died somewhere around 1947, the year of Indian Independence and Partition.

Division of the subcontinent was the consequence of several decades of tension between the two main religious groups. Despite Mahatma Gandhi's attempts to reassure them, the Muslims had become increasingly agitated by the prospect of an independent India dominated by Hindus. The Muslim League, headed by Jinnah, argued vociferously for the creation of a separate Muslim state; and the British, concluding that any agreement between the two parties was impossible, finally settled on partitioning the Indian territory on purely religious grounds into two independent countries. There followed what may possibly have been the largest population move in human history. People hurried in both directions in order to get to the country in which they wished to live: Hindus to India, and Muslims to Pakistan.

At exactly what point the title of Maharaja of Mymensingh was relinquished, or what happened to the rest of the Acharyya Chowdhuri family, Biswanath does not know. His people were high cast Brahmin Hindus. Their home and lands were now in a Muslim country and as "enemy property" would eventually be confiscated.

Biswanath's father left East Pakistan soon after Partition, if not before. As a younger son, it was his duty to accompany the widowed mother to Benares in India. To Hindus, this is the holiest place on earth, the chosen residence of Shiva. Everyone who dies within its confines is, they believe, granted *moksha*, liberation from the endless cycle of death and rebirth. So it was in that city that the old lady wished to end her days, and as a result, it was there that her grandson Biswanath was born.

The family must have retained their property in Pakistan for a little while, for Biswanath has vague memories of childhood expeditions to Mymensingh for celebrations of the Puja Festival. Part of the journey would be undertaken by steamer, and something he particularly remembers is the excitement of their arrival at a *ghat*. Long before the vessel docked, eager coolies would jump on board, clambering up on deck and shouting to make their presence known in order to secure work from the passengers.

Biswanath still retains a sentimental connection with the home of his forebears. Pictures, both of the beautiful Mymensingh rajbari, or palace, and of the older one in Muktagacha some twelve kilometres to the west, hang amongst the family photographs in his living room. The property in Mymensingh has now been turned into a women teachers' training college and is open to the public. Biswanath used to go up there with friends once or twice every year, but he no longer does so. Once word got out that he was a member of the family, crowds started to gather to see him and he felt it unwise to continue.

After graduating in physics at Benares University, Biswanath took a job in a laboratory in Bombay, and it was here, in September 1963, that his accident occurred. He had been checking some experiments. Suspecting that one was not quite right, he opened the lid to investigate and, in so doing, unwittingly exposed himself to dangerous chemical fumes. Within two hours he had developed an excruciating headache. The doctor on site, assuming stress, advised Biswanath to go home and rest. Next day he felt terrible and did not even attempt to get out of bed, but on the third day he woke up, felt a little better, and thought he ought to return to work. He tried to get up but fell, then discovered he could not stand properly. At that point the trouble seemed only to be in his right leg, but gradually it spread upwards. He was admitted to hospital, and by the following day, the paralysis had affected his lungs. He could not breathe.

A tracheotomy followed, and then thirty-five days on a respirator. He could not move his neck, close his eyes, or speak. In order to get some sleep he had to be blindfolded.

By this stage Biswanath was in despair. No one seemed to know what to do, and he himself could see no future. He could only lie on his bed, with no alternative but to allow others to feed, wash and turn him. He felt totally helpless, of no use to anyone – in fact a burden. The question rose in his mind, "How could this have happened to me – a Hindu of high Brahmin caste – a well-educated good man. And what will become of me?" A fearful mixture of anger, bitterness and hatred boiled up within him.

Then a strange thing happened. Biswanath had what he can only describe as "a very deep spiritual experience."

He was managing to read a little when the carer held books up in front of him, and one of the nurses had brought him a Gideons' New Testament. She had told him it was the Christians' holy book and then left the room. Biswanath was intrigued. He was only able to read a few verses at a time, but even so he soon found himself thinking, "I cannot reject this unless I put it to the test."

Meanwhile he was gradually getting a little better, able to come off the respirator, and to talk in whispers. Thus some days later, when he received a visit from the English husband of one of the Christian missionaries, Biswanath was able to enter into conversation with someone who, he was delighted to find, was also a fellow scientist. The Englishman answered questions about the New Testament, and subsequently suggested that they pray together. It was then that Biswanath had what he called a "strange experience".

"I felt God was present. I felt I could almost touch Him, and there followed a tremendous confidence and peace. I knew that there was a God who would accept me, and that I was His child. There was no immediate physical change, but I felt that God had a purpose for my life, and that there was something to look forward to."

After that, Biswanath's condition started slowly to improve, and his heart was still further cheered when he was assigned a new nurse from a Christian family. This was Vijaya. They shared their thoughts about God, and at the same time fell in love. Yet there was still to be seven long years in different hospitals in Bombay before there could be any real hope for Biswanath's physical condition. The breakthrough came with his transfer to a rehabilitation centre in Perth, Australia. In Bombay, there had been no opportunity for physiotherapy. Biswanath's muscles had been gradually wasting away; so that by the time he left for Australia he was extremely weak, and still unable to sit up. But in Perth, a rehabilitation plan was devised which enabled him to regain some movement in his arms. After eight months he was able to move himself around in a wheelchair, and even eventually, to drive a specially adapted car.

When he came out of hospital he felt that "God had a purpose" for him, and happily he discovered that Vijaya was of the same mind. Accordingly, after their marriage in Bombay, they both entered a missionary college in Tasmania.

Two years later, their training complete, the Chowduri's felt themselves called to Bangladesh. But it was a calling they were soon to question. Biswanath was refused permission to bring his car into the country, and subsequently turned down for a driving licence. Despite his possession of an Australian licence, the Bangladesh Authorities were simply unable to accept that a wheelchair user was capable of driving a car. And twenty-five years later, linked as it is to the general idea that disabled people cannot do anything useful, this is a view that has not changed.

"I used to go on the Microbus and visit banks and offices as much as I could," Biswanath said. I took it as a crusade, a contribution I must make to people's understanding. It is important for others to see that being in a wheelchair is not the end."

But without a car he was severely restricted; and once again Biswanath was filled with a terrible frustration. He had come to the country filled with zeal to help the village poor, but now he could not reach them. He thought back to the offer of a job received from the church in Tasmania where there would have been no problem in getting around. Had he, perhaps, made the wrong choice? It was sometime before he realised that there was another way of carrying out his mission, one that might actually be more effective than travelling out to the villages himself.

Meanwhile Vijaya had taken a job as a nurse at a mission hospital for Bihari refugees, a people suffering greatly as a result of their collaboration with the Pakistanis during the War of Liberation. It was to be expected that they should be out of favour with the local people, but they probably had not bargained on desertion by Pakistan. With no one prepared to give them citizenship, they had been left stateless and had to live in very poor conditions in refugee camps. Vijaya, at least, had a worthwhile job to do, and she stayed at the mission hospital until her first child was expected.

At this point in his story, Biswanath turned to the subject of his three children, in each of whom he has a justifiable pride. All have studied in New Zealand and gained degrees. It was only his wife's call to the lunch table that stopped their proud father from talking about them further.

Vijaya, an enthusiastic cook, insisted that she had enjoyed preparing a special meal for my visit. It was a veritable feast, six different vegetarian dishes arranged in a neat row down the centre of their long dining table. I savoured with relish, crispy batter covered pumpkin, lightly cooked aubergine and a creamy lentil and yoghurt dish which served to cool the palate after indulgence in the curry. Vijaya's recipes came from South India; the spices were more subtle than any I had tasted in Bangladesh, and the rice possessed a distinctive and delicate flavour which I could not place. Biswanath was still talking of his experiences; and I found myself really struggling to memorise his words, whilst at the same time paying due homage to his wife's cuisine. Fortunately he agreed to repeat the main points after we had finished eating.

"I felt that there was a need to train nationals," Biswanath said, referring to the start of CDC. "There were no effective training facilities for them. My missionary friends were really encouraging when I mentioned this idea, and I decided that this was an area in which I could actually do something."

In 1979 he set up his first training college in a small rented house in Dhaka. There were just six students, and two dropped out before the course was finished. Twenty years later, when I went to the ceremony in Gazipur, I witnessed the graduation of forty-one students from one in-take.

For many years, CDC was the only institution offering full time, residential, non-denominational theology courses in the Bangla medium. Students have come from all over the country. Equal opportunities are offered to men and women and to people from all educational backgrounds.

Biswanath has his critics. Some argue that entrants should at least have a school leaving certificate; and others suggest that a theology course ought to include both Latin and Greek.

He disagrees. "Where," he asks, "is Bangladesh if not in the villages? Only people from the grass roots will be prepared to return to the grass roots. Unless we identify the local structure, and use that structure effectively, we will be frustrated. But that does not mean that we have to compromise quality. We just have to have our objectives clear. We cannot, in our situation, set up a measuring stick and say, 'this is the standard'. We have to accept the situation and then see how we can develop a structure."

It is, Biswanath explained, "desirable for entrants to be educated at least to school leaving level, but not essential." He could remember students who had received very little previous education, but who had ended up doing extremely well.

Sunil Das, for instance, had come from a very poor family in Bhola, and had had to leave school at a young age. But because both he and his wife were supported in their application by the missionaries, and exhibited a good grasp of the Bible, Biswanath took them on. The mission helped by supplying a tape recorder so that Sunil Das could go over the lessons again, and the college challenged other students to help him as much as they could. By the time Sunil graduated, Biswanath was looking desperately for someone to work with a poor outcaste community of sweepers. It was a job nobody else wanted, but Sunil rose to the challenge. Ten years later he and his wife are still there, and they have successfully established both a church and a school.

Then there was Ong Sung from the Chittagong Hill Tracks, a man of fifty-seven when he came to enquire about entry to the college. Biswanath mistakenly assumed that his visitor wanted to enter a son, and admits to being somewhat discouraging when he realised that it was Ong Sung himself who wished to attend.

"I tried to put him off," he remembers. "Warned him that he would have to share in all the work, clean the toilets etcetera. But he insisted on coming, said he would accept all the conditions".

Years later, Ong Sung still walks miles in the hills every day carrying his Christian message from village to village. He has set up three churches and a significant number of small groups.

"These people are a lesson to us," Biswanath commented thoughtfully, "not to judge people by the normally accepted standards."

The Director of CDC is also enthusiastic about accepting married couples onto the course, especially since training of this kind is not normally open to women on their own. And he has recently set up a new short term training programme for special subjects such as community health care and first aid.

Yet, even to this day, Biswanath and Vijaya operate on very limited resources. The majority of the new intake of students have been accepted in faith, with no idea where the finance is coming from. Biswanath will, no doubt, overcome the lack of funds; even as he has overcome the difficulties created by severe disability.

"If we allow God to use our life," he said by way of conclusion. "He will show us a plan, and He will use us. We will not be handicapped by our handicap."

Less than two weeks' later I had the opportunity to visit Biswanath's family home, the old rajbari in Mymensingh which is now a women teachers' training college.

I found the impressive ochre-coloured stone entrance gate flanked by two enormous trees. Withered vines and long dead ferns still clung to the charcoal-coloured bark, but the branches were vibrant with glossy new leaves.

A scalloped white marble wall surrounded the central pond, which might once have contained a fountain. Now the stone statue of a near-naked lady looked lonely and forlorn. She bent hovering over the water as if undecided whether to jump.

Six curved steps led up to the front verandah of the rajbari, an ornate building of crimson brick and moulded cream plaster surrounded by decorated columns. Here I met a Bengali visitor from Saidpur whose wife was studying at the training college. Humayan had good English and proposed a guided tour.

We walked round the side of the building, past boys playing cricket on the brown winter grass, and entered a secluded area at the back. Here, in days gone by, the ladies of the house had been permitted to bathe in a gigantic pool which Humayan, somewhat pleased at his own English, described as "egg-like". We descended the chipped marble steps that led down to the water so that he could show me what he meant, and he held out his arms to indicate the oval outline of the bank. To our left, date palms leant at a dangerous-looking angle over the water, and to our right, ducks, blissfully unaware of the ravages of time, glided serenely over the shining green surface. Standing under the shadow of old sculpture, I could indulge in an imagery of the stately life enjoyed by Biswanath's forebears, the only note of incongruity a ragged washing line on the far bank.

We turned round and wandered slowly towards the palace. Goats cropped the meagre grass at the back of the building; the long arched windows had many panes missing, and the green stained glass at the top of each was broken in numerous places. An iron spiral staircase, leading to the balustraded roof, looked rusted beyond repair.

Having returned to the front, I sat down on the low stone wall which edged the flower beds. It was the end of the day, and smiling, book-clutching students were leaving the building. They were a colourful crowd. Most wore the *salwar kameez* of modern youth, but some were veiled, and a few wore the full black *burka*. Amongst them too were three white robed nuns. The days of the Hindu maharaja were long past; but the old building still throbbed with life.

Much later, I learnt more about the Bihari refugees mentioned by Biswanath in relation to his wife's work.

From my reading I gleaned that they were Urdu-speaking Muslims from the Indian state of Bihar, and that they came to East Pakistan in 1947 in order to escape Hindu persecution at the time of Partition. Bangladeshi friends, it should be noted, advise me that the term "Bihari" is actually used somewhat more loosely to apply to any non-Bengali Muslims who came from India at that time, not just to those from the state supplying the name.

Whatever their origin, the Biharis were mostly traders, and they took over the vacant shops left by Hindus who had fled in the opposite direction. Thus it could be said that the Bengalis provided shelter and hospitality. But they did not speak the same language. It was the West Pakistanis with whom the Biharis shared a linguistic bond; and in due course it was this that was to prove the stronger link. During the War of Independence the Biharis acted as scouts, guides and hosts for soldiers from the western state.

As Biswanath explained, their loyalty was not reciprocated. When the war was over, West Pakistan deserted them; the Biharis were rendered stateless. And several months after our discussion, I was to meet someone whose story illustrated one particularly sad aspect of this condition: that to be devoid of citizenship is to be without roots.

Miomun arrived at CRP unannounced and unexpected. Her sudden appearance, sitting on a low trolley in the office doorway, gave Valerie quite a shock. It was thirteen years since the hospital founder had last set eyes on her Bihari friend.

"We thought she had left Bangladesh altogether," Valerie explained. "She went to Karachi. We took her to the airport, I remember it very well: Miomun sitting up at the front of the vehicle with all her pots and pans, and her little daughter beside her wearing a special straw hat for the occasion. Being a Bihari, Miomun was quite certain that once she got to Pakistan everything would be all right."

This was someone, Valerie added, whom I would really enjoy meeting. Miomun had an incredible spirit and the ability to make everybody laugh. Intrigued, I enlisted a student as interpreter and asked our visitor to tell me her story.

Miomun began her tale in 1971, the year of the Liberation War, when her father was killed as a result of a feud. The shock was too much for her mother. The poor woman became very ill and died from a heart attack eighteen months later; and the three children were left parentless. Neighbours decided that the younger ones would have to go to an orphanage, but for nine-year-old Miomun there was an option. She was given the opportunity to stay in the home of her father's erstwhile employer. Nevertheless the little girl declined. "If the others had to go to an orphanage," she pointed out to me matter-of-factly all those years later, "I had to go with them."

I could imagine her taking a stand, for I had been watching Miomun as she talked, and was aware of an enormous strength of character. Her face was well-worn but strong, and her voice conveyed an innate determination.

The establishment to which the three children were sent was in the Mohammadpur area of Dhaka and was supplied by the Red Cross. It was not the grim sort of place that it might have been.

"We had a good time there, and good food. If we had fish for lunch, we had meat for dinner. We shared out the work, someone to sweep and someone to cook, and received an Arabic education so that we could read the Koran."

The orphanage also arranged marriage, and in this, too, Miomun considered herself to be fortunate. "All of us were married when we became thirteen, and some had to go far away to different parts of the country; but I was lucky and was able to stay in Mohammadpur near to my brother and sister."

Her husband's name was Yusef, and he was a nickel polisher, cleaning up spoons and pots and pans in order to give them a new shine. From this he earned an adequate income, and for the first year of their marriage the young couple were quite happy.

Then something strange happened to Miomun. She was pouring water down the toilet one day when, quite suddenly, she fell over and could not get up. They took her first to Dhaka Medical College Hospital and then to Mirpur, but it was a long time before anyone could provide a diagnosis. Finally, in Suhrawardi Hospital, Miomun learnt that she had TB of the spine, and, after a couple of operations, had to come to terms with the fact that she had lost the use of her legs.

"I kept trying to walk but I fell down every time. And when they attempted to sit me up on a chair or a bed, I just tipped over."

It was then that she had met Valerie, and I interrupted the story at this point to mention what I had been told about Moimun making them all laugh.

"I found the situation in hospital very sad," she explained. "Everyone was suffering, so I realised that it would not be good if they saw me looking miserable as well. I decided to make them laugh, and to try to make the time better for everyone."

"I did also get angry sometimes," she added with delightful honesty. "But most of the time I tried to be cheerful and to share the mood with others."

Miomun did not explain how she did this, but I remembered one particularly poignant story provided by Valerie.

"While she was in the hospital with us, Miomun used to be looked after by her little sister who was only about eight or nine years old. Then one day the sister went across the Mirpur Road to buy some lemons, and as she was coming back, was hit by an oncoming truck and killed outright. Miomun was absolutely devastated; this was her only sister and they had been very close. For a little while no one could comfort her. But then, about ten days later, she suddenly pushed herself through to our office, picked up a motorcycle crash helmet, and went off down the ward on her trolley with the helmet on her head, making everyone laugh. Once again her incredible spirit had triumphed."

Subsequently Valerie arranged for Miomun to take up some work, making dolls and sewing bed sheets, and then also sent her to the Cheshire Foundation in order to master the activities of daily living.

In the midst of telling us this, Miomun let out a hearty laugh. She had been watching me scribbling away in my notebook. "If you start to write my life story," she said with a chuckle "you will be here all day." Then she plunged straight back into telling me details of her exploits in dealing with the unwanted advances of guards, and of holding her own against the Management. The Sister at the Cheshire Foundation was apparently very strict, and if residents failed to carry out instructions, which might even include demands that they sing, then their pocket money was withheld. "But," said Miomun, when

117

referring to the requirement for vocal rendition. "If I don't feel so, then what can I do?"

And she had reason "not to feel so". For, at the same time as visiting frequently, and bringing gifts, her husband was demanding a divorce. True to character, Miomun was not prepared to give in. After all, she insisted, she had signed a piece of paper; and that had to be worth something.

Finally though she relented, and, having done so, found that it was not too difficult to find another husband. Miomun's sewing could now make money, and disability or not, she was considered worth marrying.

With the new spouse, she settled in Geneva Camp, an area set aside for the Bihari refugees, and here one disaster seemed to follow upon another.

Information regarding the first of these I obtained from Valerie. The details were engraved upon her memory, for it had occurred at a time when the future founder of CRP was still working at the hospital near the Camp. One day she had heard a strange popping noise like a series of explosions, and on looking out of the window, had realised with horror that she was listening to the sound of a fire. The "explosions" were none other than the cracking of bamboo as the flames raged through the Bihari settlement attacking one house after another.

The conflagration had been started accidentally, but the result was devastating. Valerie rushed out in search of Miomun and found her sitting amongst the ashes which were all that remained of her home. She had lost nearly everything. Her friends found just four big pieces of metal, and with these they managed to construct a temporary shelter.

Shortly, too, Miomun was to loose one of the few things that had not been in the house at the time of the fire. Her precious sewing machine was kept at the hospital where it should have been perfectly safe.

"I used to sleep at home and go into the hospital every day," she explained. "Then one day I discovered that my sewing machine had been stolen. I knew who it was, because I saw it later in his shop, but

I was afraid to report it to anyone."

After their marriage, Miomun's second husband had told her that he had been married previously, and that his wife had died leaving him with a young son. Miomun felt mildly surprised that he had not mentioned this earlier, but now happily took on the care of the boy. Some five years later Miomun herself gave birth to a daughter and their family was complete.

When the little girl was about two years old, Miomun's husband suggested that they should all go and live in Karachi. He had some nephews there whom he thought would be prepared to help. So saying, he set off in advance in order to send money back so that Miomun and the baby could follow. It was the occasion to which Valerie had referred: the time when they departed in the CRP vehicle, loaded with all their pots and pans plus an over-optimistic belief in the future.

Miomun now reported nothing of her initial reaction to life in Pakistan. Instead, she jumped, some seven or eight years in her narrative, to the point at which her husband decided to return to Bangladesh in search of work. Without telling her, he took his son with him. And only later, did Miomun hear from friends that her spouse had left her for good.

Miomun received from him neither letters nor funds. She had to leave her house because she could not afford the rent, and subsequently got a very small place from which she tried to earn a living by decorating glass bracelets. Her health was deteriorating, and without money for treatment, the situation could have been desperate had it not been for the support of a new son-in-law.

The solution that he recommended was that they should all move once more, go back to Bangladesh and see if they could get Miomun's husband to help her. But the sad truth, that they were about to discover, was that Miomun had been cheated all along. The first wife was still very much alive, and her husband had now decided to return to her.

It was not the first time that I had heard a story such as this. In the slums of Dhaka, it is apparently quite common for a man to marry several wives, simply because they are earning. He can then take

119

money from all of them, and live reasonably well off the combined income.

Despite the laughter with which she accompanied her story, Miomun had, in reality, returned to a fairly desperate situation. She was back in Geneva Camp; but living now with her brother's family in circumstances that were far from easy. "It is a very small house," she explained, "and my brother has three children. Also, when it rains, everything gets flooded."

It rained a great deal during the next few weeks. I thought of her often, and seized the first chance to visit.

The location was pointed out to me on the map, and I found myself directing the *baby taxi* down a road ridden with potholes and choked with rickshaws. We were now on the outskirts of the Camp, and drawing up at the first junction, I struggled with my Bangla in order to explain that I was looking for a woman called Miomun who could not walk and who had recently returned from Karachi.

Everyone gathered round, eager to be helpful, but my description drew blank faces. There was some discussion, and then someone was allocated to take me to "the office". I paid-off the *baby taxi*, and followed my guide down a narrow road which quickly disintegrated into a rubbish-lined mud track. Goats and chickens picked their way delicately over the mire; I sank. The track got narrower until we had to literally squeeze between the houses; but here, at least, there were a few brick stepping stones. My guide led on until suddenly we turned into a slightly clearer area. In the centre of it, men were at work weighing sacks of grain on enormous scales. And in a corrugated iron shack, under a notice declaring it to be the "Office of the Chairman of the Relief Committee (Non-Local)", a man with heavy spectacles and hennaed hair sat entering figures in a large book.

By-sitters vacated a chair for me, and I sat down and repeated my halting description of Miomun. The Keeper of Figures hardly looked up, but his response was immediate. The guide was sent away to check, and returned to lead me to the house in which my friend was staying.

The path was so narrow here that it was impossible to pass people coming in the opposite direction without flattening oneself against a

120

house wall. But the faces staring from the doorways always smiled; and from one entrance, the strains of Hindi music released an infectious cheerfulness which bowed to neither damp nor squalor.

Miomun lived with her brother, his wife and their three children. Six of them, in a house which, I calculated, cannot have been more than ten foot by eight at the very most. It was built largely of concrete, but the roof was of corrugated iron and lined with paper sacking.

The whole of the space to one side of the door was taken up by a high, table-like bed, and it was upon this, that Miomun was perched. She was busy threading gold sequins to help her sister-in-law with a dressmaking job, and with her usual cheerful smile, invited me up beside her. Hesitating at first, I seated myself rather awkwardly on the edge of the bed, but was soon instructed to pull up my feet and sit cross-legged opposite my hostess. The surface beneath me was hard, and I was glad, for their sakes, to see that the family had a small pile of bedding on the shelf above our heads. Here, too, were some aluminium pots and an oil container, while smaller items – cups and saucers, a non-functioning alarm clock, a blond doll and a clutter of medicines – were stored on a rack-like set of shelves against the far wall. A few clothes hung from a string beside us. Everything else, including Miomun's wheelchair, was stowed neatly away under the bed.

Miomun received my gift of fruit enthusiastically, and immediately sent one of the children to purchase coke and biscuits with which to entertain me. Three small photograph albums were then produced from the below-bed store, and our conversation was greatly helped by pictures of weddings and grandchildren.

Meanwhile, the sister-in-law, squatting on the concrete floor below us, got on with her work. She was peeling the large shining nut-like seeds of the jackfruit, and preparing other vegetables for the midday meal. Children played in the one tiny space remaining, and outside, a small oil stove flickered fretfully under the windbreak provided by an aluminium plate. As usual the doorway had filled with onlookers.

Lack of a common language limited our conversation, but I still found it difficult to depart. Feelings born of a fresh and painful awareness, both of the sameness of us all and of the enormous difference, caused me to feel like a deserter. That, like so much of the rest of the world, I was walking away to the anaesthetising comfort of my own existence, distancing myself from those we leave to struggle unaided up the long hill ahead.

CHAPTER SEVEN

A NATION'S STRUGGLE FOR INDEPENDENCE – HOSSEIN: FREEDOM
FIGHTER – SAIDUR: RICKSHAW WALLAH – GRAMEEN BANK –
EMADUL HOQUE: ACCOUNTANT

The Daily Star – Dhaka Thursday December 16, 1999. Page One
The nation today celebrates with festivity and vivacity its
victory in the War of Independence 28 years ago.
Homage will be paid on the day —Victory Day — to three mil-
lion martyrs of the nine month war against Pakistani
occupation forces in 1971. The nation will gratefully recall their
supreme sacrifice to liberate the motherland and pledge afresh to
materialise their lofty ideals and dreams.

Victory Day – the many sided National Assembly building was
festooned with fairy lights. The red and green of Bangladesh fluttered
high on flag poles all over the city. It is a green chosen to represent
the lush countryside, whilst the red circle speaks of bloodshed at the
nation's birth. Memories of the long and desperate struggle for
independence remain central to the nation's psyche.

It is difficult, in retrospect, to understand how those responsible for
the partition of India could ever have believed that the borders they
created would lead to peace and harmony. The new country of
Pakistan was divided into two states, East and West, separated by over
a thousand miles of hostile territory: and, it would seem, by as many
metaphoric miles between its people.

The West Pakistanis, tall, military and business oriented, spoke
Urdu, a language related to Arabic. The Bengalis, small, lithe,
agrarian and poetic, took a special pride in their Sanskrit-based
Bengali tongue. Islam, the reason for attempting to unite the two races
was, in fact, their only bond.

From the outset it was evident that East Pakistan would be the looser. Unification under a West Pakistani administration could only increase the serious economic disparity which already existed. Although the East had more people, and produced most of the cash crops, the majority of foreign aid and revenue was now directed to the West. A lopsided system of tariffs and controls also benefited that state; and even individual opportunities for advancement and study were disproportionately distributed.

The downtrodden Bengali people became restless. In 1952, infuriated by a Government announcement that "Urdu and only Urdu" should become the national language, they broke into revolt. Riots in Dhaka resulted in the death of twelve students who subsequently became known as the Language Martyrs. The Bangla Language Movement had become the Bengali National Movement.

For a further eighteen years the young nation simmered uneasily under the constraints of Martial Law. The situation of the Bengalis worsened. By 1969 even official reports admitted a 61 per cent difference between the per capita income of the two states.

General elections were promised and delayed. In part, this could be blamed on the disastrous cyclone which hit the area in 1970, although the Government's apparent lack of concern for the Eastern state at this time only served to further aggravate Bengali feelings. When the election was finally called in December of that year the ruling military junta were in for a shock.

They had assumed that Sheikh Mujib, leader of the Bengali Awami League, might possibly win about 100 of the 169 seats allocated to East Pakistan. But in actuality, he won 167, a clear majority in the 313 seat National Assembly. Constitutionally the Awami League had a right to form the government of all Pakistan; and the horrified West Pakistani President could only respond with a boycott. He reneged on all pre-election promises and postponed the opening of the National Assembly.

The Bengalis were justifiably incensed. The hostilities of decades began to erupt in strikes and riots. Full scale civil war was only days away, and finally came when Sheik Mujib was arrested and taken to West Pakistan. The *Mukti Bahini*, Bangladesh Freedom Fighters, captured the Chittagong radio station and announced the birth of a new nation. It was to be a birth steeped in blood.

It is horrific to read or listen to the accounts of Pakistani atrocities in the period that followed. Their soldiers appear to have indulged in a systematic programme of slaughter, looting and rape. Relief for Bangladesh was achieved only at the expense of many thousands of her people.

Due acknowledgment of the contribution made by poorer families was slow in coming. In 1999, while the front page of the Victory Edition of the Daily star employed the usual rhetoric of "homage" and "supreme sacrifice", an inside article told a rather different story.

The Daily Star – Dhaka Thursday December 16, 1999. Page Five
It is now conceded on all hands though that the sung heroes' achievements are but a culmination of the "unsung heroes" signal contributions to the Liberation War effort. Our minds have been so taken up by the refrainous recital of acts of valour by persons readily recognisable for their socio-political standing and access to publicity that the "nondescript" freedom fighters at best tend to draw a sympathetic reference, and only in passing.

Though I could not believe I would find him "nondescript", I felt spurred to meet an "unsung hero". And for that purpose returned once more to Shamoly, the noisy, dusty area which I remembered well from the many times I had circled it when looking for the home of Abu Taleb. It was a place which never seemed conducive to my efforts.

"Traffic jam, traffic jam," came the apologetic moan from my contact on arriving nearly two hours late. Having sat all that time on a concrete seat by the busy roadside, and been subject to the endless curious stares from which no lone western woman can escape, I was more than pleased to see him.

Salam was Head of the CRP Social Welfare Department, and I had recently discovered that he had been a Freedom Fighter. In fact he was one of the many to have just received a commendation from the Government some twenty-eight years after the event.

Together we crossed the road and arrived at the gateway of a hostel for paraplegic Freedom Fighters. Two or three of the residents were sitting outside, and willingly they escorted us to a reception room.

It was a place both drab and dim, with shabby chairs, two very rusty metal cupboards and little comfort. Yet I detected also an ambience of fortitude, a degree of spirit. On the wall was a well-marked map showing the location of the various sectors of the *Mujahadin* during the War. Beside it, hung a black and white portrait of their commander in chief, M.A.G. Osmani, shown with huge white handlebar moustache and a lightening of the background behind his head which had the effect of a halo. But the essence of the atmosphere undoubtedly emanated from the occupants, both residents and visitors, who were now gathering round to support the comrade we had come to visit.

His name was Modassar Hossein Modhu; and, so they said, there was still a Pak bullet inside him. You would not have guessed it from his face. A slender man with lightly hennaed hair and neatly trimmed moustache and beard, he had dreamy eyes and lips around which a smile seemed constantly to flutter.

I started by asking what East Pakistan was like before liberation, and why Hossein had joined the Freedom Fighters. And everyone wanted to contribute to the answer. From the beginning, they said, from 1947, the Pakistan Government had done a lot of bad things to the Bangladeshi people. Then there was the threat of making Urdu the national language.

"We wanted democracy," they added. "Bengalis had no rights. We produced things, but the benefits went to Pakistan. We had no independence, no rules or laws of our own."

I tried, then, to find out more about Hossein who was, at this point, saying very little. He hailed, I now learnt, from Rajshahi in the north-west; and when war broke out he was only twenty-one years old, still at college.

"We were very angry," he explained. "The Paks were killing our people, raping our mothers and sisters."

In response he joined his local group of the Freedom Fighters, and subsequently went to Shiliguri in India for twenty-eight days training. This completed, he returned to the local headquarters at Nawabgang, a secure base near the Indian border from whence the *Mujahadin* could advance on their enemies.

As I drew Hossein out, the little reception area gradually filled with people, all of them eager to contribute to the story. There were two more residents in wheelchairs, one wearing a *topi* and working his prayer beads; and another, an enormous dark-skinned man with frizzy hair, whose presence in the room unintentionally dwarfed the one I had come to see. Yet another of the inhabitants gave rise to the impression of a biblical character on crutches, an effect achieved by flowing hair and beard and particularly long punjabi. Then there were the visitors. A rather self-important looking man, carrying a briefcase and wearing a bright pink-striped shirt and woollen waistcoat, came and sat on the sofa beside me; and thus placed, delivered a speech intended, I suspect, for inclusion in my book. And standing over him was a Bengali from Holland who handed me his visiting card and explained that his job was to coordinate the effort to help those ex-Freedom Fighters now in other countries.

Together the assembled company started to tell me with considerable pride about the Non-Cooperation Movement. Information was coming at me from all directions, and only later, and with the help of my reading, did I finally succeed in piecing it together. The Non-Cooperation Movement began on 2 March 1971 following the announcement by Radio Pakistan of the postponement of the inaugural session of the National Assembly. From that day the civil administration of East Pakistan came to a standstill, and members of the East Pakistan Rifles, together with the police force, announced their refusal to fire on demonstrating Bengalis. On 3 March, Sheik Mujib called on his people for their support and directed that no one should pay rent or taxes, or cooperate in any way with the government. More detailed instructions were included in the historic speech made by the Leader at Ramna Race Course on 7 March shortly before his arrest. From then on courts, government, and semi-government offices ceased to operate. Banks no longer transferred money from East to West. Long distance tele-communications shut down. Transport facilities were denied to troops, and workers boycotted any branches of the media who failed to cover the Bengali resistance in full. Educational institutions closed their doors.

"Even our primary school children took part," residents and visitors at the Freedom Fighters Hostel impressed upon me. The Bengali people had acted as one, and no one could dispute that every effort had been made to achieve a solution through peaceful protest. Indeed some Bangladeshi historians now argue that Sheik Mujib waited too long: that his followers should have been permitted to resort to arms earlier, and that his policy of non-violence served only to give the West Pakistanis time to assemble their troops.

With some difficulty I got back to the story of Hossein. Once trained, he had soon found himself in action. "The Pak Army wanted to attack the village," he explained, "The Freedom Fighters challenged them face to face". On that day in early October, less then six months after the war had started, Hossein received a bullet in the ribs which paralysed him for life. Four of his comrades were killed; the Head Quarters were saved.

Hossein was sent to hospital in India and he was still there in December 1971 when Independence was declared.

"Everyone in bed was cheering and crying," he recalled. "I had a bullet in my side, but it didn't matter. My country was free. There were tears in my eyes."

It was not until September 1972, nearly a year after his wounding, that Hossein was able to return to Bangladesh. Even then he had to stay in hospital and to come to terms with confinement to a wheelchair. I asked about his life now, but he tossed his head slightly as if to throw off the idea.

"I am not thinking about my life," he said. "I am thinking about our country."

And the dream for which he fought, had it been fulfilled?

"My dream," he replied, "was that one day Bangladesh would be independent. We wanted happiness for the people of our country. But this is not fulfilled. We wanted peace, and a developed country, not a poor country. Our country is independent and yet it is still dependent financially, economically and politically. When we are independent in all these ways, then our dream will be fulfilled, not till then."

The interview was over. The big, frizzy-haired man pressed upon me an article about himself and lifted his shirt to reveal the enormous scar on his stomach. Hossein said no more.

I had read about the single-legged rickshaw wallah some nine months before I met him. An article in the Daily Star had detailed the experiences of a group of young people travelling round the country showing a documentary film about the Liberation War. In the process they had met many former Freedom Fighters willing to talk of their experiences, and one of these was Saidur Mia. Immediately interested, I added the names of the film makers, Tarique and Catherine Masud, to my list of leads. But during the months that followed I found my time consumed by our own CRP production. I might never have managed a meeting, had not fate decided to take a hand. In order to edit our film, the Director had to hire equipment, and thus, much to my surprise, I found myself actually working in the Masuds' office. It was then but one easy step to get introduced to Saidur.

He arrived, tall and quiet on his crutches, and waited patiently for me to leave my work and join him in the other room. One could not help but be struck by Saidur's unusual appearance. Prominent cheek bones, close-set eyes and a patrician nose served to elongate a thin face – an effect heightened by the manner his hair was pulled away from the brow to be tied at the back. A wispy beard added a touch of the whimsical. But his expression exuded calm and spoke of inner strength, a stoicism developed, no doubt, by the amazing set of circumstances which the possessor was about to unfold.

It was Saidur's mother who had insisted he join the Freedom Fighters. The atrocities committed by the Pakistan army had reached a point at which normal life was no longer possible. No more could the people stand by and accept what was happening to them. Saidur, aged about nineteen and newly married, left for the front.

He was to come back just once, before the start of a major military operation. And he remembers now, with painful clarity, how his mother cooked a special meal for him. It was duck, his favourite dish; and she begged him to take time to eat it; but he felt compelled to leave without doing so. Little did he know that it was to be the last time he would see her alive.

The ensuing battle was both bitter and bloody. Many Freedom Fighters were killed, including one with exactly the same name as Saidur. Thus in the confusion which followed, news was carried to his mother that her son had died. Normally prone to high blood pressure, she immediately had a heart attack and passed away herself.

Saidur had loved his mother greatly. When the Commander told him to go to her, his reply was a cry from the heart.

"There is no point. I will not see her. I will see only mud. I will liberate the country; then I will go to my mother. Then I will visit my mother's grave. It was she who inspired me to go to this war, but now she will never see her country free."

It was the following December, and only a few days before Independence, that Saidur became so grievously wounded. They were fighting near the railway line at Khulna, and he had to crawl over a big pile of sand in order to get across the track. First one bullet hit him and then others.

"It felt as if my leg was being pushed and pushed, and then I realised that it was almost gone."

Victory Day came on the 16 December 1971; but Khulna was still in enemy hands. Celebrations in the hospital were muted.

"The country was liberated but I had become a cripple and lost my personal freedom. My mother, too, was gone. She was not there to see the result she had longed for."

The remains of Saidur's leg had to be amputated. He was transferred to a hospital in Dhaka, and later, to an adjacent hostel for disabled Freedom Fighters. There, in 1975, the comrades heard that their beloved leader, President Sheik Mujib, had been assassinated along with all his family.

"We were devastated. We thought to ourselves, 'He was in Pakistan for nine months while we were fighting, but even they did not dare to kill him. But today he has been killed by these murderers. If they can kill him, they will kill anybody.' Everybody, even the staff, was frightened. As committed Freedom Fighters we had received great blessings from Sheik Mujib's government. So now, we thought, we would become the target."

They all fled. Saidur set off, with only one good leg, to walk all the way from Dhaka to Aricha. It is a journey which, I know myself, takes more than two hours by fast bus. For Saidur it took all day. Not daring to use the main road for fear of the army, he chose a side route which was even longer than the norm. His artificial leg was new and untried. It rubbed horrendously against his wound, and at Aricha he was forced to leave it behind. But from there, at least, he was able to use the ferry and a bus to get to Khulna. It was the only place where he felt safe.

Saidur's village had been totally burnt down during the war. But his family had been rehabilitated in 1972, and he was now able to join them. Sadly, though, his father died shortly afterwards, and Saidur suddenly found himself responsible for a stepmother, as well as for his own wife and, in due course, some children. Determined to support them, and not to be dependant on charity, he hit on the idea of becoming a rickshaw wallah. By tying his one good foot to the pedal, he found he could manage. But in his own area, Saidur felt embarrassed. He decided to take the whole family to Dhaka and start afresh.

The most lucrative area to ply a rickshaw in Dhaka, Saidur soon discovered, was Motijheel. But it had it's problems, especially for a puller with only one leg. Accidents were frequent; and with his foot tied to the pedal, he was unable to exert much control. He decided to move to the much less busy, residential area of Dhanmondi.

Saidur and his family had settled in a *busti*, or slum, and he hired his rickshaw from a wealthy man near New Market. Getting from one place to the other was not easy. To leave his busti he had to cross a bridge made of a single bamboo. With only one leg it was a tricky process, and it normally took him three or four hours to get to his rickshaw.

Tarique and Catherine Masud, meeting Saidur about this time, were so troubled by his situation that they enlisted the support of friends and managed to find him alternative accommodation.

In my ignorance, I had, until this interview, always imagined that no payment was necessary for setting up shelter in one of the appalling slum areas around Dhaka. Now I learnt from Tarique, that the "position" which they had bought for Saidur in this second *busti* cost them twenty-five thousand *taka*, (approximately equivalent to two years wages for a domestic servant). Even worse, was the fact that this price provided no legal entitlement. In the Government's heartless programme of demolishing slums, Saidur could be evicted at any time; and he would not have the right to any form of compensation.

Both the system, and the conditions to which it gives rise, seem tough and unjust. How did Saidur feel now, I wondered, about the country for which he had fought?

"We had only one expectation: that our country would be free. And we are happy now that it is liberated. But in my case I am suffering, while those who were not Freedom Fighters are benefiting. I am being treated almost as if I had been a collaborator. The Government does not support those who became disabled whilst freeing their country. I do not even have a right to a home."

Saidur's health has now deteriorated. Dhaka is a highly polluted city, and rickshaw wallahs, constantly breathing poisonous exhaust fumes from the vehicles in front of them, are particularly at risk. Our own CRP doctor once told me that the average life expectancy of a rickshaw puller in the city, regardless of age, was only ten years from the day on which he started work. Saidur himself managed twenty years before he was forced to give up by the onset of resperatory problems and tuberculosis.

His spirit, as opposed to his body, appears undiminished.

"I have," he said, "Great, great respect and admiration for physically challenged people who do not give up, or go for begging: for those who work and earn, and live a life of respect. I do not like those who give in, and become a subject of pity."

He gave me his gentle smile and said good-bye.

There are many in Bangladesh today, and not just the disabled, for whom to "work and earn, and live a life of respect", is extremely difficult. And if they are to be helped with a sensitivity to the kind of feelings expressed by Saidur, it cannot be by simple charity. Imaginative solutions are called for; and one such is that of the Grameen Bank.

Even their Headquarters came as something of a surprise. I had not fully appreciated, prior to that visit, that Dhaka has so few skyscrapers – a fact which came forcibly to my attention whilst standing at the tenth floor window of the bank complex. I was only half way up the building, but was still far above everything else in the vicinity. The roofs of the city were laid out beneath me. Only in the distance did I perceive one or two other isolated towers on the horizon, and even these terminated at a height roughly level with my eyes. Here there were another eleven storeys to go.

The edifice I was visiting was certainly an appropriate one for an organisation which has been described as "possibly the world's leading proponent of trickle up development", and "the most successful self-sustaining anti-poverty programme in the world".

The Grameen Bank was founded in 1976, and now operates in half the country's sixty-eight thousand villages. It has five hundred million US dollars in assets, and its ideas have been copied worldwide. Yet, like so many other successful organisations, it started as the dream of one man, and as a result of a casual encounter.

Mohammed Yunus, an economics professor, was out walking in the country one day when he met a poor village woman trying to make a living through the production of bamboo stools. On seeing how hard she worked, Yunus was concerned to discover that the stool-maker earned very little for her labours. The reason, she explained, was that the only person prepared to lend her money to buy the bamboo, was the trader who purchased her final product. This man was thus in a position to set the price he paid, and it barely covered her costs. On hearing her story, Yunus' first instinct was to give the woman some money, but then he realised that if he did so, his help would be short-lived. What if he gave her a loan?

Yunus started to investigate, and the result is the Grameen Bank, based on the simple proposition that access to credit is a fundamental

133

human right. From the beginning, he strongly opposed the concepts that a borrower must be educated to be risk worthy and that micro loans cannot be profitable. Instead he insisted, and still does, that if financial resources are made available to poor landless people on existing commercial terms, then millions of small families, with millions of small pursuits, can create a development wonder.

Grameen Bank concentrates much of its effort on helping destitute women. It makes money available to them at low interest, and further opens the doors of opportunity by enabling each of its customers to gradually increase the amount of their loan. The success of the scheme depends on the fact that borrowers are formed into neighbourhood groups, jointly responsible for vetting each other's loan requests and ensuring weekly paybacks. If one member fails to pay, the group receives no further loans. And peer pressure seems to work; for according to the Bank's own figures, the default rate is only about 2 per cent. Typically the money is used for such purchases as livestock, a sewing machine or a silkworm shed. And by this means, the Bank claims that about one third of its borrowers have transcended the poverty line.

Certainly Yunus and Grameen have their critics. There are those who claim that the Bank's statistics are unreliable and the repayment arrangements unreasonably hard, there is no let up, even in times of natural disaster. Notwithstanding, there are few who would deny that the Grameen Bank is a remarkable organisation which has achieved great results.

It has not finished yet. Grameen is still developing and diversifying, and it has given rise to a number of other projects which also bear the Grameen name. At the time of looking out of the tenth floor window, I was in the General Manager's office of the Grameen Fund, a social venture investment company set up in order to finance those entrepreneurs whose commercial ideas appear likely to benefit society as a whole.

The General Manager, Mr Emdadul Haque, was sitting in his wheelchair behind the desk. A handsome, immaculately groomed man, with short back and sides and a smart khaki shirt, he had a distinctly military air, and ran his office with appropriate efficiency. A bell at his right elbow enabled him to summon assistants to fetch and carry files, while at the same time, he dealt in an organised fashion with the demands of the three telephones on his desk and the stream of visitors who took their seats before him.

Very soon after my arrival, Emdadul asked whether I spoke Bangla, and being reassured that my comprehension was poor, he felt able to continue business throughout my two hour stay. In so doing, he constantly amazed me by his ability to pick up our conversation wherever he had left off. In addition, and in order to ensure that I was fully employed when he had to talk to somebody else, he called for an enormous blue spiral bound file which he placed before me. This contained everything relating to his accident and subsequent medical care, understandably seen by him as "the most significant occurrence" of his life. Accordingly, and rather hesitantly, being used to the mores of western confidentiality, I found myself perusing medical reports, contract related documents, correspondence with insurance companies, newspaper cuttings and all the personal letters sent to Emdadul Haque during his long sojourn in hospital.

Emdadul, who is a chartered accountant, had a brief spell at Grameen in 1982, but subsequently went on to work for the Bata Shoe Company, where he stayed for three and a half years. He realised then that he was not really "commercially minded" but more what he himself described as "missionary minded", someone who is much happier working for a social development organisation or something similar. In 1985, he therefore rejoined Grameen and became their Chief Accountant. But his marriage in 1986 was to bring about a change in direction. His wife started to tell him that with his qualifications, he could, and should, get a much better job.

"It was making conflict in my mind." Emdadul explained. "One side missionary and one side commercial."

Perhaps, he thought, the way to solve the problem would be to take a short term consulting job. This would enable him to give his wife a reasonable sum of money, and he could then ask her to let him return to the work he preferred.

"I asked Dr Yunus to give me leave of two years. And I told him I would go to this job in Zambia. Then I would come back to Grameen."

Yunus agreed; and Emdadul and his wife, who was now pregnant with their second child, moved to Zambia where he became Audit and Systems Manager for the National Breweries, a State owned enterprise. It was thus in Africa, on the Ndola-Kitwe Highway in November 1991, that Emdadul, swerving to avoid a pedestrian, became involved in a disastrous traffic accident.

He had a major operation and was then transferred to a hospital in South Africa, where he was confronted by the fact that his paralysis was irreversible. Eight years later, Emdadul could still recall the surgeon's words. "Mr Haque, you will have to take rehabilitation training. I do not want to open the spine again because I do not see any good signs."

Continuing his story, Emdadul touched obliquely on a circumstance which I was later to understand as constituting his greatest sorrow. "All this long period my wife was not with me. She was in Zambia with the children."

The experience in South Africa, and later in a Rehabilitation Centre in Zimbabwe, constituted what Emdadul described as a "very tough period". And it was a time when the terrible loneliness, which still haunts him, first raised its ugly head.

Even so he did not give up fighting. His next move was to get himself transferred to the USA where he had some relatives. But the verdict of the doctors was the same. He must, they said, come to terms with permanent paralysis. Again the surgeon's words burned themselves into Emdadul's mind. He quoted them for me now, adding at the same time, his own reply.

" 'You must not be frustrated. A lot of people move around in wheelchairs in America.' But I replied, 'I am not American. I have to go to a very poor and densely populated country. I do not know how I will survive.'"

There were no answers. Emdadul returned to Zambia and resigned his job. He could have stayed on with National Breweries, but only for a short while, and in the meantime he had received a letter from Dr Yunus. "I wanted to come back; and Dr Yunus had already written saying, 'Come back as early as possible, join with us again.'"

On doing as Yunus suggested, Emdadul found himself in the

position of the first General Manager of the Grameen Fund.

At this point in his narrative, I made a mistake which Emdadul, putting my confusion down to ignorance rather than mishearing, considered extremely funny. I had thought he said something about "an adventure".

"If I want to cross a river with you after the flood, that is an adventure," he laughingly explained. "But if we start a commercial company, that is a venture."

He kindly interrupted his story then in order to explain patiently and helpfully about venture capital and the work of the Grameen Fund, which now includes supporting projects in electronics, cybernet and internet.

When we returned to more personal matters, I asked Emdadul about the main problems he had faced as a disabled person in modern Bangladesh.

"The worst thing," he said. "Is that people don't understand. People generally don't have extra sympathy for handicapped people. Suppose I am moving in the marketplace. Suppose I am facing some problem in a sloping area. No one will say, 'Can I help you?' ".

With hardly a pause he went on to the second problem.

"Doctors don't know how to treat a paralysed person. I was admitted to the sophisticated Diabetic Hospital recently for a minor operation, but after it was done I discovered that the nurses did not know how to care properly for someone who is paralysed. I asked to be released so that I could go home and look after myself."

Then came the third problem, and it was the one that consumed Emdadul the most.

"My wife stayed eight months, but she was gloomy, upset and frustrated. Then she went back to America. Dr Yunus said, 'Maybe she cannot accept it. Don't criticise her. Keep a good relationship.' I kept a good relationship, and after one year she came back to this country – but not to live with me.

"You see, I am staying with my brother. The house is small, so my wife says, 'I want to stay with my parents. When you go to the office I want to go to a job and the children can be in my mother's care. When the children are grown up then we can get together again.'"

"That arrangement made me alone, and if I was not a paralysed person that would not have happened. You see, the finance I have is not enough, the sex I offer is not enough; there is, for her, no sexual enjoyment. I can give, but she does not like it."

Emdadul's face had darkened. There was a terrible hurt and pain in his eyes; and for a dreadful moment, I thought this powerful man was going to cry.

"I am devoting myself to my work," he said. "When I go home I am lonely always. I need love. I need affection. I need company."

There followed another work interruption. It was getting late, and I think the person on the telephone reminded Emdadul about the time. He looked at the clock and put down the receiver with the words, "In just fifteen minutes we must finish."

Later I learnt that the lifts are turned off on Thursday evenings. On this day every week, Emdadul was forced to go early to his lonely existence at home. On others he stayed at the bank to keep himself busy.

Anxious to turn the conversation, I asked about changes he would like to see in Bangladesh.

"Our Government," he replied. "Our Social Department. It is not conscious of the need. It is not doing anything. Not creating any insurance for crippled people. If my job comes to an end where will I go? Maybe, since I am an educated person, I can earn my bread. But a less educated person, what will he do? Where is his shelter? Our Government and society does not care for people. This is a densely populated country. The people are too many. If they die, the Government does not care."

Did he, I asked, have any special message he would like to convey to others who become disabled like himself.

The answer was immediate. "Don't lose courage. What I believe is this: I have lost my lower part, but if I want to survive my upper part is sufficient. The main thing is to keep your vision upright. That is the main thing."

Emdadul was talking fast now, as he raced against the clock; and I was scribbling madly in order to keep up. But he called me in check. "Look at me," he commanded with urgency. He was clearly desperate

138

that I should take in the full impact of what he was saying.

"You could be going somewhere in a car, in a van, with all your family: wife, children, brothers, sisters, uncles, aunts, cousins. And suddenly they might decide to put you out and leave you by the road-side. And what would you do then? You have to start all over again. Make contact with those around you. Make new friends.

"So make a mission, make a job. Concentrate on that job. That will keep you alive. When you make a success in your job, a lot of people will come to you."

Then, once again, Emdadul recalled words that had been spoken to him in hospital, but this time by a counsellor, "Think for the future. Think for the present. The world is yours. You have a right to go there."

Still thinking about his message, Emdadul switched from second, to third, and finally to first person, so that his words seemed to become a lecture unto himself.

"He must make his mind up. I will have to walk and run alone. If I get success the people will gather round. If I fail I will be alone."

Our time was up and the meeting was over. I got up to leave, and, as I did so, glanced again at a big poster hanging on Emdadul's wall. Bold writing proclaimed the words, "Attitude is Everything in Life"; and underneath was a picture of four beer mugs. I had idly copied these into my notebook whilst waiting for Emdadul to finish a business conversation, and later when I came to type up the interview, I looked again at my sketches. The first mug, half empty was labelled: "Pessimist"; the second, with the froth overflowing down the side: "Optimist"; the third, with a froth which had come right off the top: "Spiritualist"; and the fourth, full to brim: "Realist".

Emdadul himself, I suspect, came into the last category. He recognised the limitations, especially in his personal life, which made excessive optimism impossible. But it was by perceiving and realising the opportunity for a full life at work, that he had achieved such amazing success. When later I told my Bangladeshi friends that the General Manager of the Grameen Fund was in a wheelchair, my remark was met with incredulity.

139

CHAPTER EIGHT

MADHAB: COUNSELLOR – CHRISTMAS IN MYMENSINGH – **POLASH:**
STUDENT – THE GAROS – DEATH OF A FRIEND

Madhab held the party in his garden; and we sat under a sky rich in
stars. The chairs had been arranged in a semicircle around an
ingenious central decoration of plants and candles. Mohua was still
putting the finishing touches to this as Madhab directed the
distribution of dishes from the heavily laden tables behind us.
Children darted amongst the guests, and a medley of Asian and
European music provided the background for their laughter. Mohua's
little niece danced in the candlelight.

It would have been a magical scene on any occasion, but this was
the seventeenth of March, the anniversary of Madhab's accident, and
we were involved in his annual celebration.

Though a moving idea, it also seemed a strange one. The serenity
around me was undoubtedly genuine, but why commemorate such a
terrible event?

Madhab had only been sixteen or seventeen years old when, on
trying to climb a mango tree in order to retrieve his football, he
slipped and fell. Twenty-three years later, apart from a very small
amount of movement in one shoulder, he was still paralysed from the
neck down. How could anyone wish to celebrate this? The memory of
the party stayed with me, and with it the question. It was the first thing
I asked, one December day some nine months later, when Madhab
gave me the opportunity to talk about his life. Proper understanding
of the answer, we had both realised, required a lengthy explanation.

"Generally, people do not like to remember horror," Madhab said
slowly by way of introduction. "They like to avoid it, forget it.

"When I was a boy I went to school, and when I was in the mood
I helped my father with the family business. But at that time I was not
very serious about either family or country. After the accident, things
suddenly changed – everything, both physical and mental, because the

two are very much connected.

"At first I was very distressed about the physical aspect, and very frustrated. Lying on the bed with plenty of food, and everyone visiting me and caring for me, had been all right. But gradually I realised that things were changing. My family were not able to come so often. I got fed up.

"In my boyhood, I had faced every kind of physical sickness. I had had typhoid and chickenpox, falls, a bullet injury during the liberation time, a snake bite and, on several occasions, had nearly drowned in the river. Always I had got better. But now a few months had gone by since this accident, and nothing was changing. I was just lying on the bed: lying..... lying.... lying.

"Then I did it. I put my question to Valerie Taylor who was my physiotherapist. I asked, 'When will my finger start to move?' And she replied, 'Your finger will never move again.'

"That was a great shock for me. Still I cannot forget that word or that day. I cried a long time. I felt there was no longer any point in living. 'Better to die,' I thought. But that was not easy for me either.

"Val encouraged me to keep trying. She made me practice writing and drawing, using the power in my shoulder and a splint on my hand. But I found it boring.

"Always in school I had been a poor performer in art. I had been very good in other things – always first, second or third. In fact it was impossible to even think of being fourth, or failing. But in drawing, I regularly got a very poor mark, only just a pass. So when Val gave me the materials with which to draw, I was not very happy. But I tried to draw a flower and a leaf; and using the colour frame, my efforts gradually took shape. Then one day, I found Val hanging bits of paper round the room and on the office wall, and she was showing them to other people and saying how excellent they were. That was encouraging. I tried to give more and more time to my painting. I wanted to do something she could really be proud of. I tried enamel and oil, but it is watercolour that I love. And one day I realised that, 'yes', I could paint. And if I could paint, I had the opportunity to do something."

As Madhab talked my mind wandered to his paintings. Although he now had very little time for art, his pictures were popular with all who saw them. Several had recently been commissioned for an exhibition in England, and others had been used on greetings cards. I remembered some lovely river scenes and sunsets.

"Then," Madhab was saying, "I found a lot of other tetraplegics suffering from depression, and I thought it would do me good if I could help them. I suggested to Val that maybe, when they came for treatment, I could assist them to build up their confidence. She agreed and I started work. I had no academic training at the time but I used my personal experience, and later, I took a short course and got the advice of experienced counsellors. Helping others helped me. I began to see a lot of paraplegics and tetraplegics improving after our discussions. Maybe what I said was right, maybe it was wrong, but they were listening.

"For example, there was one paraplegic, a well-off educated boy, who was very upset. He didn't want to show his face to anybody. I tried encouraging him. I said, 'Let's go outside for a change' but he always refused to go with me. He didn't want to continue his life. He wanted to finish it as soon as possible. Yet his disability was not as serious as that of others, and he came from a rich family. He had opportunity. So I tried again. I said, 'Let's go at night time. No one will see us', and to this he agreed. So we went out in the dark, and he insisted that we sit right in the middle of a field, out of sight of everyone. And we sat in the middle of that field and had a long discussion. Then at 11 o'clock we turned to come home, and on the road he covered his face. He said that the headlights were disturbing him though I knew that he was hiding in case any of his friends were in the cars that went past. But he had been out, and it was a turning point for him. And after his discharge we kept in touch. We went to the cinema and to a Chinese restaurant, but the big move was that first field. Now he is a man who has a full time job with another NGO. His name is Ashraf.

"Apart from this sort of thing, I have also had the opportunity to meet many important people. For example the Oxfam Director, the Head of the British Council and other very responsible people have become close friends. And I have met Mother Teresa, Edmund Hillary and Princess Anne. There was also Brother Roger, founder of Taize. Mohua and I visited his community in France, and while we were there, he invited us to have dinner. He even tried to persuade us to stay an extra month.

"All this is so different from the future I saw before me as a boy. As the eldest son, I would have been responsible for helping the family, and I would simply have gone into business. But now, as things have turned out, I can supply a service to a large number of families. Most of the patients who come here after an accident are alone in their trouble, none of their relations having suffered anything similar. They need a lot of moral support to start again and to fight their new lives; but if they get this, they can be successful. Of that I am very much sure. Many ex-patients are now running their own businesses and supporting their families. And they are helping others as well, lending support whenever they hear of an accident happening.

"So now, I am involved with many people. And in this I have been given a big happiness. How is it that I have this kind of opportunity? It is because I had an accident. So my accident actually increased my opportunities, and gave me a brighter life. That is why I do not like to forget. I try to celebrate, to remember. I feel I have more responsibility: I can do more for the poor people around me. It is my job to help them."

The previously unstoppable flow of Madhab's words came to an end. His answer was complete and we were both silent. To continue our discussion seemed almost superfluous.

Yet there remained a few general questions which I had noted down to ask. As Special Projects Officer for CRP, and the main counsellor for patients, Madhab had acquired a unique understanding of the disability issues in his country.

What did he see as the biggest problem facing disabled people in Bangladesh?

His reply was instantaneous, "Undoubtedly it is the attitude to disability. Our Health Service is very limited in the countryside. Also, over 30 per cent of disabled people cannot read or write, and the general public have no idea about treatment facilities. They will go to any so-called doctor or 'quack' who offers a service, and because they believe in ghosts and bad winds, they will believe anything the 'quack' says. Often, they do not receive proper treatment, and in a very short time many of them die. Then the 'quack' has to say something, so he says that the patient must have done something wrong in a previous life and that this was his punishment. And the people believe what he says; so when they see another disabled person, they think that that person also must have done something wrong: that the disability is a punishment from God, and will be followed in a short time by death. They think to themselves, 'If we help him or her, then maybe God will become angry with us as well, and then the problem will spread to our family'. So they do not help.

"We need first to change the attitude to disabled people and, yes, there are already some good signs that attitude is changing."

I asked Madhab to elaborate.

"Twenty years back," he said, "there were only four or five NGOs working on behalf of disabled people in Bangladesh. Now there are more than one hundred. People are trying to do something, and as a result, more people are coming to the hospital for help. Previously for example, stroke cases very rarely came for admission, even when they had enough money. The family would say, 'He got up to go to the toilet in the night and a ghost pushed him in the back and broke his neck.' They had no idea what had actually happened, so they called the 'quack'. But now the stroke patients, including women, are coming for proper treatment. It is a big jump, for the women especially, because previously they were not allowed to go outside. They never came to the city. Thousands of people in the countryside have never been to Dhaka."

Warming to his theme, Madhab went on to explain why the situation for disabled women in Bangladesh is so much harder than it is for men. According to him, when a man marries he does so for three purposes: one, to acquire a slave; two, for sex; and three, to produce children to look after him when he becomes old.

"In Bangladesh a man can change his wife. He can have any number up to five. It is no problem, and if the first one becomes disabled, then the husband may feel that she is 50 per cent dead anyway. No longer can she help with the family, satisfy him in sex, or produce children. God is punishing her, the man concludes. So why spend money on her? Better to let her die and then get a new wife."

Watching Madhab as he spoke, I could sense how very deeply he cared about the plight of such women. And when I asked what changes he considered most necessary in Bangladesh, he continued in the same spirit.

"I would like to see more educational opportunities for disabled women, including professional training which would give them the chance of independence."

Then there were other things he wanted: more organisations and government facilities for disabled people generally, legislation, not just written but also practised. Drafts for this, he said, had already been prepared.

"We have spent the last ten years trying to make it (the legislation) happen. In a short time now it should become law. Even then, there will still be a long way to go before it becomes practice, but the opportunity will be there. The opportunity for disabled people to claim their rights."

I turned to the subject of employment. Did Madhab consider it possible for those who were as severely disabled as himself to get work in Bangladesh?

"Not easy," he replied, "but possible."

There was, he said, a very big employment crisis in his country. There were simply not enough jobs. Hundreds and thousands of educated men and women were without employment, and every day this figure was increasing. "When we advertise for a cleaner at CRP, we ask for a Class 8 pass but we actually get people with degrees applying for the job of cleaner. Just recently, we have appointed a receptionist who has a Master's degree."

"Then, when a person with disability applies for the same job as an able-bodied person, there is also the problem of accessibility. Bangladesh is very poor in this respect, so it is difficult for disabled people to travel between work and home. The employer has to think about this, and as a result, even when he might have offered a job to the disabled person, he will often change his mind and take someone else instead."

145

As a concluding question, I asked Madhab if he had any unfulfilled ambitions. And it was typical, I later reflected, that he should reply not in terms of desires for himself, but of his dream for society as a whole.

"One thing I would like to see, is a situation in which those who are disabled like me have the opportunity to survive on their own resources. With proper support such a person can do a lot, not just for his own family, but also for his country. Without help he will suffer and die. It is the support that matters."

To rise from a hard bed at 6 a.m. on a chilly morning and to wash in a bucket of cold water, would not normally be my idea of a good Christmas. But on this occasion, it seemed actually to heighten the feeling of pleasure. As a guest of the Taize Brothers in Mymensingh, I was about to enjoy a memorable 'Big Day', or *Boro Din*, and was to start by accompanying Brother Frank to early Mass at the convent of the Sicilian Sisters.

The old Brahmaputra was still misty in the early morning light. In leisurely fashion, our rickshaw made its way around the outskirts of the stirring town, and took us to a large Catholic church standing amongst palm trees in a green and peaceful compound. The service had already started. We discarded our shoes at the door and entered quietly: Brother Frank turning to sit amongst the men on the left of the aisle, whilst indicating that I should join the women on the right.

The Church interior was bright with lights and colour, red and white predominant. Scarlet decorations hung over the white cloth of the altar and cascaded from walls and ceiling. I was surrounded by snowily-habited nuns, but there stretched behind a brilliant mélange of saris, wave upon wave, in every hue and shade. To the front, a group of young musicians sitting cross-legged upon the floor, welcomed Christmas with cymbal, tambourine and drum; and red beribboned girls circled incense through the air. Music ebbed and flowed, revolving round the words of the Mass. Sight and sound coalesced to form a unity of the devotions of many. The Host was lifted heavenward. Under the direction of the Bishop, a kindly-looking man dwarfed by his mitre, the congregation filed quietly forward to take Communion. And each, after the final blessing, knelt before the crib in order to kiss the image of their infant Lord.

Outside in the sunshine I rejoined Brother Frank, who now stood chatting to some of the workers from the Taize Community Centre and also to Polash, a blind Garo student supported by the Brothers.

Brother Frank took Polash's hand and we walked along the cloister to visit Sister Lucy, now ninety-one, and the last of the foreign sisters to remain at the convent. Ahead we heard the sound of tambourines, and on turning a corner, came suddenly upon a courtyard full of dancing figures.

Brother Frank did not hesitate. With shoulders hunched, his white head bowed and a shirt tail escaping mischievously from the bottom of his pullover, he fell into step behind the dancers. Still holding the Brother's hand, Polash had little option but to follow, and before I knew it, I too was drawn into the circle.

Round and round we went, clapping in time to the cymbals and *khol*, a small drum held horizontally across the body. No matter now, that my two male companions came to a standstill. I had been sucked into the festivities, and felt happy to stay. Many of the dancers were nuns, their white habits flapping gaily as they smashed any illusions I might previously have entertained regarding the staid nature of monastic life. Saris and habits swirled together, faces broke into delighted smiles, and cheerful Bengali voices filled the morning air. As we circled, a Sister standing to one side, popped morsels of some unknown titbit into each and every passing mouth.

One song followed upon another but the steps changed little. This was the popular *kirtan*, a song-style dance of Hindu origin now adopted by all groups in Bangladesh and frequently kept going right through the night. How exactly they achieve this I do not know, for after only twenty minutes I felt ready to welcome the completion of the performance. The end, on this occasion, came with much handshaking and an all round exchange of Christmas greetings, and we were then led to the refectory to consume a breakfast of homemade cake. Sister Lucy was required to wait a little longer.

Sitting at the dining table, beneath a large map designed to show the distribution of the Order, but now partially eclipsed by seasonal decorations, I learnt a little more about Polash.

There are, apparently, relatively few disabled members of the Garo community. And those who do exist, have largely reached their predicament as a result of illness or accident. To be born with a defect is rare, a fact possibly linked to the tribal kinship rules which, in forbidding marriage to anyone of the same lineage, effectively reduce interbreeding. Polash went blind at three years old as a result of typhoid, a disease responsible for many such problems, including the deaf mute state of his tribesman Kleopa, carpenter of Taize.

With relatively few disabled people in a community, the able-bodied may be even less understanding. Little Polash soon found himself abandoned to the care of the Salvation Army; and he did not take his fate easily. "Our young friend," Brother Frank informed me only half jokingly, "was a very naughty child". I stole a glance at the adult Polash now sitting beside me. He was cheerily dressed in warm tartan shirt, tucking with relish into a plateful of cake, and nonchalantly nodding his assent.

Polash had run away from the Salvation Army and ended up begging on the street. He followed the vagrant life for a year, but then decided he liked it no longer and tried to return to his former carers, not expecting, perhaps, that the doors would be closed against him. They had had enough.

The Taize Brothers stepped into the breach. They adopted Polash who then, Brother Frank commented teasingly, proceeded to give them trouble as well. But they managed to get him into a hostel run by Aid to Blind Children, and subsequently enrolled him in Edward's School in Mymensingh. Soon they were to discover that they were sponsoring a very bright student. By the time I met him, Polash was in his second year at Dhaka University.

Intrigued, I asked how he coped with his studies, for I had not expected any Bangladesh establishment to be equipped to serve the blind. And indeed it was not. Brother Frank explained that they had bought Polash a typewriter and paid a stipend to other boys at the college in exchange for their reading aloud to their blind companion. The information he thus received, he had to memorize.

I turned to Polash in amazement. "Can you remember everything that is read to you?" I asked.

He answered matter-of-factly, apparently unable to understand my bewilderment, and as if he thought I had not heard Brother Frank's preceding explanation. "They read to me," he said. "And I put it in my memory."

Back at Taize, I borrowed some books from the Brothers in an effort to discover more about the Garos.

There are more than 1.2 million tribal people in Bangladesh, approximately 10 per cent of the population, and they come from over forty different ethnic groups. Although each group is numerically quite small, it still has its own identity, history, culture and language.

The Garo people, who prefer to call themselves Mandi, a name meaning "human being", are indigenous to the hills of Meghalaya and the plains of northern Bangladesh. They live amongst Bengalis and other tribals, but in an area where practically all their non-Bengali neighbours have opted for Hinduism, 90 per cent of the Mandis have converted to Christianity; and they attach a great deal of importance to it.

Mandi history depends largely on the oral tradition; and this maintains that their people came from Tibet and ended up in the area now known as the Garo Hills. It would seem that they have always been divided into a number of different sub-groups, and each, with its own dialect or language, continues to live more or less separately from the others.

At Partition, in 1947, the area escaped the mass migration and riots which ravaged other parts of the subcontinent; but the creation of East Pakistan had serious long-term consequences for the Mandi people. The new border divided them, and those to the south became a tiny minority in a country dominated by Muslims.

As the years passed, the Mandis were harassed increasingly by Muslim migrants, and in 1964 the situation erupted into violence. There were serious communal riots and nearly all the Mandis in the border area fled the country. But gradually, as a consequence of the terrible conditions in the Indian refugee camps coupled with a longing for home, most of them returned. By 1971 they were to be found fighting beside their former enemies in the hope of a free nation and a brighter future.

The Mandis were to suffer grievously at the hands of the Pakistan army who, it is alleged, particularly hated the Christians and Hindus. But amongst the Freedom Fighters, there was no discrimination or racism. They shared the same food and fought together. Side by side they faced thirst, starvation, bullets and death. It is sad, therefore, that the country which has emerged from their efforts has, for the most part, failed to recognise the sacrifice made by its indigenous people. Few have received the recognition due to the *Mukti Bahini* (Freedom Fighters) and many are today destitute and sick without any help from those with whom they fought. But their plight does not go entirely unnoticed. On Victory Day 1999, I found several articles in the national papers on this very subject. Things may yet change.

The Mandi kinship system is one of the aspects of their culture which most sets them apart from those around them. They are matrilineal, which is not to say that women rule the domain, formal roles of leadership and authority are normally assumed by the men, but rather that each person belongs to the kinship group of their mother, not to that of their father. Inheritance practices are linked with this system, and traditionally property is passed from a mother to her daughters. Often one daughter will be the main heiress with special responsibility to look after her parents, and consequently it is normal for husbands to move into the parents-in-law's household, something which is totally opposite to the practice of most Bengalis.

Sometime later, whilst travelling amongst the Mandi community in the Madhupur Forest, I was told a story which illustrates exactly what this tradition can mean in practice.

Chengu was a "Borman" (a Bengali speaking tribal Hindu), but at seventeen he ran away with a Mandi girl. The young couple returned together and the village forced them to marry. It was a stormy partnership, and one which came prematurely to an end when the wife died in the course of her fourth pregnancy. According to Mandi tradition, the husband loses everything on the death of his wife unless the family of the deceased formerly recognise him by instantly

150

marrying him to another Mandi girl. In Chengu's case the family were not prepared to do this. For him "everything" was very little, but most distressingly, it included his three children who were required to remain with their grandparents. On being forced to leave the household, Chengu effectively lost them.

The responsibility which rests upon a deceased person's own kinship group, to find another spouse for the widowed partner, works both ways; and has some outcomes which seem extremely strange to those of us from other cultures. If, for example, a woman is widowed, her husband's family are considered as "owing" her another husband. The problem is that men of her own age are usually already married, and therefore the only solution lies in finding her a younger man and in somehow persuading him to take on the role. The method frequently employed is to offer him two wives, not just the widow but her daughter and heiress as well. Even if the child is very young at the time, the promise is still be made; and in due course the girl becomes the co-wife of her mother. If, on the other hand, the heiress daughter is already married, no new husband has to be found. In that case the husband of the heiress is already living in the household and able to do the man's work. All he has to do now is to marry his mother-in-law!

Another way in which the Mandi women differ from their Bengali sisters, is that they are much freer to travel, and purdah is totally unknown. Mandi boys and girls are never segregated, and although the Mandis love all children, they tend to have a slight preference for girls. It is a most unusual attitude for Asia, where the birth of a female is so often seen as a disappointment, if not as an outright disaster.

In one respect, however, the traditional custom and belief of the Mandis does have similarities to that of their neighbours. Their previous religion, *Sangsarek*, taught that the world is populated by *mite* (unseen beings, generally translated into English as spirits), and that these caused illness by biting people. The only hope of a cure for the sufferer was ritual sacrifice of an animal, usually performed by the *Kamal* or priest. The severity of the illness determined the size of animal, and local men assisting in the ritual were required to build a new altar on each occasion. The *Kamal* killed the offering, daubed its

151

blood on the altar, and recited a chant urging the mite to leave its victim alone.

On reading this, I was reminded of the "evil winds" described to me by the Muslim healer on Bhola Island; and of the expensive sacrifices of chicken and goat undertaken by Joynal's parents in the hope of curing his club feet. In both *Sangsarek* and Muslim religions, the sick and the disabled, it would seem, are subject to similar superstition and misunderstanding.

Problems which may result from these sort of beliefs had been one of the main concerns raised by Madhab during our long talk just before Christmas.

Looking back, the timing of that discussion was to seem sadly opportune. Although Madhab had been one of the people to provide the initial inspiration for this book, I had delayed his interview. He knew so much about disability issues in Bangladesh, that by planning to leave him until last, I thought I could put to him any additional questions that might have arisen during my visits to others. Then something changed my intention, an instinctive feeling of urgency, a certainty that I had to talk to Madhab sooner rather than later. Strangely too, it was a feeling he shared, and being extremely busy at the time, he gave up much of his precious lunch hour in order to talk to me.

Only three weeks later, I was to return from Christmas in Mymensingh, to find Madhab seriously ill.

He had been in a clinic in Dhaka, but now, at his own request, had been brought back to CRP. His lungs, it seemed, were failing; and so were all his other vital organs. Tetraplegia creates a tremendous stress on the rest of the system, and as all his medical friends knew, more than twenty years of life after an accident such as his, was quite a record, even in western terms. Madhab's body now was horrendously swollen; and he lay, struggling to breathe, in a special care bed next to the nurses' station. To go near him, was to feel deep inside oneself the fearful presence of death. But it was only the visitor who seemed

152

thus shattered. Madhab, himself, was as perceptive and humorous as ever. Quickly and kindly he jolted me out of the cloud into which I had descended. "Your Bangla," he said with a gentle gasping laugh, "Is really terrible. Now repeat after me ...."

Alternately he teased us and then returned to serious matters. Acknowledging and confronting the inevitable, he asked Mohua to settle some outstanding financial affairs; but laughed at anyone who sounded too concerned. I sat with him late that night and found him anxious to know how the film was progressing. As an instrument designed to change social attitudes towards disability, it was a project close to his heart. It was Madhab's efforts that had finally got it off the ground, and even now he wanted to quiz me on the details of the contract.

Next morning he was still interested, but indicated he no longer had breath with which to answer. "The plane is on the runway," he told a colleague, "but it won't take off."

I had to go into Dhaka that day, and returned to hear a voice from the mosque loudspeaker wafting over CRP in a sad monotone of supplication. "They are praying for Madhab," a student told me dolefully.

It mattered little now that Madhab was of the minority Hindu religion, the whole of the organisation was united in one prayerful feeling. I found a considerable crowd around his bed and a constant stream of others moving in and out of the room, staying just for a few minutes in order to say goodbye. Madhab was no longer conscious. They were keeping him alive on a manual respirator, and we all knew that the muscles of his diaphragm could not sustain the stress for long.

I left him about 10 p.m. but was woken in the small hours by a lone masculine wail from the neighbouring house. Madhab had gone.

CRP was totally stunned. It came to a halt. In the clear light of morning everyone was to be found standing around in small groups. Most, including the men, were crying openly.

And then they came – the outsiders. On foot, rickshaw and by motor vehicle, pouring through the gates, people from far and near and from all walks of life, anxious to share feelings of love, loss and gratitude.

Madhab was laid in an open coffin, garlanded with flowers and carried to Reddaway Hall where Mohua's father read from the Hindu holy book. Silently we filed past to pay our last respects, laid our flower amongst the others, and signed a book of remembrance.

Madhab had enriched the lives of all with whom he came in contact. And his achievements lay, not only in the successes of his lifetime, but also in the determination he left behind – a determination to improve the quality of life of all those whom we so wrongly call "disabled".

Our inspiration lay in a man who had triumphed over paralysis and actually turned it to good effect. A few days after his death we planted a tree in his memory. It was a mango, the same species as the one from which our friend had fallen some twenty-four years earlier.

CHAPTER NINE

The second Eid of the year, Eid-ul-Azha, is a time of sacrifice. Time
to recall the piety and obedience of Abraham: a man prepared to bow
to divine command, even to the point at which he must kill his own
son. In the Koran this story varies in at least one important detail from
the version found in the Bible. For Muslims, it was not Isaac,
patriarch of the Jews, over whom the sacrificial knife was raised, but
Ishmael, son of the handmaid Hagar. Though not the child of
marriage, Ishmael was Abraham's first born, and it was he who
fathered the Arabic race.

For every family in Bangladesh, the Eid celebrations must be
marked by sacrifice. The number and size of animals involved varies
according to means, and as such often becomes something of a status
symbol. A well-off family in Dhaka will typically purchase one bull
and two goats sometime during the preceding Wednesday or
Thursday, keep them in a garage overnight, and kill them outside the
front door on Friday morning. According to Koranic law, the meat is
then divided into three parts, one third for consumption, one third for
gifts to family and friends, and one third for distribution to the poor.

The Eid sacrifice thus becomes a philanthropic event. Even so I
preferred to avoid it. Bangladeshis may justifiably accuse me of
hypocrisy, and public slaughter is no worse than any other, but I had
no wish to be a witness. It seemed a good idea to escape to a Christian
community, and to use the Festival as a time to increase my
understanding of the tribal people.

Madhupur Forest, I was told, was one of the Mandi areas; and a
Christian mission was willing to put up visitors. I sent e-mailed
enquires but drew no response. Once again it became a choice
between not going at all, or going without any clear idea of
destination or place to stay. It was with little difficulty that I decided

upon the latter, and a good deal of luck that I managed to talk Patricia, the new English teacher, into coming with me. With scant comprehension of what we were doing, we went into Dhaka on the Wednesday afternoon with the intention of making an early departure on the eve of festivities.

The New Zealand couple with whom we stayed the night shook their heads doubtfully. In truth it was a crazy plan. The whole city was in a frenzy; and even the short rickshaw ride to the bus station proved an impossibility. The only way was to dismount, and commit oneself to the flood of pedestrians overflowing pavements and seeping amongst the traffic. Everyone was hastening home for Eid. A train rattling along beside the road must have had as many people on top as it did inside. A colourful tightly packed jumble of bodies swayed precariously along the entire length of the roof.

The buses, brought to a halt at angles all around us, were similarly laden. And then, of course, there were the animals: animals everywhere, beautiful bulls and well-fed goats, owners of sleek coats and patient eyes. Each and every one was walking to his death. Ironically, too, owing to orange garlands, and horn decorations of crepe and tinsel, they appeared to do so with a jaunty, almost cheerful demeanour. My heart ached; and, perhaps fortunately, the determination to escape increased to a level which was shortly to become necessary.

The bus station itself was like a mad house, so crammed with people and vehicles that it was impossible to see the stand for which we were aiming. Heading in what we hoped was the right direction, we were forced to hold our bags immediately in front of our bodies in order to squeeze between buses. Constantly we were challenged by touts who tried to persuade us to board alternative transport. ENA, the company we wanted, they repeatedly insisted, was either closed or non-existent.

There was some truth in what they said. When eventually we reached the ENA stand we found that the booth was non-operational. There were no tickets to sell: every bus was fully booked. We joined the female side of the long line of would-be passengers and embarked on a three-hour wait.

Despite the chaos around us, we soon discovered both system and concern. A quota had been fixed in order to prevent the people in front from buying large quantities of tickets. And ahead of us, a kindly lady with excellent English, called me up to join her. She had, she said, only one ticket to buy, and could therefore acquire our two as well. Later she just as miraculously disappeared, but not before instructing the girl behind to look after me. And the latter did so with extraordinary diligence. Seeing a one hundred *taka* note held carelessly in my hand she remonstrated firmly. Then took the money herself, folded it small and replaced it in my palm with mimed instructions to close the fingers. Whenever, too, some movement ahead required us to shuffle forward, she insisted upon lifting my bag.

Long waits for the traveller may be very wearying, but they are rarely dull. There was a fascinating variety of people to watch in the melee around us. This being one of the more expensive type of bus company which permit advance booking of seats, the queue itself consisted mainly of young middle class people heading home for the holiday. But plying their trade amongst them, was a motley collection of hawkers. Face flannels were going well, for with these the sweating passenger could wipe his brow, or even try to prevent some of the effects of heat by covering his head. Shell jewellery was also popular for it made inexpensive and pretty presents for the children. However, potential buyers seemed less convinced about the appropriateness of underwear and kitchen utensils.

For two whole hours the queue was both patient and ordered, and then suddenly it sprang into action. The booth started to dispense tickets, people shouted excitedly, and we pressed forward. I was concentrating on keeping my position, and for a moment, did not notice an older man, with long blue *punjabi* and grey beard, who was beckoning me over. Even when I did so, I hesitated, for I was not prepared to lose my place at this juncture. Neither were the well-wishers around me willing to have me cheated. They questioned him hard before indicating that I should do as he advised. Somewhat bemused, I beckoned to Patricia, who was waiting beside the queue, and we followed the tall blue figure round behind the booth and into a waiting room. Here we found shade and comfortable seats and, in

157

due course, were presented with the two tickets we needed. It was totally undeserved treatment, bestowed on us, presumably, simply because we were "*bideshis*" or foreigners.

Eventually, nearly four hours after setting out on our journey, we finally pulled out of Mahakhali Bus Station and headed north. Soon we left behind the dust, noise and confusion of the capital, and entered upon a world of verdant paddy and pleasant tree-lined roads. Soothed by the sights around us, and exhausted by the long ordeal, our minds sunk into careless reverie. Despite the warning of Dhaka, we were but little prepared for the reality of Mymensingh.

In one step, we were off the bus and onto one of the waiting rickshaws. It was our plan to go first to the Taize Community for tea and advice, for we had no idea of the time required, or the best means of transport, for proceeding to the mission in the Madhupur Forest.

Mymensingh, like the capital, was in a pre-Eid fever of excitement, and as we got near to Taize it reached a crescendo. On the normally peaceful football ground outside Circuit House, hundreds of people were gathering; and all led animals for slaughter. A loud-hailer rent the calm with which I had always associated this corner of Bangladesh, and for the first time ever, we found the gates of the Community securely locked against intruders. A staff member did open when they saw us, but none of the Brothers were at home.

With Alex, a kind young Bengali student who made us tea, and Else, a visiting Dutch girl, we discussed our situation. Patricia's face looked shattered, and I feared that perhaps she had had enough, but I longed to press on to fresh territory and to the peace of a Mandi community. Time was against us. The clock had crept round to 3.30 p.m. and Alex was describing a journey which might take three hours, a significant portion of which was to be spent on a flat-bed rickshaw, or *vangari*, struggling along a rough road deep into the forest.

I looked across at Patricia. Was she willing to proceed? Confessing she really did not know what to do, my weary friend nodded an uncertain assent. We picked up our bags and I felt the responsibility fall firmly on my shoulders.

A rickshaw took us to the Tangail bus station, where as usual, someone tried to snatch our custom, this time by offering a truck and a driver for the rather substantial sum of one thousand *taka*. It was tempting, but we desisted, bought the fifty *taka* bus tickets and got on the local transport. Unfortunately it was only part full, and we knew that it would have to be well and truly crowded before the driver would consent to leave. In the meantime we were to be the target of beggars, all of whom looked desperately in need. Shortly after 4.30 p.m. we pulled out, and for fifteen minutes bowled along a quiet country road, then inevitably joined another traffic jam. Nevertheless, it was only an hour before the conductor motioned us to get off in the tiny village of Rosulpur guarding the entrance to the Madhupur Forest Reserve.

A little shop provided buns and bananas, and with a white moon already clear in the sky, we wasted no time in negotiating with the owner of a *vangari*. This, we discovered, was a hoodless, flat-topped rickshaw, usually used for conveying goods (and corpses), rather than people, but a version considerably more stable than its ornate upright counterpart. The long forest road to Pirgacha was known to be extremely rough.

No sooner had we passed through the gates of the Reserve, than we entered a different world, a sweet-smelling jungle of fascinating foliage. Vines embraced stout old trunks, broad fronded ferns grew out of the bark, fringed cane saplings rose delicately upward, and enormous crinkly leaves mixed with others of every colour and shape to surround our path. Ahead of us, the departing sun had turned the sky to gold, and high above, the white moon gradually assumed a silver glow.

Appreciatively we sniffed the fresh forest air, and looked around with a sense of wonder. A handsome Golden Tufted Monkey watched unmoved as we passed; and further along his kinsman sat high in a tree, a lengthy rope-like tail descending invitingly. Two large cats, possibly civets, crossed our path in the dusk.

Our *vangari* bumped and swayed, but we were engulfed in a deep peace. Constantly our barefoot rickshaw wallah had to dismount to negotiate pond-sized puddles and particularly difficult potholes. As darkness fell, the thought did pass through our minds as to whether he knew where he was going; and whether there were beds to spare at this unknown and isolated mission. But the question caused little more than a momentary ripple on the pool of our serenity.

And indeed there was no need to have worried. Father Homerick hardly blinked when two dishevelled, middle-aged English women materialized out of the darkness. A stout practical American Jesuit, who has been in Bangladesh over forty years and weathered the Liberation War, he simply requested that we shut the door quickly because of the mosquitos, then led the way to the dining room. Apart from asking whether we happened to be either the Germans or the Swedes he had been expecting, he in no way questioned us.

At the table we met Libby Laing, a diminutive New Zealand nurse in her sixties, who welcomed us enthusiastically. "So lovely to have some female company," she said; and settled down happily to doing all the talking whilst we hungrily consumed our meal.

In the "Villa Maria", nicknamed by Father Homerick "the convent", we slept well. The place was clean, and the hated mosquitos kept at an almost acceptable level by the vicious use of spray. We hardly stirred until the 6 a.m. bell reminded us that morning Mass would commence in only half an hour; and even then, both unashamedly turned over and went swiftly back to sleep.

Breakfast, one and a half hours later, was toast, scrambled egg and fruit; and once again we made the acquaintance of Father Homerick, Libby Laing and also Father George, a newly ordained Bengali priest here to serve some twenty communities scattered around the Pirgacha Mission.

There was little doubt that everyone worked extremely hard. The Fathers each undertook a seven-day week; and Libby Laing, based at the adjacent health Centre, had willingly committed herself to a regular six-day stretch, with only the occasional three-day break in Dhaka. We were to get to know Libby quite well during our short stay at the Mission. She had really meant it, when she said she was starved of female company. Now was a chance to pour her heart out, and to share the full details of an eighteen-month struggle.

The more Libby talked, the more we admired her. She was incredibly isolated, possessed the minimum of western comforts, and coped admirably with her medical boss who sounded to be one of those inspired and dedicated people with whom it can be extremely difficult to work. By her own admission, this brave little lady had reached rock bottom halfway through the previous year, and even now she appeared to be under immense strain.

During the first morning we looked round the mission clinic and weaving workshops, and succumbed to some of the lovely tribal fabrics in the showroom, before setting off on a beautiful twenty minute walk through the paddy fields to find the Health Centre where Libby worked. Sweet-smelling white flowers fringed our path. Brilliant scarlet blossoms etched themselves against the blue sky overhead. Broadly smiling Mandis, in colourful skirts, bent low over the emerald paddy or led their goats lazily along the causeway. It was a million miles from the chaos, noise, pollution and bloodshed of yesterday's Dhaka.

The Thanerband Health Care Centre consisted of a few simple mud brick huts scattered amongst the trees; and Libby's desk, decorated with fresh flowers, was set on an open verandah overlooking the fields. Here at least, she could find both peace and beauty.

The Centre exists to provide treatment "of the poor by the poor"; and with the exception of the doctor and Libby, the staff are all impoverished local people, many of whom have little education. Offered the opportunity of training, they have progressed rapidly; and Libby spoke proudly of a sub-centre already nearing independence. Not only does the organisation provide treatment, but also health education for patients and carers, a service which extends out into the villages.

At the long mission dining table that evening, Father Homerick regaled us with his experiences during the Liberation War.

"The Paks took me out in order to shoot me. But in the middle of the field I turned to the Brigadier and asked where he had received his training. And when he replied 'New Jersey', I pointed out how bad the story was going to look in the press: someone who had received their education in the USA ordering the shooting of an American priest. So he let me go."

Such stories poured fourth from our host with little prompting. He spoke in still-shocked tones of a night when the Pakistan army killed a total of 132 women and children in a single village. And, more amusingly, of a time when the Freedom Fighters had taken over the Mission. The Indian Army were supplying them with ammunition, and in one of the rooms of his house, Father Homerick had discovered a young Fighter sitting idly smoking on top of a pile of dynamite.

Other memories were stirred. A visiting Pastor, Father Eugene, had been only a child in 1971; but he remembered well the Non-Co-operation Movement which preceded the outbreak of war. One of the Pastor's older brothers had worked for the national electricity company, and the employees there had been unanimous in withholding electricity from all but the hospitals. The water suppliers had done likewise. But Father Eugene shook his head sadly in reminding us that although such peaceful efforts had succeeded in paralysing the country, they had failed totally in their attempt to extract justice from the opposition.

"When the Freedom Fighters seized the radio station in Chittagong and declared independence," the Pastor said. "We were determined that this should be our final war. We would either achieve our freedom now, or die."

Later the conversation turned to snakes, and Father Homerick conjured up some frightening tales of his encounters. This man, it appeared, had not had nine lives, but something nearer nineteen. He had already survived twelve motorcycle accidents: a fact which did not stop him from lecturing his young pastors on the slowness of the speed at which they chose to travel. "Why," he demanded, "did they take forty-five minutes to ride a distance which he could easily cover in only quarter of an hour?"

He spoke lightly of death. There was, he informed us, a lady dying in his clinic even while we spoke. Patricia and I had seen the patient that morning and thought her to be very old, but we now learnt that she was only in her mid-forties. "She stopped eating a couple of weeks ago when her husband died," Father Homerick explained. "They brought her to us too late. We are feeding her through a tube but she will die." It was not, he said, unusual for the bereaved to react in this way, and was a practice similar in some respects to the outlawed Indian custom of *sati*, where the widow lies down on her husband's funeral pyre. That however, is a very dubious practice: one which may, in some circumstances, be imposed upon the woman, rather than brought about by her own wish. Here, at least, there was no doubt that the impending death was voluntary.

The next day we were afforded a glimpse of some of the problems which confront disabled people living in the villages.

I had been talking to Kalik, a young therapist working at the Mission, and had told him about my book. In response he looked inquiringly across at Stephen, a paramedic who served as Father Homerick's right hand man. The latter turned to me and spoke in English. "Will you ride a bicycle?"

Four old-fashioned cycles made in China, were produced almost immediately. We pedalled out through the mission gates with Kalik leading the way, and Stephen bringing up the rear as if to pick up the pieces. Certainly the contraption beneath me sounded as if it might disintegrate at any moment. It rattled and crashed along in such a way that I wondered which would be the first to come off – a wheel or the rider.

Leaving the short stretch of tarmac provided by US Aid, we pushed our way up a brick-surfaced incline, and onto a rough and potholed dirt track. This, I was later to learn from Libby, was considered by her to be the "good bit" of road.

It was a beautiful morning. Bamboo bent gracefully overhead, and a Blackheaded Oriole gave his lovely flutey call from the adjacent trees. Crickets sung in the undergrowth. I bumped, rattled and shuddered.

We left the track and rode straight through a compound, scattering, as we did so, a flock of bantams on the thatched roof over our heads. Then we squeezed our way through a narrow gate, skirted a pineapple crop, and entered the clean, well-swept home of our first patient.

A man who should have been in the prime of life, lay huddled and motionless under some torn covers on the floor. Kalik spoke to him; but he neither opened his eyes nor moved, responding only with an unwilling mutter. Gently the two workers removed the covers, and revealed a dark shining body locked into crippling paralysis. The clenched hands had to be forcibly opened, and the legs with difficulty straightened by the therapist, whilst the broad tribal face of the patient contorted with pain.

He had apparently been referred to CRP last September, and had been told that the only form of treatment was exercise. It was uncertain, though, as to how well he and his family had been able to follow the advice given. A younger brother had the duty of caring for the invalid, but had obviously failed to turn him regularly. There was now a serious danger from bedsores.

The elderly mother came in to join us. Hitching up a long tribal skirt, she squatted down on her haunches to discuss the situation with the two men from the Mission. Meanwhile they continued the treatment, carefully sitting the patient up and working through a series of exercises, before laying him down again on the opposite side to the one on which they had found him. We then all watched helplessly as one of his legs went into spasm. The poor man was indeed in a bad way; and his situation prompted me to ask about the help available generally.

In some respects, this patient could be said to be lucky. He had the two health workers to watch over him, and would probably be referred back to CRP, with the Mission paying part, if not all, of the expense. For most disabled people in the villages there is no access to qualified medical help, and no one to support and train the carers. I remembered going out with the Flood Relief team way back in September 1998. Our doctor was the first medically qualified person to visit that particular community in ten years: and he was required to see 302 patients in just six hours.

Even for villages situated reasonably near to a hospital or clinic, the cost of a consultation with a qualified doctor is way beyond the reach the majority of the inhabitants. And there is unlikely to be any physiotherapy or occupational therapy available. These two services, which can do so much to help the disabled, have until recently, been virtually non-existent in Bangladesh. Information written in 1998 records a total of three occupational therapists, and about twenty physiotherapists, for a population of 120 million people. And although the Training Institute at CRP is working hard to rectify the situation, it will inevitably be many years before the full benefit of their effort is felt.

Our visits to the next three patients on Kalik's list only consolidated my impression of the lone battle to be fought, in this country, by those faced with ill-health. There were two three-year-old girls, both of whom had walking difficulties; and an eleven-month-old baby, with bulging eyes and distended stomach, unable even to sit up.

I rested on the edge of the verandah in one of these compounds, and considered the plight of the mother engaged in talking to the mission staff. Several months ago, whilst visiting Zakaria in Dhaka, we had discussed the lack of medical help for the disabled in Bangladesh; but I had failed to really empathize with the problem until now. This village seemed so far from anywhere. The kind and dedicated health workers had little training; and, it seemed, nothing to suggest for the case presented to them. The woman before me was confronted by the situation that all mothers most fear, and she had to face it in a kind of isolation, devoid of any truly informed assistance.

Death itself is never far away; and perhaps for this reason, is treated far more simply, and with a comforting familiarity which we seldom experience in the West.

We were finishing lunch that same day when Father Homerick announced the funeral of the widow whose self-starved plight we had been discussing the night before. We should hurry, he said, if we wished to attend. I was surprised at the invitation, and in two minds about accepting it. Surely the presence of strangers and foreigners at a time like this would be seen as an intrusion? But even as I sat undecided, Father was arranging for someone to show us the way.

We hastened down the road and over the rice causeway to a cluster of dwellings on the far side. In one of these, bench seats had been set out in the compound, and the male mourners were already seated. Something to drink was being ladled from a large cauldron into a collection of metal beakers. We didn't partake, but I guessed correctly that it was the smoky Mandi rice wine which we had first tasted at dinner the previous evening. The experience had taught me to avoid it; although Father later told me that the villagers preferred a

165

more diluted version to that enjoyed by himself.

The women mourners were, for the most part, huddled on their haunches round one of the houses; but some were in a separate room keeping vigil with the deceased.

Father George arrived on his motorbike, and on dismounting, donned white surplice and purple stole. Almost immediately, a loud wailing accompanied the body into the open. And with everyone gathered, the face of the dead was uncovered. She looked serene.

Father recited the prayers, and at the appropriate point, bamboo matting was reverently folded round the deceased. Then, securely tied and attached to a long green pole, it was hoisted on to the shoulders of a couple of bearers, and they led the procession out of the compound.

We all followed; and leaving the road, wound our way down a narrow track to a secluded spot on the corner of a pineapple field. It was a pleasant place, raised somewhat above the paddy, and providing a peaceful green vista. Here the villager would rest, truly at one with the ground that had supported her life.

A grave had already been dug out of the rich red earth. The deceased was lowered, and with great care the men proceeded to build a matting roof deep in the ground. As they did so, Father intoned the final prayers; and two women circled the grave anti-clockwise seven times. With bamboo fronds they sprinkled the covered body with Mandi wine, their holy liquid used both for the baptism of infants and the anointing of the dead. And as they did so, I remembered the gentle visage from which all emotion had been erased, and wondered about the forty-odd years of life, which despite the respected position of women in Mandi society, its owner had chosen to terminate.

It was a simple, dignified ceremony; and the ease with which it was carried out caused both Patricia and I to reflect adversely on the more protracted proceedings required in the West. For all its benefits, development too often brings the imposition of bureaucracy, and with it the destruction of much that is soothing to heart and mind.

166

CHAPTER TEN

"The big move was that first field," Madhab had said when telling me about his young friend, the one whom he had had such difficulty in persuading to emerge from the hospital and with whom he had finally succeeded only under the equalising cover of darkness.

By strange coincidence, I met Ashraf quite shortly after hearing his story. Like a sequel he arrived at CRP in person; and although his real purpose had been to visit Valerie, he was happy to stay and talk about his work.

Ashraf was now employed by the Voluntary Health Services Society (VHSS), the only health networking and support service in Bangladesh. He had been there for more than five years, and worked on their Special Needs Desk.

Reiterating what I had already heard from Madhab, he explained that Bangladesh now has more than one hundred NGOs working in this field. The purpose of his own section of VHSS was to coordinate and streamline their different efforts and to provide assistance where necessary. For this purpose, it had initiated the National Forum of Organisations Working with the Disabled (NFOWD), and for five years provided the new coordinating body with office premises, secretarial activities and other support. As a result the Forum was now off the ground and had offices of its own in Lalmatia.

Much of Ashraf's work so far had revolved around awareness raising, and the effort to achieve legislation. First, he explained, they had to get laws that would establish equal rights and opportunities; then they could "knock and hammer" at more specific issues. Though he would place accessibility as the most serious problem facing disabled people in Bangladesh, Ashraf considered the difficulties surrounding employment to be of almost equal concern.

We talked about the jobs of some of the other people I had interviewed, with most of whom Ashraf seemed well acquainted. I referred to Abu Taleb and the high post he held in government service; but my new friend looked unconvinced. Abu, he pointed out, had been working in that department prior to his accident. The Government, to Ashraf's knowledge, had never employed anyone at an executive level subsequent to their becoming disabled. Though conceding that the authorities had now taken on a few technicians with disabilities, he felt that having done so, they seemed to consider their small gesture as more than sufficient.

"They think they have done a lot," Ashraf commented wryly. "That they are giving some charity we have not earned.

"People with disabilities don't deserve this treatment," he added with feeling. "If someone has capability, they should be recognised for that capability."

I mentioned, then, that nearly all the disabled people I had met so far had been employed by NGOs. Did Ashraf, I wondered, know anyone working in the world of big business? He thought hard for a moment, then recalled a friend in a travel agency, another in a bank, and a third, Sugralakhani, who was an executive with Apex Tanneries. Yes, these people were successful, but it had been a hard struggle, the degree of prejudice with which they had to contend being best explained by an example.

Sugralakhani had been educated at the prestigious Holy Cross College and left with a Higher School Leaving Certificate. Her disability was not severe. She limped quite badly but did not need any form of mobility aid. Even so, when Sugralakhani had gone for a job as a telephone operator she was turned down because of her impairment. In vain had she pointed out that they were not requiring her to do anything with her leg. That, of course, was not the point. Ashraf explained that one of the main problems is that business employers in Bangladesh still think that the employment of a disabled person will impair the image of their organisation.

Something that made him particularly sad was the fact that, despite the large number of NGOs working with disability in his country, there were less than ten actually prepared to employ the people for whom they were arguing.

"Most NGOs are looking to other organisations to employ disabled people," he said. "But they do not do so themselves. NGOs should be setting an example. What they say should be reflected in their activities."

I asked Ashraf what he thought was the best way to increase awareness.

"It's very difficult." he acknowledged. "People with disabilities need to talk about their experience. Campaigns should be run involving all the print and electronic media. Awareness campaigns have to go on."

But he was not optimistic, and after a momentary pause added grimly, "We can achieve very little."

I tried to return to the positive. Surely he had seen an improvement in attitude in the seventeen years since he first became disabled with AVM (arterial venous malfunction)?

"Yes," he agreed. "When I became a disabled person I kept myself indoors and could not talk with other people. My problem was psychological. People whom I knew usually ridiculed those with a disability. They used many unpleasant words. As a result the disabled could not go out, could not meet with others, could not take part in cultural and social activities. Now it is much better, and this change has come about because of the work done by NGOs and the media."

We went on to discuss how entire families could be adversely affected by the existence of just one disabled member; and Ashraf told of how even a person prominent in the field of disability had been known to prevent the marriage of a male relative for no other reason than there was a disabled child in the bride's family.

Ashraf felt strongly that disability should be seen as a development issue, rather than one of charity. He was restless now with his desk job, merely coordinating and advising. He had plans that he wanted to initiate.

"Unless a person can become economically independent, then education and training are in themselves of no use. And through economic activities we can also address other development issues in the community. Thus, moving forward step by step, we can contribute to community development, and eventually to national development."

The economic independence of which he spoke was to be the result of income generating schemes. Currently in Bangladesh, there were no significant business entrepreneurs with a disability. And this fact Ashraf attributed, not only to the belief that people with disability could not achieve, but also to a tendency on the part of other business partners to deprive people with disabilities of their fair proportion of the profits.

"We need to establish small enterprises that can act as models. If these succeed more people will be interested, and integration can begin. If our businesses operate only with disabled people then the result will be segregation. We need to bring about integration, but only after ensuring that those with disabilities have the necessary leadership qualities, and that systems are implemented to prevent domination by the able-bodied."

Ashraf spoke with conviction. It would, I thought, be only a matter of time before he succeeded in getting some such scheme off the ground. The man who had once been frightened of anyone even looking at him was on the point of becoming a leader.

I sat in the cool, marble tiled interior of the Arab Bangladesh Bank. They had received me graciously and supplied a cup of tea while I awaited the arrival of the Foreign Remittance Officer, Antora Ahmed.

She had agreed to meet me on her day off but, because of my interest in her employment, had chosen to do so at her place of work. It was Antora to whom Ashraf had referred when he told me he knew someone who worked in a bank. And of all the disabled people I met in Bangladesh, she was one of the very few to have a job in the commercial sector.

Severely crippled by polio, Antora entered slowly but punctually through the main door. She was bent low over a pair of crutches, her movement laborious but determined. The daily journey to work had to be undertaken by rickshaw and must have involved enormous difficulties.

Shyly now she led me to her work station situated to one side of the bank in a sparse and orderly cubicle. I followed her bent back. Antora had to struggle to move; and at this point, conversation was not appropriate. Neither was it possible to see her properly. Only when we sat down, did I have an opportunity to realise Antora's beauty. Upright at last, and relieved of the crutches, her slender body, tastefully clad in a navy and white *salwar kameez*, conveyed an elegance all its own. She had lovely long hair gathered at the back of the head in a brown bow, and from her ears shone delicate little silver heart ear-rings.

With attention to detail, Antora ordered tea and cake and introduced me to her colleagues. Her English for business and work-related matters was more than adequate, as indeed our previous telephone conversation had already demonstrated; but it had been a mistake to assume that I need not bring an interpreter. When we started talking about her life experience I realised the degree of my error. Antora could understand the questions, but felt unable to express answers to her own satisfaction. We struggled for a little while, and then agreed that I should indicate my areas of interest and allow her to go home and write out what she wished to say in her own language.

Her charm simply over-rode any apologies I tried to make for creating extra work. Instead, she turned the conversation around and expressed unearned appreciation of my interest. Then very courteously led me to meet her Manager before saying good-bye. I was cursing my own stupidity. I knew too well how easy it is to say you will do something like this, but not actually do it. And I could not help wondering whether Antora would really get round to sending the material promised.

Such thoughts were ill-judged. It was but a brief delay before I received a lengthy e-mail. The following is a shortened version of the translation we made at CRP.

"My name is Antora Ahmed. I was born in 1965, the youngest of seven offspring of a middle class family in small town Bangladesh. One of my sisters has told me that as a small child I was very active. It seems I used to spend my days romping, dancing and playing all over the house. Then, when I was only three, I was attacked by polio, and all of a sudden all my fun and endeavour came to an end.

I remember that it felt as if I had I become a captive within the four walls of my room. The only way I could observe the outside world was by sitting quietly at the window, and I tried hard to understand what had happened to me and to make some meaning out of the environment all around. I watched the other children playing, but could not join in.

My family made an effort to acquire treatment for me, but our finances were limited, and they found that the cost was more than they could afford. My parents, I know, felt deeply frustrated. It was very difficult for them to accept my illness. My brother and sisters could not help me either, and they just left me alone. It was as if all the members of the family found my presence a disturbance. Nobody seemed to realise the importance of my education; although my brother and sisters all went to school, to college and to university. If it had not been for my mother I do not think I would have been educated at all. The lifestyles of my brother and sisters became so different from my own. It felt sometimes as if they were playing hide and seek with me, for when they used to go to school, or play, or visit relatives or friends, they dodged me. I did not understand their behaviour and it used to hurt a lot.

I would sit by the window and watch the other children going happily to and from school, or playing together as a group. When I saw them playing in the field I wanted to go and join them, but of course I could not, and even if I had, they would have rejected me. As I watched, my heart wept and my spirit was in agony: tears flowed down onto my lap. Sometimes my mother would insist that the others take me with them, but when they did so it was against their will and they would behave in the same way as before, just making me sit in a corner of the ground and instructing me to watch quietly. They really could not tolerate me, and most of the time they would try to leave without making any noise in order that I did not hear them.

Thus, when I was only three or four, all the doors to the outside world became virtually closed to me. None of the members of my family wanted to go out with me. They would not even talk about me, and they never introduced me to their friends. Often they seemed to pretend that I was not there. As I grew older I realised more and more what they were doing, and I felt unwanted and unimportant.

Newspapers, magazines and books became my only friends. They opened my eyes to the broader world beyond my four walls. I learnt that many disabled people like me could read and write, and with the help of others, could carry out their everyday activities on crutches. So I started to revolt, and to make my own demands on parents and family. I insisted on going to school, and finally got my own way.

The Headmistress gave me a really warm welcome. She seemed to understand my feelings, and in so doing, changed my world. I started to feel as if I was a human being. Some of my classmates actually wanted to associate with me, and for the first time, I could taste the enjoyment of life, and experience the help of others. So many of the feelings of disability and handicap were relieved by the friendship which I received at that time. And I gave myself wholeheartedly to my studies. I completed school and college and even graduated from university without difficulty. It was physically stressful attending my classes on crutches, but all my pain was relieved by the mental satisfaction I received from getting an education with my friends.

After doing a Masters Degree in Psychology at Rajshahi University, I started looking for employment. I attended interviews for jobs in both the government and private sectors. My physical disability proved to be a hindrance in getting a job with the government but I went on trying in other areas. I left no stone unturned.

Thus, in due course, I passed the written test for the Arab Bangladesh Bank. But the interview was problematic. Every member of the board expressed anxiety about my being employed. However, I managed to persuade one of them that I would be able to perform all of the duties and responsibilities related to the job, in just the same way as I had completed my education in school and university. Finally it was decided to employ me on the condition that I undertook to resign in the event of being unable to carry out my duties like other members of staff. In that way the bank authority would not be held responsible for my redundancy. I am very happy to say that I have now been working here conscientiously and efficiently since 1990.

But despite the fact that the authority is satisfied with me, I often find that I am discriminated against in relation to official duties. For example, as I have to sit at the desk all the time, I am frequently required to do the work of other colleagues. The reason they ask me to do this is because I work efficiently, and meanwhile they can move here and there, or go and chat with the boss. As a result I get a very heavy workload but the management usually pretends not to notice. My main responsibilities include facilitation of foreign transactions, and the preparation of statements and their analyses. And I have to operate telex and computer in order to carry out such duties efficiently. I am able to perform all these tasks without difficulty and I face hardly any trouble. Moreover I am happy because in many ways my colleagues are very helpful.

I came to Dhaka with this job in 1990; and at that time I had several close relatives living in the city. They all had their own houses in Dhaka and enjoyed every comfort and facility, but even so, because of my disability, they did not help me with accommodation. I had to live on my own and to stay at the Working Women's Hostel in Baily Road. Now I have a small flat and live with dignity and social prestige, a situation I have achieved largely as a result of my own effort. It is, though, the support and companionship of friends that has given me strength.

I spend my leisure time doing housework and cooking, listening to music, reading books and chatting. I hope also to improve the quality of life of the disabled by working to increase understanding, and to help people like myself become self-sufficient in the future.

To improve the life of women with disabilities one thing needs to be done immediately, that is to raise awareness amongst other family members. If parents, brothers and sisters were to show a positive attitude towards the disabled, give tender love and assistance and help them towards independence, then the life of those like myself would be much easier and happier. Most important of all, they would then be able to develop confidence and self-respect. Families of people with disabilities should be the first to receive social awareness education.

For my part I have reached my current position by patience,

enormous effort and sheer determination. I firmly believe that the success of all human beings depends on their own integrity and determination, and it is no different for people with disabilities."

I sat up reading into the small hours of the morning: the cause of my fascination a "Directory of Organisations Working in the Field of Disability in Bangladesh". A user friendly manual, it has clearly displayed entries and useful charts with detailed statistics on well over one hundred organisations. But some of the information puzzled me. Like so much else that I had been told or read in Bangladesh, it contradicted reports I had received from elsewhere.

It was a statement made by Ashraf that had caused me to turn to the Directory in the first place: the worrying figure of only ten NGOs prepared to employ the people for whom they were arguing.

The Directory told otherwise. Of the 120 organisations on their main list, ninety-six claimed to have at least one disabled staff member, thirty-seven reckoned that more than 20 per cent of their staff had disabilities, eleven put the figure at around 50 per cent, and three even boasted 100 per cent.

A closer look revealed that the three organisations with 100 per cent of staff disabled, were all very small. And it seemed quite credible that if a school for the deaf, for example, had just three staff, they might all themselves be hard of hearing or coping with other impairment. But what about an organisation which claimed to be working in several different regions of Bangladesh, to have both community-based and institution-based programmes running a wide range of activities, and to be benefiting thirty thousand disabled people? The Poor and Helpless Development Organisation (PHOD) claimed to be doing just that, and to be achieving it all with fifty-eight staff of whom thirty were themselves disabled.

There were one or two other organisations with similar records, but PHOD was of particular interest because it was situated in the Dhamrai area, only a short distance from Savar. Yet neither Valerie Taylor, nor her Social Welfare Department had ever heard of it. And one of the doctors, who actually lived in the Dhamrai *thana*, looked at the Directory in disbelief. "A hospital for the poor in that village," he said. "It is not possible. I would be surprised if they even have a house at this address." And when I pointed out the official nature of the Directory he only laughed, "You do not know my country!"

There was only one way to find out. Kabir, the public relations officer, agreed to accompany me, and though thwarted in our efforts to make an appointment, for both telephone and fax numbers in the Directory proved inaccurate, we arranged to go to Dhamrai on the following Thursday.

Meanwhile I had time to find out how the Directory had been compiled, and accordingly paid a visit to the offices of ActionAid who, together with the National Forum for Organisation Working with the Disabled (NFOWD), were responsible for publication.

ActionAid, I discovered, had done considerable work in the fields of research and documentation. National data on disability in the country was previously very scarce. Even incidence per capita was in considerable doubt; and in the absence of accurate information, most commentators used the international average of 10 per cent. Detailed surveys undertaken by ActionAid, however, now pointed to a more likely figure for Bangladesh in excess of 14 per cent, and suggested that over 50 per cent of households had at least one person suffering from some form of impairment.

Having talked about the degree of need, Dr Nafeesur Rahman, Unit Head at ActionAid, proceeded to describe his organisation's approach to a solution: a method based on something they call Participatory Rural Appraisal (PRA).

The process starts with mapping. The villagers are asked to take a stick and draw a detailed chart of their village in the sand. Everything is included – not just roads, mosque and school, but also every house and well. Then, into each dwelling are put different stones, seeds or leaves; these to indicate number of occupants, their sex, and any disability. It is, ActionAid have found, an incredibly exact procedure. The villagers have no hesitation in accounting for the slightest change in numbers. Once resources have been identified, they can look at aspirations. What, the team ask, do the villagers consider to be an

176

Boy washing at a well
Roger Varney

Robi cooking
Elspeth Waldie

Hossain in his shop
Elspeth Waldie

Village homes
Roger Varney

Garo mother and child
Elspeth Waldie

The Puja Festival
Elspeth Waldie

The Bandarban Hill Tracts
Elspeth Waldie

Maker of limbs
Elspeth Waldie

"ideal village" and what a "very bad village", and where would they place their own community on a scale between the two? With this decided, they can enter into discussion about methods for improvement. What are the problems and possible solutions? How should the latter be prioritised, how can the roles and costs be shared out, and at what time of year is the work best undertaken?

Such a method is nothing if not thorough; and it therefore came as something of a surprise to learn of the rather different approach taken, by Action Aid, in regard to production of the Directory. Two advertisements were placed in the national dailies; and all the organisations who responded, as well as those already known to NFOWD, were sent a questionnaire. Information collected from the completed questionnaires was tabulated, and then sent back to the NGOs in order to be verified. Dr Rahman admitted that the editors had done nothing to check out the validity of the information for themselves.

I mentioned then that it had been suggested to me that many NGOs in Bangladesh were not genuine. But the Head of ActionAid's Disability Unit merely smiled. There were, he pointed out about thirty thousand NGOs scattered across the sixty-four districts of the country. That was approximately five hundred in every district, or one NGO for every two villages. "If they were all working efficiently," he paused laughingly to give me time to reach the logical conclusion, "there would be no poverty."

It remained for Kabir and I to investigate PHOD. We set out by bus, and on dismounting, showed the address to the rickshaw wallahs gathered on the edge of the Aricha Highway. "House 86", it should be, "at Munto Nagar, P.O. Jalsha, Via Manikgangj". But not a single puller knew of it. There was much shaking of heads, and then after some discussion, the decision that one of them would take us to the village of Jalsha where we could make further enquiries.

A narrow, bump-ridden track under the shade of banana, palm and bamboo led straight into the heart of the country. Instantly we entered that world of emerald beauty and deceptive tranquillity so typical of rural Bangladesh.

The first people we met had never heard of Munto Nagar and

certainly did not think there was a hospital anywhere in the vicinity. But as we moved further into the depths of the countryside, our enquiries drew more response. Eventually, an elderly man, with long white beard and ornamental armband, pointed us in the right direction. Munto Nagar, it appeared was not the name of a village. Munto was a man.

We stopped at a tiny shop and were invited to sit down on a bench in the shade of a verandah while someone went away to fetch Munto's daughter. She was only a schoolgirl, and greeted us shyly, before leading the way past a notice proclaiming the entrance to PHOD, and so into her small tin home. It was dark inside. I could just make out an amazing collection of calenders. They spanned many years and appeared to have been retained as wall decoration. The girl seated us in front of a table piled high with school books, then stationed herself awkwardly at our side. Meanwhile the usual audience crowded behind her into the room and, by gathering in the doorway and at the windows, effectively blocked out the few rays of sun which might otherwise have illuminated the scene.

Munto's daughter explained that her father was away. He was in Canada and had been gone for nine months. She thought he was doing some sort of training in connection with PHOD but did not know exactly what it was.

I asked about the hospital described in the Directory as one of the main strengths of the organisation; but the assembled company immediately disappointed me by saying that they did not have one. Yes, they had started building, but the village politicians had not allowed them to continue. No further explanation was forthcoming.

By now, a member of the audience had identified himself as Munto's brother; and an elderly man, introduced as Munto's father, had taken his position on a stool in front of us. The brother took over responsibility for answering our questions.

He spoke of the organisation as having "branches", although he did not know where they were, and he thought Munto had bought a cow for blind people somewhere. Maybe there was a building for blind people, but he did not think it was open and had no communication with those involved.

178

After explaining my interest, I asked about the fifty-eight staff mentioned in the Directory, thirty of whom were said to be disabled. Everybody looked blank. Well, perhaps I could meet some of the disabled beneficiaries? I paused hopefully. This should not have been a difficult request. In the directory PHOD claims to have helped thirty thousand people, all with some problem of impairment. But I was waiting in vain; Munto's brother could not think of a single disabled person to whom he could introduce us.

Later, when the brother reiterated the information about those who were blind, I asked if I could visit some of them. But this only produced the hurried response that the beneficiaries lived a long way off, that the road was very bad, and that anyway neither the brother nor the daughter had any real acquaintance with the people concerned.

It was quite a relief when our hosts offered to show us the tube wells they had installed. They were eager for me to take photographs; and for our part we felt that any evidence of PHOD's work would be welcome. We went out past the small locked tin shed, briefly exhibited as the organisation's "Head Office", and got back on our rickshaw. Directions were given, and the brother, producing a bicycle, followed on behind.

The path narrowed until it became only just wide enough for our two back wheels. Beside us stretched massive fields of cucumber, and our host plucked us each a fresh green sample. He was eager now to impress and not a little distraught when the first tube well proved to be out of order. They had supplied forty wells, he told us proudly, and at absolutely no cost to the recipients. And with that he led us on to see some others. Free of charge the wells may have been, but I had considerable doubts as to the genuine poverty of those who had received them. The source of funds had been foreign donors.

Next they led us to a school: one which, externally at least, was impressive. Bright new paint covered the three-roomed block, and a notice outside proclaimed the work of PHOD in establishing the institution a year previously. But inside yet another disappointment awaited us, the classrooms were completely bare. Not a desk nor a book was to be seen, nor any other evidence of teacher or pupils. "It's the fault of the Government," our guide said without further explanation.

179

As our rickshaw struggled back along the path, Kabir and I looked at each other in dismay. There could be only one conclusion: that, name of the contact apart, every single piece of information entered under PHOD in the Directory had been invented.

It was a long way to the main road; but news can travel fast. When we got to our destination, somebody was waiting for us. As our rickshaw pulled up near the bus-stand, a distinctive looking character in dark sunglasses and white *punjabi* pointed us out to his companion and they both closed in. We had, they noted, been visiting Munto's place. It was a good organisation, they said, to which we should give money, and they wished to talk to us. Would we come to their house for a cup of tea?

The invitation did not require translation, but Kabir had a message of his own to convey. Narrowing his eyes and looking hard into mine, whilst at the same time shaking his head wildly, he repeated the stranger's words in English. He need not have worried. I had already decided that Sunglasses looked to be a suitable candidate for any bad man role on the Bengali screen.

Professing our need to hurry, we took the first tempo that came, and Kabir blurted out his relief even before we had settled on its hard bumping bench. "We'll get off down the road," he said in an effort to reassure himself as well as me. "We can find a tea house. I want a drink – but not with that man!"

"I like to use Ms," Fatema Khatum said with a firm smile, as I wrote down her name. It was the first time I had heard the title used in Bangladesh, and I suspected it said a great deal about the holder. Fatema was a much praised receptionist and telephonist at UNICEF. She was also a single parent and a tireless campaigner for the rights of women. There was little need for me to prompt with questions. For her, the hurdle created by a foreign tongue simply gave way under an overwhelming desire to communicate. The words came tumbling out of her.

"The Government has no concern for women," she pronounced as an opener. I murmured something to the effect that their Prime

Minister was herself a woman, but Fatema dismissed my comment with a laugh. "The Prime Minister and the Leader of the Opposition," she said. "They are both the same, they both lead political parties of men."

Fatema had recently attended the International Women's Day Rally in Dhaka; a good event, she said, with many lights and a cultural programme of songs and drama. Over forty women's organisations had been represented. "But," she added, "I protested when I heard that Lux Company wanted to sponsor us with their name on the leaflet. They are dishonest. A girl cannot develop a fairer skin, a sign of beauty in this country, just by using Lux preparations. They say these things to sell their products and with no reference to the truth. Such creams may even be dangerous."

Fatema was actually of a fair complexion herself, although clearly not as a result of using Lux. When later she asked me whether I could guess her age, I felt unable to do so. The sky-blue sari was youthful; but her face, half hidden by dark glasses, possessed a maturity and strength of character generally slow to accumulate. Laughing at my hesitation, Fatema told me that she was forty-six, and had been visually impaired for more than twenty years.

Born in Dhaka, Fatema had studied at The College of Home Economics. "Even then," she said, "I wanted to work for women's rights but the College Principal did not allow any political involvement."

At eighteen, she graduated and hoped to embark upon her ambition. But it was not to be. She was struck down by a fever and for this was prescribed a series of injections to which her eyes reacted by closing-up. An operation one month later only made matters worse. The tear ducts ceased to function, and Fatema started to loose her sight. It was a gradual and depressing process that was to last a full six years and culminate in almost total blindness.

In 1977 she married. "Not an arranged marriage," she said, "neither was it love; I had that love before my blindness. With my husband it was just an understanding. Like me, he was a human rights activist."

Sadly, though, the understanding did not last. "After marriage he changed. Basically I do not think he is concerned for human beings.

Maybe he just showed an interest. Anyhow my sight went and I became depressed. I did not like his behaviour. Now we are separated and he has married again. This is not illegal, but he should get the written permission of his first wife and this he did not do. I could divorce him if I wished. But we do not disturb each other."

Though her personal situation did not appear to worry Fatema too much, the system made her angry.

"It is simply unfair: a woman cannot get married again without a divorce, but a man can. People say that it is the Muslim law; but in the true religious law, although it is permissible for a man to marry more than one wife, he must treat them all the same. In reality men do not do this. As in other areas, people take advantage of the things in the religious law that they like and disregard those that they do not."

Fatema was now in full spate. "In our society," she said, "sons can have sex before marriage, but if a girl does so it is immoral. Our society should be more sincere. I am not saying it is right to have sex before marriage. There are many diseases that can arise from this. But the rules should be the same for men and women."

Such thoughts led to Fatema's own teenage daughter, and to the effect which the parents' separation had had upon her.

"She told me that I had chosen a bad person. None of her classmates were in the same situation. In this country it is very rare for a marriage to break up. Many women are beaten by their husbands, but for economic reasons they still live with them."

Even when the law is on their side, victims seldom receive help. "You know how bad our police are?" Fatema queried. "Our doctors also?" I confessed I knew little.

"What! You have been in Bangladesh so many months and you do not know about the corruption amongst our doctors! Before they will provide any treatment they ask if you have any money. If you have none, they will not treat you. They charge highly for prescribing medicines and take a bribe for admitting you to hospital."

Fatema had reason to be convinced about what she said. "My younger sister went into Dhaka Medical College Hospital quite recently in order to have her baby. There was a woman there who had been sent up from the hospital in Khulna. Her condition was critical, and the people in Khulna did not have the equipment for the operation she needed. For two days that woman begged the doctors to treat her. But after they had made their examination, they said, 'The child inside you is dead, and we have a great deal of work to do. It would be a waste of our time to operate.' This they said because the woman was poor and had no money for the operation. So for two whole days she pleaded with them. Then she died."

"In these sort of hospitals the doctors often give the poor women ten *taka* in order to take a rickshaw and go away. Yet DMCH and others are state hospitals. We are talking about government doctors and nurses. The authorities should be checking what they do; but our Government thinks only of power."

Did Fatema think the situation was improving at all? I did not receive a direct answer.

"I am lucky; I have a job. And there are many sighted girls who are unemployed."

After her husband left, she said, she had been very depressed. So much so that she consulted a psychiatrist. "My father was dead, and now I had only a stepmother and stepbrothers and sisters. I stayed with them but I hid in a dark corner of my home. If I had to go out, I tried to do so at night. I was ashamed of my blindness, and did not want to show myself. I thought my life was over.

"Then, after sixteen years without sight, I started to think differently. Everybody has family crisis, I told myself, and my family is not rich, so they will see me as a burden. I have to get out and do something. But where shall I go? How can I learn to adjust? Then I started going twice a week to BAFA, the Bangladesh Academy of Fine Art; and I learnt songs and I practised them in order to become more cheerful. Then after about four years, I got in touch with FAVH, the Fellowship for the Advancement of the Visually Handicapped. There I learnt Braille, and got to know other blind people; and they encouraged me."

"In 1994 I went for an interview for a job as a telephone operator at Helen Keller International. I did not get the job, it went to a sighted person, but later that year the organisation contacted me with an invitation to join their new project for the visually impaired. They took nine or ten girls and gave us a three-month training which included mobility and telephonist skills. And after the course, the Director wrote to twenty-eight organisations telling them about the training provided and followed this up by putting us in temporary employment in order to show that blind people can do a job. I was sent to an organisation which already had one sighted operator, and the trouble was that she would not allow me to touch the equipment. There is a great deal of unemployment in Bangladesh, and I think she was frightened that her own job might be at risk. After a couple of days the PBS board developed a problem, and they sent me away temporarily, telling me that they would contact me again when the equipment was repaired. Then they talked to the other operator to find out how I was working. And she reported that I could not do anything, that I could not see the lights etcetera. So as a result, the organisation wrote to Helen Keller saying that I was not fit for the job."

It was a sad story, and one which demonstrated very clearly that employment of the disabled depends not only on employers but also on fellow employees. The Director of Helen Keller, it seemed, had no doubts about Fatema's efficiency. He sent her next to a German consortium for a three-month stint while the regular post holder was on maternity leave. The new employers also expressed some initial concerns and even wrote to their partners explaining that they had a blind girl coming, and that they did not know how much she would be able to do. But at the end of the three-month period, they were so enthusiastic about Fatema that they asked her to stay.

She chose, instead, to return to the Helen Keller Organisation, and remained there until she joined UNICEF in 1998. Whilst at Helen Keller, she took a computer course and subsequently worked as a translator before joining the education programme as a resource person providing training on mobility issues.

In 1996 Fatema, with one other blind colleague, went to Canada to participate in the Blind Women's Forum.

"It felt good," she said, "that so many visually impaired people were there and were letting everybody worldwide know about their problems.

"In Bangladesh, families do not want to educate their blind

children. Many visually impaired people cannot read or write Braille. Some parents even use their blind children for begging. Human rights activists are arguing that we should not spend money on weapons, that we should spend it on the less fortunate. But it does not happen. We still lack equipment such as braille typewriters.

"In Canada, 25 per cent of visually impaired people are employed, and those who are not get an allowance. In this country there is no allowance; and I suspect that less than one per cent of us have a job. There is also a problem here of attitude. Our middle class do not want anyone to even see their disabled children."

Fatema's mind was still racing on. Now she was talking about the NGOs, many of whom, in her opinion, were not genuine, although they succeeded in getting money from abroad. She explained that, with the help of bribery, it is easy in Bangladesh to register as a voluntary organisation. It could be done, she reckoned, for just ten thousand *taka* (about £120); and it was easy to get someone to write a project profile which would bring the donations from overseas. As an example, she cited an organisation which, according to Fatima, received large sums of money from Norway but did nothing to help those on whose behalf they appealed. All the funds, she maintained, had been consumed by the three or four people in charge.

"But who will speak out? Who will tie the bell on the neck of the cat? You know this saying? The rats met together and debated as to what they could do to stop the cat eating them. One rat had an idea. 'Let us tie a bell onto the neck of the cat; then when we hear the bell ring we will know that the cat is coming, and we will be careful.' 'But,' said the other rats. 'Who will be brave enough to put the bell on the cat? That rat will surely be eaten.' "

"So it is with the situation in this country. The people know what is happening, but they don't have any power."

Less than two weeks after my talk with Fatema, an announcement by the World Bank, that future development assistance would depend on how effectively the Bangladesh Government succeeded in curbing corruption, caused a flood of comment in the national press.

In a Daily Star article entitled "The Culture of Corruption – Endangered Existence", the writer, Mansoor Mamoon, makes some significant points.

The United Nations Development Programme (UNDP), World Bank and Transparency International all place Bangladesh as amongst the six most corrupt countries in the world. Billions of dollars change hands every year through bribery, kickbacks, underhand payments, favouritism and cronyism. Corruption is the country's number one problem. Yet political leaders and all concerned seem to be tolerant and lackadaisical about it. The UNDP Report 1999 suggests that if corruption could be effectively curbed, poverty would be reduced by 25 per cent, and per capita income doubled to something in the region of seven hundred dollars, considerably more than that of India.

With reference to health services, Mamoon notes that a survey, undertaken by the Human Development Centre of Islamabad, found one out of every three hospital beds in Bangladesh subject to bribery.

The World Bank Report, he says, blames both ruling and opposition mainstream parties for using their powerful trade unions and student and youth fronts in resorting to widespread extortion. Income of police officials, he adds, is skyrocketing. Most expensive houses in "posh" areas are owned by political leaders, police officers and members of the civil and military bureaucracy. Bank loans are issued without scrutiny in exchange for bribes. Huge loans remain unpaid.

Another worrying figure, drawn from the World Bank Study of 1999, is the statement that 30 per cent of development funds are syphoned off through corrupt means. "Foreign aid," Mamoon feels drawn to comment, "has become known as what the poor people in rich countries pay for the rich people in poor countries." Despite huge amounts of foreign assistance received over many years, nearly half of Bangladesh's population remain in abject poverty.

For the time being, the cat steals the booty – but a few small bells have been successfully placed. They are starting to ring.

CHAPTER ELEVEN

BY TRAIN TO BRAHMANBARIA – **SHAHALAM: ART TEACHER** – VIOLENCE
ON CAMPUS – TELEPHONE MARRIAGE – SAD STORY OF THE SPECIAL
OLYMPICS – **MIZANUR: PRINTER** – CHASING JUSTICE

My weekend visit to Brahmanbaria suffered a slow start. It took one
and three quarter hours for the bus to reach Dhaka, instead of the
usual sixty minutes. Workman had long since converted the highway
into earthworks, and now a few days of heavy rain had reduced it to a
gleaming slurry of ginger mud.

Amidst the dust and smog of brick kilns, young road workers, with
lungis hitched high above their knees and feet caked in sticky earth,
were engaged in an apparently interminable task. Armed only with
shallow dishes, they scooped up the thick brown water and
repetitively tossed it to one side. All around them life went on as
usual; and in spite of the chaos, the little wayside shops continued to
do brisk business. Numerous traders and customers passed busily to
and fro around our stationary vehicle. A woman with dust-
embroidered black *burkha* picked her way over the mud with a huge
bunch of vegetables. A delivery man squelched across the road under
several sacks of potato crisps. A shopper attempted fruitlessly to clean
his sandals with a scrap of waste paper no less muddy than the shoes
themselves. And only a little further on, we could see the entrance to
a dingy alley glamorously converted into a wedding gate by means of
generous folds of white and purple cloth. Meanwhile we sat hot and
impatient inside our sophisticated microbus: birds of passage, unable
to adjust to conditions which, for the local residents, had become the
norm.

On reaching Dhaka, Pia, who was one of my students and on this
occasion also my hostess, had to go first to the hospital. I had two
hours to wait before we embarked on the next stage of our journey;
and we seemed to be in an unfriendly part of the city with little of note
except for the Dhaka Sheraton. Perhaps it was a good excuse to treat

myself. Within the hotel's rarefied environment, behind a high and neatly trimmed world-excluding hedge, I might, for a short while at least, be permitted to forget that I possessed the twin curiosities of white skin and womanhood.

In the Lobby Cafe, I chose the cheapest item from the menu, two fabulously expensive Danish pastries (you had to have them both) and a small pot of tea into which three tea-bags had been wastefully submerged. With this in front of me, I sat beneath the chandeliers and Dutch-style paintings, but failed in my quest for relaxation. I knew that, just outside the gate, beggars were squatting on the pavement waiting for a few guilt-relieving *taka* to fall from the departing hands of clientele like myself. And for the umpteenth time in Bangladesh, I struggled unsuccessfully to come to terms with our disparity.

The train from Kamalapur Railway Station was seriously delayed, and once again we had an enforced break, this time in the dark, red den of a station restaurant. Heavy crimson curtains shut out the daylight, and crimson plastic cloths adapted the tables to match the red-backed chairs. A limp bunch of red roses drooped before us, and electric light shone dimly through red-painted bulbs. Over the counter a digital clock silently indicated the passing minutes in shiny scarlet figures.

At last the train was announced, and in true English fashion I hurriedly gathered up my bags. Pia, on the other hand, appeared quite unconcerned. After two hours of sitting at the table, she now felt the necessity for another glass of water and to ascertain the name of a tape which had been blaring tediously at us for ages. She knew what she was doing. Approximately forty minutes later, and two hours forty minutes after its scheduled time of departure, the three o'clock Intercity Express to Brahmanbaria pulled out of the Dhaka terminal.

The slum area just outside the rail station had previously marked itself indelibly on my mind. But I was surprised, after the Government's much publicised and considerably criticised programme of demolition, to see almost as many sad hovels as before. The inhabitants, Pia explained, having nowhere to go, had simply returned. With typical resilience they had rebuilt their tottering constructions, and once again found shelter beneath the distinctive blue plastic sacking.

Inside the train, across the aisle, a fat man in western clothing conversed with a thin man in a *punjabi*. Their voices rose in apparent acrimony belied by the wide smile across both faces.

Like all Bangladeshi trains there developed, within its confines, the feel of a community. Up and down the aisle moved water carriers and traders. Did we require tea, books, combs, sweets, *chanachur*, bananas? All were available. Prayers were broadcast over the loud speakers, and confident beggars held out hands in the name of Allah.

Outside, the odd bits of land taken over for cricket turned from city dust to rural green. We left the slums and entered the up-market areas of Banani and Uttara. Then Tongi Junction slid past and the paddy took over. The sun gradually sank beneath the horizon; and the great patches of water on either side of us turned a leaden grey.

We reached Brahmanbaria just before 8 p.m. and took a rickshaw to Pia's home. It appeared empty. The family, presumably, had despaired of our arrival and gone out. In the dark we climbed the open stone stairway and settled in Pia's roof-top room. And here, for the first time, she started to tell me about some of the people I was to meet.

"I haven't spoken to my father for more than six months," she said by way of introduction.

"Oh dear. Where is he?"

"He is downstairs. But none of us speak to him. He has done many bad things in his life, and he realises that now."

One of the four sons of a wealthy tradesman, Pia's father had, like each of his brothers, inherited a thriving retail business as well as a house. Unlike the others, though, it had not taken him long to get into debt. With a penchant for going off to India, for forgetting about his family and spending all his money, he was soon forced to dispose of the shop at a ridiculously low price. And as if this were not enough, he then decided to take a second wife. The new lady came to live with the rest of them; and of Pia's mother was required a considerable degree of generosity. Already forced to develop a tailoring business in order to feed her own children, she now found herself providing for the offspring of her husband's other marriage as well.

189

Thus Pia had three brothers, one stepbrother and one stepsister. The oldest two were already married, but via strikingly different arrangements. The first brother, who now ran a video shop, had depended on his mother to find him a bride. Ever faithful to her maternal duties, the good woman had walked from village to village to seek out just the right girl and had apparently been extremely successful. The newly-weds moved into a room downstairs and, though strangers at first, quickly conveyed their happiness to all around them. The second brother, on the other hand, had fallen hopelessly in love whilst still a student and had somehow persuaded both sets of parents to agree to the marriage. Now the young couple, though wed, had to suffer an enforced separation whilst the bride returned to university. Tenderly, and with passion undiminished, the lonely husband showed me her photograph.

This same brother carried the scar of a serious wound on one arm. He had become involved in politics at University, taken a minor position and, as a result, been shot by the rival party: an incident which somewhat incredibly took place while he was in the Principal's office. This sort of thing, Pia explained, was not uncommon, and was the reason why she so greatly hated politics. Her favourite cousin had actually been killed on campus as a consequence of his political activity.

The next morning Pia led me onto the roof as soon as I emerged from the bathroom. Then she looked at yesterday's clothing hanging over my arm and stopped.

"Your *salwar kameez* isn't wet," she said in amazement "I thought you would need to hang it out to dry." Then after a moment's pause, added wonderingly, "You must have taken it off to wash."

She explained that in Bangladesh the Muslim religion forbids women from removing one set of clothing without putting the other over the top first. It is considered wrong to reveal the naked body, even to oneself.

A little later we set off to explore Brahmanbaria. The sun shone but weakly; and there was a cool breeze resulting in a pleasant temperature in which to rattle and sway our colourful rickshaw way through the town.

Our first port of call was the District Hospital which I had asked to visit in order to get some idea of medical facilities available outside Dhaka. The initial impression here was of a respectable looking edifice put up only a few years previously and embodying the occasional modern attribute. It was the first time in Bangladesh that I had seen a ramp to the first floor in addition to a staircase. But Pia seemed depressed. She had watched the building going up, and was greatly dismayed at the speed with which it was already deteriorating.

Certainly the premises were far from clean, and strangely seemed to lack sufficient beds, almost as if such things were considered unnecessary. The children's ward was enormous, yet contained only twelve iron bedsteads: half the number it could surely have taken with comfort. All around us patients lay on dirty blankets on the floor; and mothers crouched sadly beside tiny prostrate figures attached to saline drips and oxygen cylinders.

One infant gave reason for particular anxiety. With bulging eyes and waving limbs, he was struggling desperately to breathe; but the ball on top of his gas cylinder failed to move. An eager and concerned student, Pia felt convinced that the baby was not getting enough oxygen, but could not persuade either of the two nurses on duty to take any interest. They both stayed behind the desk in the office, well away from their patients; and it was only with the greatest difficulty that my young friend eventually succeeded in getting one of them to check the equipment.

Another baby was in need of blood, and the anxious father approached us in the hope that I was a doctor. Having expressed himself willing to be a donor, he was concerned about the protracted delay. The need, he had understood, was urgent; yet no one appeared to carry out the necessary procedure.

In the Sister's office, a newborn infant lay unattended on the desk. Its life had started a few hours ago in another hospital, and failure to cry within the allotted span had led to referral. But here, it seemed, nothing was being done. Medicine was needed, they said, and this the parents would have to buy for themselves. While relatives went out to make the purchase, a tiny anxious granny kept nervous vigil. The nurses did not appear to be the least bit interested.

191

Feeling increasingly depressed, we moved on to the adult wards where, in bleak surroundings, patients lay on dirty sheets with filthy uncovered pillows or on bamboo matting brought in by themselves and layed out on the floor. Both Pia and I felt we had seen enough.

The Brahmanbaria Deaf and Dumb School is housed in a long green and white building set well back off the road. Using bricks as stepping stones, we traversed the enormous puddles at the gate in order to find out what was happening on the verandah. For although it was the weekend, a group of children, with brushes, paints and paper, had gathered round a young man working away at a watercolour laid flat on the ground in front of him. His pupils were obviously neither deaf nor dumb, and we might have departed in confusion had not a charming young mother come forward to greet us. She led the way into the empty Headmaster's office; and with unabashed curiosity, everybody else followed.

Our hostess introduced herself as Mino. Then, indicating the thin young teacher, informed us that his name was Shahalam, and that it was he who was disabled. He was in fact a graduate from this very school, and now successfully made a living teaching art and writing signboards. "There are actually two teachers," she added, pointing to another young man hiding behind his blue baseball cap, "But Shahalam is *Ek Number*": the favourite Bangla expression meaning "Number one". Going on to convey her approval of Shahalam, who smiled enthusiastically in response, Mino explained that she brought her own two children here every Friday morning, and was well content with their progress. At a signal, a daughter of about eight, stepped forward to display her work, a brightly coloured village scene copied from something produced by the teacher. Shahalam's usual method, apparently, was to "discover" a picture in his own heart and then draw it for the children who would copy what he had done. He also encouraged them to produce their own compositions, and in both cases carefully corrected the mistakes.

As she chatted, Mino used a half-developed form of sign language to draw Shahalam into the conversation. He responded with a huge smile, waving hand gestures, and eyes which danced beneath the low set brows. I felt encouraged to ask more questions. Was he married?

Mino giggled and tapped the ring on Shahalam's hand, thus causing him to laugh delightedly. The wedding, to a fellow student from the school, had taken place only two or three months previously.

Noticing that Shahalam appeared able to comprehend some of Mino's words, I asked whether his deafness was complete. He answered with forefinger and thumb almost touching, thus to indicate a very limited amount of hearing. So what about a hearing aid? Yes, he did have one, but had left it at home because it made such a terrible noise. Aids were not supplied by the Government or anybody else, and he had been able to afford only a very cheap model. Though it had come from Dhaka, it was far from satisfactory.

At this point we were joined by the Headmaster who had just arrived back from the bazaar. Mr Giasudden was a kindly-looking man with tight curly hair starting to turn grey and eyes fringed by the imprint of many smiles. He took his position behind the desk and prepared to answer my questions.

The school was private, but received some government support and a very small grant from the Bangladesh National Federation of the Deaf (BNFD). It had been founded in 1942 by a Mr Bhattacharii who had received his training in Calcutta. Parents mostly paid a small fee, although it was possible for very poor children to get a scholarship. Finance was always a problem. The school could not, unfortunately, afford to build a hostel for pupils from the rural areas, nor did they have any money for hearing aids.

I asked about Mr Giasudden himself. How had he become interested in working with the deaf?

He laughed. "That is a long story but I will try to cut it short. I had a girl cousin who was deaf; she had been attacked by typhoid as a child. Her parents moved from Comilla to Brahmanbaria so that she could attend this school, and I used to come here to see her and to accompany her home. Gradually I became more and more interested. Inspired by the Headmaster, I started to help. So it was that Mr Bhattacharii sent me to do a six-month training in Dhaka, and finally appointed me to this post."

"We have sixty boys and girls here now," he continued. "The age range is four years to fifteen, and we can take them to Class 8. The education we provide contains a vocational element, such as tailoring, and we also practice voice culture and teach sign language."

The success of this last subject was clearly evident. The two young artists, Shahalam and Shonjib, now seated diagonally opposite one another at distant corners of Mr Giasudden's large desk, were chatting away incessantly with their hands while the rest of us talked more conventionally. Mr Giasudden produced the Bengali Sign Language Dictionary and provided us with a brief introduction to their method.

A request for more information about Shahalam, brought another smile to the Headmaster's face. "Six or seven years ago this boy won a prize at the Shonkers International Children's Art Competition in New Delhi," he said. "It was an enormous competition, open to both able-bodied and disabled children from all over the world, and yet Shahalam won."

Tea was brought; and Pia and Mr Giasudden continued their conversation in Bangla. Then suddenly the Headmaster became very heated and I wondered what was wrong. But it was only that Pia had suggested that she thought it worse to be blind than deaf. Mr Giasudden, a man deeply committed to his students, could not let such a comment pass unchallenged.

It was time to go; but I had one last question. "What happened," I asked, "to the girl cousin?"

Mr Giasudden gave an embarrassed laugh and the answer I half expected, "The girl cousin? Oh – she is my wife."

A huge storm had broken during our visit. While we talked, it had cut off the electric current, banged doors and caused corrugated iron to clatter. Now, as we emerged from the building, we found the brick stepping stones to be completely submerged; and in the effort to reach a rickshaw, our sandals filled with water.

Next stop was to be an orphanage for destitute rural boys; and then, Pia insisted, we must visit a couple of Hindu temples. She had made a list of places she considered it important that I see, and was determined to delay lunch until the tour was complete.

Later in the day, we went to visit more of her innumerable relatives. Uncles and aunts all lived in close proximity, and in every household, parents shared their home with married sons and other members of the immediate family. Each couple had their own room, similarly furnished with double bed, a few easy chairs and a large glass fronted cabinet, the latter always containing a collection of ornaments plus a large quantity of extra cups and saucers.

In one such household I was introduced to two people with particularly interesting stories.

The first of these was one of Pia's male cousins who, in similar manner to her brother, had been shot by political adversaries at college and had lost a finger and part of his hand.

The other was a new cousin by marriage who was introduced as having "not yet met her husband." He was in Japan; and she had been married to him over the telephone. Like all other brides, she had, for her big day, worn a scarlet sari together with the ornate wedding jewellery now displayed before us. A registrar had been present in order to record the wedding officially, and a video made of the whole proceedings. The bridegroom, it would seem, had been the only item missing. But now he was her husband and would shortly secure her entry into Japan where she could meet him for the first time.

Later in the evening one of Pia's college friends came round to meet me and, to my horror, told yet another story of how a friend had been killed by political rivals. I could not help but express incredulity at so many incidents, but the two young people just shook their heads sadly. Brahmanbaria, they said, was infamous for this sort of thing. The killers, desperate impoverished youngsters, were employed by both political parties. In return for money, cars and arms, they would integrate themselves into university life, identify their target and then shoot. In 1999 there had been many such attacks, and six had proved fatal. Bribes to the police ruled out any possibility of convictions.

Next morning we set off once again through the awakening town. I had promised to buy one of Shahalam's paintings.

Brahmanbaria presents the visitor with a fascinating mixture of old and new. For the most part, our road was lined with small corrugated iron shops erected quite recently; but here and there the eye alights upon a dilapidated old Hindu facade with elegant arches, or glimpses a colourful minaret peeping over the rooftops. I tried asking Pia about the age of the Hindu buildings, but met with little success. "That one is very old," she said pointing to my left. "It must have been built before 1971."

By the time we arrived, the school premises were a hive of activity; and we remembered that the Headmaster had told us that there were, in fact, two establishments on the same site. We had an opportunity now to learn something of the other, a school run by the Society for the Intellectually Disabled (SWID).

I was particularly pleased to find them here, for it was an organisation which I had already planned to visit in Dhaka. They had come to my attention the previous year when a triumphant Bangladesh team arrived back from the Special Olympics in North Carolina. The victors had brought with them no less than forty Olympic medals, including eighteen gold. In an upsurge of national pride, the media sung with praise for all concerned. Television News included a shot of the Prime Minister presenting each competitor with a special medal from the Bangladesh government. And a letter in the Daily Star was typical of the surrounding comment. "These children," it read, "have enhanced the image of our country in the public eye of the globe."

SWID had been responsible for selecting, training and organising Bangladesh's entry into the Games; and now, sitting in the Headmistress's office of their small school in Brahmanbaria, I was able to ask for more information.

After talking about the event in general for a little while, I enquired whether any of their own students had been involved, and in response the Headmistress held up three triumphant fingers.

"Three competitors came from here?" I queried, somewhat surprised. But already the lady had risen from her seat and was unlocking the metal stationary cupboard. With a clatter, four medals landed on the desk in front of us, two gold and one silver plus the Government's special award.

"One competitor, three medals," the Headmistress explained, as she started to untangle the red and blue ribbons. "Abu Ashraf won the 100 metres and the 400 metres, as well as taking part in the 400 metre relay in which Bangladesh came second."

I looked at the awards in amazement. "May I meet Abu?" I asked. "Is he here today?" Then, hearing that the lad was sick, I went on to enquire about his selection and training.

"We had just seven days training in Brahmanbaria," the Headmistress said, "and then I sent a small group of students to Dhaka where two of them were selected. The final choice was made by lottery. After this SWID provided one month's training at the Dhaka Army Stadium."

Abu Ashraf's success seemed all the more incredible when these facts were borne in mind. With so little support, far less than the children from the developed countries would have received, he had won outright in both his individual events. How, I now asked, did the school foresee his future?

My question was met by an abrupt change in the surrounding atmosphere. Verbal exchanges seemed to alter in tone and to become more rapid. Pia ceased to translate fully. It was with some difficulty that I extracted fragments of the story, and not until we were on our way home did I get the full details.

Abu Ashraf, who was aged eighteen but had the approximate mental age of an eleven-year-old, had been accompanied to the Special Olympics by his mother. She was a very poor woman, and the temptations offered by America proved too much. Jumping immigration, she took a job and stayed. Abu had to return alone to a father who was quite unable to relate to him. Deserted and depressed, left to wander the streets on his own both day and night, it was not long before the boy who had "enhanced the image of his country" was picked up by the police and put in prison. Twice the Head Teacher had managed to secure his freedom; but it was a losing battle. Abu's brothers were all involved in crime, and his own memory loss made him a convenient person to quote as an accomplice. Now the erstwhile hero, praised by all the media and honoured by his government, languished in Comilla gaol. Neglected and forgotten, he was also vulnerable to the influence of the worst sort of criminals, people who might have little hesitation in using him on their eventual release.

The basic fact of his imprisonment, I had extracted from the conversation at the school, and almost unbelieving, had immediately asked why SWID itself had done nothing to help. As an organisation they had accepted the praise for Abu's achievements, and having taken him to America, must surely also take some responsibility for his subsequent predicament. Why did they not look after him? The answer, probably, was that they did not know what had happened. The Headmistress was too frightened to report events which she suspected might reflect badly upon herself.

Later, talking to Pia, I mentioned this fear of authority, and the worrying frequency with which it appeared to determine the decisions of her compatriots.

"This is Bangladesh," came the reply. "People are interested only in making money and looking after themselves. They do not care for other people." She referred to the many organisations that I had visited, and suggested that it was never Bangladeshis whom I had found responsible for the good work undertaken.

Preferring not to agree with such sentiments, I responded with silence. But in my heart I knew Pia's country to be one of incredible contradictions. For the extended family and the guest in their house, they will care enormously and their generosity knows no bounds. But if you are not part of that close-knit group, you can be at the point of death and still deserted. Abu's story was to haunt me for weeks to come.

Fortunately our last meeting that day was a much happier one.

We were looking round the classrooms when the Headmaster of the Deaf and Dumb School introduced us to one of his more regular visitors. Mizanur Rahman was a well-groomed young man with neatly trimmed moustache, generously oiled hair and a smart black T shirt. He communicated so well that it was difficult, at first, to realise that he suffered from a serious hearing impairment. But Mizanur, we discovered, was himself a past student of the school. Now a businessman in Dhaka, he ran his own printing press and was also General Secretary of the National Friendship Club for the Deaf. He was married with two children, he added proudly, and so saying, produced their photographs. Happiness and success radiated out of him; and once again I was reminded of the ability of the so-called "disabled" to triumph over every obstacle, even those presented by a country like Bangladesh. I reflected, too, that Pia was far from right. The Deaf and Dumb School in Brahmanbaria had been founded, and continuously run, almost solely by her countrymen. Furthermore, at least some its graduates went on to help others.

All these things were discussed at length by the two of us as we trundled back to Dhaka. The train was full. As on the outward journey, it had proved necessary to purchase our tickets on the black market; and on this occasion, the source was almost certainly corrupt. Unable to get any tickets at the station, Pia had planned to get on the train, take seats in the first class and pay our fares to the ticket collector as he passed through the carriage. But when no such person appeared she became worried and asked one of the stewards what she should do. It would not be a problem, he replied, he could get tickets for us. My companion was doubtful but then spotted one of her brother's colleagues, someone more than willing to sort the matter for her. Returning shortly, he assured us that he had paid over the money and that the tickets would be supplied later. And so they were, but not until after the airport stop on the edge of Dhaka. Pia looked at them: one was from Chittagong to the capital, and the other from some-where else. They would, she realised, have been handed in at the airport station and subsequently sold back to the stewards on the train. Railway employees would themselves be pocketing the proceeds.

Innocent of all this, I lay comfortably back in a first class seat and watched the life around me. Those passing us on their way down the train were largely traders or beggars; but there came one with a difference. He moved with difficulty, down the shuddering aisle, on a single leg: the other having been amputated at the knee. With one hand, he clutched the seats for support; and with the other, held a strong stick, together with his wares – several plastic bags of sweets and chocolate bars. We made our purchase; and he smiled politely as he served us but atypically moved on before I could find the last *taka*.

Here was a man who, against all odds, was supporting himself with tremendous effort and doing so legally; but I had failed to give him the money that was his due! Great was my relief to see him once again on the airport platform and to have the opportunity to pay my debt. I called out, and he came over happily but seemed very surprised when I offered a little extra, even to the extent of asking Pia if he were meant to take it. Then, smiling and polite as ever, he moved back into the crowd. I watched until I could see him no more – the black and white *lungi* terminating in a single foot, the perilously thin body encasing a spirit of amazing strength and dignity. Though nameless, he was to remain in my memory.

Abu Ashraf continued to play on my mind. Friends told me that Bangladeshi gaols were terrible, and anyway what of the young athlete's future? He had none, as far as I could see, except to be a pawn in the hands of the criminals who were now his only companions. I discussed the matter with Pia, and having ascertained that she was in agreement with my interference, decided to visit the Head Offices of SWID.

The decision was one thing, but making myself do it, more difficult. I knew that my action might well result in trouble for the Headmistress of Abu's school; and blowing the whistle, however necessary, is never pleasant. As I approached the task, my uncertain resolve was further weakened by a number of minor obstacles. First the telephone number in the Directory proved to be incorrect. And then, the rickshaw wallah conveying me to the appointment got lost. I arrived considerably late, and found the offices of SWID housed in a grim building, in itself quite prison-like. There was little to raise my spirits.

The Executive Officer, Mohammed Nurul Islam, greeted me politely, but I knew that the time he now had available was limited. It was necessary to get quickly to the point. After a few initial pleasantries, I took the plunge and expressed my concern about Abu Ashraf. Was the Executive Officer aware that his award winning student was in prison?

Nurul Islam's reaction was ambiguous. He simply nodded, face blank. It was not at all clear whether he had understood. "Prison," I repeated again slowly. "You know what I mean – prison – gaol?" Once more Nurul Islam nodded blankly. Did he understand? Was this an affirmative? Only later was I to remember that the nod in Bangladesh means "no" and the head shake "yes".

But whatever the problems of vocabulary, tone can still convey a message. Mr Islam had undoubtedly picked up the concern in my voice; and next minute he reacted with something near to panic. All of a sudden he became very busy, looking in files, calling assistants, offering tea and suggesting I might like to look around the offices, perhaps meet the Secretary.

I reiterated, as firmly as I could, that all I wanted to do was discuss the problems of Abu Ashraf. But to my concern, the Executive Officer's response was simply to get up and leave the room. He returned, almost immediately, to insist that I must see the Secretary right away; for this gentleman, whoever he was, could only give me ten minutes. Having been given clearly to understand that it was Nurul Islam to whom I needed to talk, I was somewhat doubtful about the wisdom of going elsewhere. But the tone in the voice of the Executive Officer suggested he meant business. I followed him into another room and realised immediately that I had made the right move. There was no doubt that I was now in the presence of the "Head Man". Mr Baten, whose full title I was later to learn was Secretary General, sat comfortably behind a large desk, and Nurul Islam took a hard seat against the wall. Fortunately, too, Mr Baten spoke good English.

I told him Abu Ashraf's story in full, and at last got the horrified reaction for which I had hoped. Inevitably Mr Baten did rage at the school's failure to report, but he also expressed deep concern at Abu's fate. More importantly, he assured me he would take action immediately. I asked if there was anything I could do to help, and suggested that, if payment of a fine was necessary, I might be able to raise a little money. Mr Baten agreed to let me know the outcome; but somehow I did not feel totally convinced. For Abu's sake, I wanted to know that action would be taken, and taken quickly. I threw in my trump card. "It was lucky," I commented, that it was I who discovered the young athlete's situation." American journalists, I pointed out, might well intend to follow up the story of Bangladesh's successful Olympic team, and would wish to do so by personally visiting the most successful members, those like Abu, who had won several medals.

Mr Baten gave an uneasy and horrified laugh that convinced me that I had been understood; and I felt, perhaps wrongly, that, at last, my job was done.

"Please remember to let me know what happens," I said as I took my leave. "I have written up the whole of Abu Ashraf's story for my book, and I would like to be able to give it a happy ending."

Sadly there has been no further news.

CHAPTER TWELVE

Monsur Ahmed Choudhuri, Director of Impact Foundation Bangladesh, was born into an educated well-off family and started life without any problems.

Fate struck its blow in the form of a tennis ball which hit Monsur's left eye when he was a kindergarten pupil of seven years old. The lens was dislocated; and subsequent surgery actually made matters worse by causing an infection which, upon spreading to the other eye, resulted in total blindness. Thus Monsur became one of just two pupils at the first school for the blind in Dhaka.

Even to this day he can remember the teachers. Both were blind and were a great inspiration. They were Indian, had been trained in Calcutta and talked of visually impaired friends who were highly successful. One of these, for example, was a barrister, an achievement which impressed itself particularly upon Monsur's mind because of his father's own position in the judiciary. At this school, the boy realised, he had a real opportunity to acquire knowledge. And happily his parents and family were extremely supportive.

"Support for the disabled child is all important," Monsur told me as we sat at the big table in the meeting room of Impact Bangladesh. A strongly built man with a shock of black hair, he looked younger than his fifty odd years. They had been years packed with interest and personal achievement, but Monsur had not forgotten the debt he owed both to his first teachers and to his family.

"Over protection is harmful, under protection damaging." he said firmly. "Both my parents collected a lot of information about disabled people, material with which to encourage me. I learnt about those like Sir John Wilson, a blind person who had a degree from Oxford. By such success, I was both impressed and inspired."

"Then, when I was eight years old, the Director of the RNIB in London, who was himself visually impaired, brought braille equipment to our school. 'Now you can write in both English and Bangla,' he said. And we, the two lone students, were enormously excited."

A year after this, Monsur's father was transferred to Chittagong. His mother was naturally concerned at the prospect of her small blind son entering a hostel and becoming a boarder; but Monsur pleaded with her. Even at the tender age of nine, he knew that he wanted the opportunity of education. It was an opportunity for which he was to continue to fight on behalf of others: a battle upon which he would still be engaged nearly fifty years later.

He did well in his studies, and by 1966 was ready to take his Secondary School Certificate but found himself confronted by the first of many obstacles which authority was unthinkingly to lay in his path.

"The Dhaka Board of Intermediate and Secondary Education would not allow me to sit for the exam. 'You have become blind,' they said. 'You have no need to study. You can do music.' It was all very negative; but we were not deterred. My father contacted a friend in Rajshahi and sent me there to take the examination. I passed and with that moved from a special education into integrated education, or rather inclusive education, for in order to get my Higher School Certificate, I entered Dhaka College where there were, at the time, no other blind students."

"I remember that I had a big row with my father because I wanted to go to Notre Dame College. But Dhaka is more prestigious, and he pointed out that if I got a place there, I would be setting an example for my blind friends. Others would follow. And, indeed, he has been proved correct. The College has subsequently opened its doors to many visually impaired students."

What was it like, I wondered, being amongst sighted classmates for the first time?

"It was difficult for the first two or three days. Several sighted friends sat around me and seemed keen to talk, but they were shy and did not know how to start. The teachers, also, were concerned and wondered how I was going to manage. One lecturer raised his voice when he heard the sound of my machine. He did not know what it was, and he shouted angrily, 'Who is that boy making a noise?' I replied, 'Sir, it is me' and the poor man was very embarrassed.

"My sighted friends helped by reading the text books to me, and I had to learn to depend on my memory. Even now I can remember nearly four hundred telephone numbers. A blind person has to develop this facility because they need it so badly. You, for example, can see all around you. Your eye alights on the table here and the television there, but you do not concentrate on these things very seriously. You can look at them at any time. I, on the other hand, have to remember where they are located. Once something is shown to me, I have to register in my mind exactly where it is positioned, otherwise I will fall over it. Those of us who are visually impaired have to work from childhood to develop and enhance their other senses – sound, perception, smell – all of them.

"Take the tactile sense, we have to feel size and texture and to be able to differentiate by weight. The weight of a mango leaf, for example, is different from that of a jackfruit leaf.

"Then smell, that is very important. Recently I spent some time with my son in London. We got down off the underground at Victoria and walked for a while, and then I pointed out to him an eating place on our left. I had smelt the food and knew exactly where it was coming from.

"By a developed sense of hearing I can also recognise people by their voices; and 99 per cent of the time I am right."

Monsur stopped himself talking. It was more important, he felt, to show me a video interview with the man who had become his role model, the blind Englishman Sir John Wilson.

The significant part played by other people in Monsur's life was a fact he was to reiterate continuously. "My friends," he commented a little further into our discussion, "have always been very important to me."

Initial relationships were not always easy; but, in spite of this, the blind student was well supported by his peers. "At Dhaka College I was exposed to girls as my classmates for the first time and in the beginning we all experienced a shyness, but after a while it was all right. In the second year I was elected unopposed as the Class Representative to the Student's Union, and later I was made responsible for organising a three-week study tour for thirty-two students going to West Pakistan.

"I had already had my first experience of an international gathering when I attended the first World Convention of the Blind in Colombo. We sailed from Chittagong and had a four-day voyage by ship. En route I was introduced to alcohol and for the first time was invited by a girl to dance. The Convention itself was very helpful, and I met many distinguished blind leaders."

In 1971, having completed his honours degree in law at Dhaka University, Monsur decided to study Public Administration. But in the aftermath of war there were many interruptions, and the course took longer than usual. By the end of it, he was eager to go abroad, for there were few good employment opportunities in Bangladesh, and many of his classmates had already left to seek their fortune elsewhere. Encouraged by his elder brother, who was then in England, Monsur applied for admission to the Inner Temple. To his delight, he was accepted, but only to find his hopes dashed by the intransigence of a British Immigration Officer. It was a bitter blow, and some twenty-five years later I could still sense the depths of Monsur's disappointment. "Immigration people act according to their discretion and whim," he opined sadly. "Because I was blind, and my brother was in Coventry not London, they could not believe I would be able to manage. I explained that I was going to live in a dormitory, that I had two university friends already there, and that we would study together. But my appeal received no consideration."

Later, en route for Oslo, Monsur felt compelled to visit the Inner Temple, and, standing at the entrance, reflected sadly on the extent to which the opinion of one individual can affect the life of another. Blighted hope still lingered, although when the event occurred, there had been little opportunity for self-pity. His parents had urged him to get on with life, suggesting that he do something to help other blind people, a view reinforced by Sir John Wilson.

"Sir John told me to give myself for the betterment of the blind community. He pointed out that he had sacrificed his own career in this way. When he was at Oxford he had been offered a teaching job but had not taken it because he wanted to help others who were visually impaired. 'Now,' he said to me, 'it is your turn. You must do the same for your people.' "

In 1967 Monsur went to Oslo for a six-week course in International Relations. It was, he commented wryly, his first introduction to European culture, and it occurred in a very permissive society!

He was also somewhat daunted by his fellow participants. "On the first day everyone introduced themselves, and two or three got up and said they were from Cambridge. I thought, 'My God, what jewels!' But it didn't matter: in no time at all, we were close friends."

In a lifetime of travel, Monsur has visited thirty-three countries and collected several amusing anecdotes.

There was the time when he was with some friends climbing the tower in Cambridge. His friends looked down and were overcome by the height. They shivered with fear, removed their shoes and descended very carefully in the sitting position. Monsur, unable to see anything, came down upright.

His blindness also gave him the edge nearer home at a restaurant in Dhaka which he visited with Sir John and Lady Wilson and the Head of UNICEF. Soup had just been served when, quite suddenly, the lights went out. Laughing, Sir John and Monsur refused to wait: for them it was no more difficult than usual to start their meal. But their friends, meanwhile, sat helpless in the darkness.

In January 1978, Monsur became the Chief Executive of the National Society for the Blind in Dhaka. Once again he felt daunted. He was without any management training but now found himself responsible for twenty-five people, including medical staff. As at so many other points in Monsur's life, it was his father who came to the rescue.

" 'Be very careful,' my father advised. 'Listen to your people, ask them to read everything to you. Then you can make your judgements.' "

Monsur succeeded; and his success led to more opportunities. After making a presentation at a conference for the blind in Antwerp, he was invited to America for a sixteen-week training on rehabilitation. And in Stockholm, he was able to undertake a Blind Leadership Course.

"What is important," he said to me now, "is that we develop our own indigenous leadership and cease our dependence on the expatriots".

He found travel a most enriching experience. "I believe that whatever I have learnt by reading, I have learnt three times as much by travelling." He turned again to anecdote, this time a story about his use of British English in the West of America.

"I was in a cafeteria and asked for some biscuits. The girl handed the packet over, and I was really surprised to find it was hot. I turned to a supervisor, 'Why has she given me a hot packet of biscuits?' I asked. The supervisor laughed. 'You are from the British Commonwealth,' she said. 'Here biscuit means sandwich. If you want your type of biscuits you must ask for crackers.' "

In 1981, Monsur moved to another NGO, Assistance for Blind Children (ABC) where, for nine years, he held the post of General Secretary. What, I asked, did he consider to be his greatest achievement during this time?

"My achievement? Perhaps it was to develop the programme for education and rehabilitation. Many blind people are from the poorer sectors of our society. The Government has set up an integrated education scheme; but there are no hostels, and blind students in the rural areas cannot travel to the schools. We need good hostels where they can live with a houseparent. I extended our programme to include seven of these, six for boys and one for girls. I also started two centres to provide training in orientation, mobility and daily living activities for the blind. I organised and planned these myself and subsequently took part as a resource person.

"It was a tough time. Today there are many disabled people around me, but then I was alone. In 1981, I was the only disabled person on the fifty-four member committee for the International Year of the Disabled. Today our numbers have gone up and our voice is stronger. I know my time is coming to an end, but I believe that the initiative and the thirst is there; and that we will achieve our goal."

In reply to a question about this goal, Monsur answered at length and with barely concealed anger.

"Our target is a law giving equal rights to people with disabilities. The Constitution has already made provision for this; indeed there exists a national policy on equal opportunity, passed in 1995. But it is an executive decision only and, as such, cannot be legally enforced. We need a law. Only yesterday, at a meeting with one of the Government Secretaries, we pointed out, yet again, that the Prime Minister promised this to us way back in 1997; and that as many as five members of the present cabinet have reiterated her promise at public meetings. Yet still there is nothing. Only a draft which moves from one Ministry to another and is held up by dishonesty and corruption amongst the bureaucrats. Every year, on the International Day for the Disabled, we raise our voice. We remind the Government that there is a UN Resolution binding every member country to ensure equal opportunities and rights for their disabled citizens. This country is a signatory to that resolution, but our leaders have signed it without realising the consequences. They do not give us a law. I am not going to benefit now personally: I am over fifty. For the younger disabled people coming up, it is for them I am fighting. They should enjoy equal opportunity."

Monsur speaks eloquently and with strength on behalf of all people with disabilities; although, during the early part of his career, he was really only aware of the needs of the visually impaired. It was in 1981, when he attended the first World Convention of Disabled People, that he had, in his own words, his first "exposure to people with other disabilities."

Ten years later frustration took over. The Government had not changed their policy at all, and Monsur thought about leaving the country. He took a job in America but stayed only a short while. Swayed by the advice and opinion of friends who felt he was needed in Bangladesh, he returned to take a job with the Helen Keller Organisation and subsequently to become the first Chief Executive of the new national branch of the Impact Foundation. It is a job into which he throws heart and soul, and to which, since the death of his wife, he considers himself to be well and truly married.

The work of the Organisation centres around the "Jibon Tari" floating hospital, a ship especially designed and equipped to carry out minor operations and other treatments, and also the Primary Health Care Programme for the prevention and cure of avoidable disability.

The latter includes such projects as a Home Gardening Scheme, set up after it was discovered that Vitamin A deficiency is the prime cause of blindness amongst children in Bangladesh.

"We were utterly frustrated by the Government's inability to distribute the millions of Vitamin A capsules provided by UNICEF," Monsur explained. "So now we are encouraging people to produce the vitamins for themselves. Our scheme helps rural villagers to grow up to eleven different types of leafy vegetable by rotation, in order to ensure that something is available all the year round; and we also show people how to cook so that nutrients are not lost. Now, thankfully, we can see a change. In 1982–83 some thirty thousand children below the age of six were becoming blind owing to vitamin deficiency; but we now feel confident that the number is falling. Poverty and disability have a direct link as cause and effect."

Undoubtedly Monsur and his friends have already achieved a great deal, but I suspected that the driving force within him was not yet satisfied. What, I asked were his remaining ambitions?

He enumerated them carefully. One, to achieve a law on equal rights; two, to bring about a change in attitude; three, to update resources for the disabled. All were enormous ambitions which I assumed he intended for society as a whole rather than for himself personally. However, it sounded as if he, as an individual, was quite prepared to take them on. The slightest mention of the subjects awoke again the political speaker within him.

"In this country, 13,034 crore *taka* (approximately £1.75 billion) has been put aside during the current financial year for the Primary Education Programme. Yet not a single *taka* of this will be spent on the education of those who are disabled. They come under the Ministry of Social Welfare, not under the Ministry of Education, and that, in itself, is an indicator of the lack of importance attached to the academic well-being of those for whom I speak. There were five special schools established in the 1960s, and not a single one since.

Instead there is lip service to an integrated programme. Sixty-four ordinary schools have been selected by the Ministry, and in each there is supposed to be at least ten disabled students; but in reality there are often none. Blind children do not have the opportunity to travel from the villages, and there is nowhere near the schools where they can stay. Moreover each of these schools is supposed to have one trained teacher to support the blind, but for the most part these teachers are absent. Some just draw the salary but do not attend for work. Nor is there any special educational apparatus. Without anyone willing to teach them, or any appropriate equipment, those blind children who could actually reach the schools fail to make the effort."

The whole subject of education and training was clearly very close to Monsur's heart; and the underlying reason for this became apparent when I asked him for a concluding message.

"I urge disabled people and their families to help the disabled to develop skills so that they can live their lives with dignity, rather than being dependent on charity."

Typically, too, Monsur had a few last words for the politicians.

"I, a disabled citizen, strongly believe that people with disabilities in Bangladesh should enjoy human rights. To achieve our goal of equal opportunities we need political commitment from the highest authority, the State. Every political party should make that commitment and reflect it in their manifesto. They need to pronounce and write down what they will do for disabled people. In seven elections not a single political party has given us any commitment at all. I am a voter, a taxpayer and a citizen and yet they still ignore me."

A few weeks later came news that must have excited Monsur, although it was given significantly low priority by the National Press. I happened upon the information by accident. Even my activist friends, I think, would have forgiven me had I failed to notice the following announcement in the Daily Star.

The hills around Chittagong, though expected, come as a shock after six hours of staring through a train window at the flat watery landscape which constitutes the greater part of Bangladesh.

Patricia and I had seized the chance of a holiday and were making first for the Bandarban Hill Tracts in order to visit the site of a new resort planned by a friend who was in tourism. Mr Hasan, waxing lyrical about the beauty of the countryside and keen for us to inspect his chosen location, had booked the train tickets almost before we knew what was happening; and at the same time, he had fixed a car to take us from Chittagong to Bandarban. Thus it was in style that we settled back to enjoy our climb into the steep terrain adjacent to Myanmar.

Our transport dropped us at the Purboni Hotel, where Hasan's brother, Kokhon, was temporarily residing whilst overseeing work on the project. We recognised him instantly. Like his sibling, he possessed sharp expressive features decorated with a mass of smile lines, and was able to equip himself with the same natural twinkling charm.

Kokhon seemed to consider his own accommodation unsuitable for English guests. Instead, he took us round to The Green Hill Hotel. And yet, despite this concern, I awaited the viewing of our room with some trepidation. Patricia had warned me with delightful honesty, but worrying overtones, that she did not like "slumming it"; and my experience of the more inexpensive Bangladesh hostelries told me that we might well be on the verge of doing exactly that.

We walked past a gaggle of youths reclining in the dingy reception and, pursued by their unflinching gaze, climbed the stone staircase to Room A1. It was locked on the inside. The hotel porter knocked and called out, and to our surprise, the door opened in order to eject a young man. He was followed instantly by another, and then another and another, until I lost count. When finally we were able to enter, it was to find the sheets dirty and dishevelled, and the air thick with cigarette smoke.

There was no explanation, and Kokhon did not seem particularly surprised; but he gave his orders, and action was swift. The beds were stripped and remade, and the room sprayed with a deodorising perfume. But it was not a good start; and when we were finally left alone, Patricia sat down on her bed, brave but disconsolate. I decided not to mention the mouse.

Next morning Kokhon knocked promptly on our door at 8 a.m. as promised. He was attired now in his work clothes, an american baseball cap and baggy trousers with enormous pockets in which he located what he called his "mobile office". In his hand he carried our breakfast, small green bananas and marmalade sandwiches specially prepared by himself. "Dhaka bread," he said proudly, as he held out his offering. I ate hungrily: the local restaurant we had visited the night before having served nothing but a very unappetising version of the usual rice and curry. But the relish, with which I appreciated Kokhon's efforts, might well have diminished had I encountered any one of the family of ants that apparently crawled out of Patricia's portion!

Kokhon was to prove incredibly helpful throughout the whole of our stay. He seemed to consider us quite a responsibility and made it his first job to discuss our plans and arrange a later meeting. Obedient then to his instructions, we spent the morning visiting Meghla, a partially man-made, but delightful, local beauty spot much beloved by film directors, no doubt as the location for their most romantic shots.

Later, in the afternoon, we sped in a local vehicle behind the wind-filled shirt of Kokhon as he rode his motorbike with reckless speed into the hills and thus to the site of his "new project". It was with considerable excitement, that, dismounting from his machine, he led us off the road and up steep steps cut in the bank. We had arrived at an area of incredible natural beauty, the place where Guide Tours planned to build their new resort.

"Here," he said proudly, "will be the car-park. Down there a dormitory for students. Here the restaurant; and it will have glass all round. Just look at the view!"

"Then higher up," he was dancing now up the steep slope ahead of us, darting amongst the banana trees like a mountain goat and throwing his arms in all directions. "Here the chalets – one here, one there, another over there, more higher up. And the beauty of it is we have our own natural spring water. Come and look." He bent low beneath the branches and skipped on, "Feel it, feel how cold it is. It is like that all year round." We gazed down into a pool where a local tribal woman was bathing her child. She did so against a backdrop of jungle-clad hills, and amidst a colourful surround of Chakma skirts hung to dry from a pole above her head. Kokhon really had no need to enthuse us. It was a location of true beauty.

Guide Tours were employing several tribal women on this site, Kokhon explained. Suddenly the aesthete was transformed into a hard-nosed entrepreneur, his next words expressing a grim satisfaction. "They are so poor they will work a nine hour shift for only one dollar."

Turning, he led us further up the hillside to an open-sided bamboo house raised high on stilts in order to provide a breathtaking view right across the Hill Tracts. And, as if affected by his surroundings, our guide changed chameleon-like back to the Kokhon we preferred. "It is so silent here," he said. "So beautiful – no pollution, no noise. This is where Hasan and I like to sleep, on this platform, out in the open."

We moved on next day. And Patricia, who had survived the Bandarbans episode with wry good humour, made no attempt to deny an audible sigh of relief as soon as she saw the gates of our new abode. Two buses and a baby taxi had brought us from an area in which she felt not a little uncomfortable; and the mission hospital at

214

Malumghat was greeted as a haven.

It had been described to us by one friend as "little America"; and by another as a place "where the American missionaries certainly know how to do it": words which seemed quickly justified by our initial impressions.

At first sight there appeared to be an almost unacceptable disparity between the dark, crowded hospital buildings clustered tightly round the gate, and the luxurious American-style staff houses dotted spaciously around the beautiful tree-clad grounds. Amongst the latter, also, were to be found a swimming pool, playing field, and a well-fed palomino riding pony tossing happily on his tether.

Maybe these things were necessary. Margaret Archibald, who greeted us, had lived here with her husband Jack for twenty-eight years. To this place they had brought many touches of America, and had thus achieved a situation in which they felt perfectly at home.

Consciously or unconsciously, most expatriots staying long-term in Bangladesh develop their own way of coping. For the doctor up at Madhupur Forest, this had involved immersing himself in the local culture and integrating as far as possible with the Bangladeshi people. He slept on the floor, wore a *lungi* and ate only local food. But for the thirty or so American missionaries at Malumghat, survival meant importing as much as they could of their own culture and building for themselves an American community within Bangladesh. For them it had worked. The more we got to know Margaret Archibald, the more we admired the positive attitude displayed to her country of residence and noted the friendly concerned relationship she had developed with all those around her – a relationship quite possibly sustained by the ease of escape into her imported surroundings.

As we reflected on this, we realised, also, that our dislike of the hospital might well be based on a very western viewpoint. We considered the buildings dark and cramped, but in this respect they were probably not unlike the houses of many of the patients. To place the sick in a more spacious environment might well give rise to an undue sense of exposure. In this type of accommodation they could, at least, feel at home and derive the security most beneficial to recovery.

During our stay we were able to see both hospital and houses in more detail and had time to learn a little more about the people whose lives they sheltered.

Jack was an administrator, and Margaret a teacher, leader of women's groups and writer of a book about the fear and superstition encountered in the course of her work. Their big comfortable home was copiously furnished with accessories from the United States of thirty years ago: a brick fireplace, locally made reproductions of American furniture, a piano, window drapes caught centrally into many folds, frilly-edged cushions and dried flower arrangements.

Margaret invited us round there on our first evening, and led us through to the enormous television in her air-conditioned bedroom. But the world news did not attract. We were much more interested to hear about her findings with regard to local superstition. For me her words provided further confirmation of the very real fear attached to the lunar and solar eclipse and to the evil eye. The black dot which we saw painted on the forehead of so many babies was, she said, a third eye to ward off the evil one. And the *tabij*, worn for a similar purpose by adults on an amulet or necklace, most commonly enclosed verses from the Koran although it might, instead, contain a few threads from the cloth of a corpse, or even earth from the grave of twins.

Next day we visited the hospital and found it, in Bangladeshi terms, to be extremely well-equipped. We toured the out-patients department, examination rooms, medical records office, and male and female wards; noted the signboards to operating theatres, pathology and x-ray; and chatted to an ex-CRP student in physiotherapy. But most of our time was spent in the Limb and Brace Department: for it was here that we met Shadhan Nomo.

He had come into work despite a heavy fever. Sweat glistened on his neck, and, above his broad features, the short hair was pushed hotly back. Shadhan wore the departmental uniform of brown shirt and black trousers and stood, with legs slightly apart, shifting his weight from one white trainer to the other while he carefully wound strips of pink rubber round a half-made prothesis.

This was the "Jaipur Foot", a type relatively new to Bangladesh,

216

and particularly valuable because of the low cost of production. The main component was rubber, obtained both locally and cheaply from two main sources, sandal soles and tyres. These were fed into a machine in which they were melted, dyed a variety of different skin colours, and finally pulled out into strips.

When we arrived, Shadhan was winding these sticky, pliable slices round the frame of a foot: one which he had previously made himself from wood strengthened with a central metal rod. Next he would clamp the prothesis into a mould and fire it in the machine. The final touches would not be added until the new owner was found, at which point Shadhan would trim it to suit, and carefully paint the toes so as to appear realistic. He carried out his work with loving care and deep insight – for Shadhan, himself, had one artificial leg.

I tried to keep my questions short, for it was clear on this occasion that he was not feeling at all well.

He had, he said, been born in a village north of Chittagong, and had trained as a carpenter prior to sustaining his injury at the age of twenty-four. That had been twelve years ago, but Shadhan obviously remembered it as clearly as yesterday. He had been riding on the back of a friend's motorbike when a truck from behind ran into them. At Chittagong Medical College Hospital his leg was amputated; and he returned home with feelings of utter despair.

"What am I going to do?" he thought to himself. "My life cannot go on like this."

His family were not happy with him either. He was no longer earning, and they considered him a burden. Described in his own words, he was "just sitting around and consuming".

Help came from a friend in Chittagong who owned a *pan* shop. He invited Shadhan to work with him; and the disabled man was able to earn just enough on which to live. This was tremendously important to him. "Even if the day came when I couldn't eat," he told me now, "I would never become a beggar."

It was while he was working at the *pan* shop, that Shadhan first met Mr Golin. The physiotherapist from Malumghat saw the young man going along the street on crutches, and called him over. Then, presenting his card, uttered words which Shadhan found unbelievable,

"You come and see me, and I will give you a leg."

"At first I did not believe him," the builder of prothesis told us now, "I thought to myself, 'It is not possible'".

It was not until sometime later, and after a reminder from one of his regular customers, a driver from Malumghat Hospital, that Shadhan was finally persuaded to take up the offer.

"The driver said to me, 'Didn't Mr Golin give you a card, and tell you to come and get a foot? Here is a hundred *taka* for your bus fare to the hospital'." It was money, Shadhan later found out, that Mr Golin himself had provided. And when he got to Malumghat, he was to receive another hundred *taka* from the same source in order to pay for lodgings across the street.

But when, for the first time, Shadhan saw a prothesis, his hopes were dashed. He could not "figure out how he was going to walk with the thing". He would be taught, he was told; and from then on things moved amazingly quickly. His own leg was measured and the prothesis made up in less than a week. Only fourteen days later he was walking.

Now at last, life started to move again; and Shadhan was eager to commence earning. "I really need work," he said to Mr Golin: a plea to which the hospital responded by sending him to Dhaka to do a further three months training in carpentry. But by the time he returned, Shadhan knew that what he really wanted was to work at Malumghat. He made his request more direct. "It would be really good if you gave me a job. Is there something I can do?"

His persistence paid off. At that time, Mr Golin was still going regularly to Jaipur to bring back suitcases full of the famous Indian foot. He was planning, however, to start production at Malumghat; and for this, two of the staff had already received training. Just one more was needed.

"By God's grace I got the job." said Shadhan. And it proved a turning point in his life. In due course he got married and is now proud to be supporting a family. But this is not all. Shadhan is also changing the lives of others. He can turn out five new feet a week, and he has been doing so for over eight years. He only laughed when I asked if he had ever worked out how many people this had helped; but I did the calculation for him. There must, I think, be somewhere between one-and-a-half and two thousand disabled people, now able to walk as a direct result of Shadhan's efforts.

We left Malumghat next day and travelled on down to Cox's Bazaar, the tourist capital of Bangladesh, which, with 120 kilometres of sandy shoreline, claims the prize for having "the longest beach in the world". With so many of my students telling me that I must go there, I had feared commercialism and crowds; but this was the off-season, and we enjoyed relative peace and quiet.

My time in Bangladesh was running out; and it was with gratitude that we collected here a particularly lovely memory to take home. On our last evening, we beheld perhaps the most spectacular of the many wonderful sunsets I had seen in that country. Behind dark palms, the sky was ablaze with the most brilliant pink imaginable; and so perfect was the reflection in the water beneath, that it seemed as if all the world was suffused in glorious colour.

Despite the odds – dirt, noise, pollution and suffering – with which Bangladesh is beset, nature had once again triumphed. So also does the spirit of many of the country's most challenged people.

FURTHER INFORMATION

Centre for the Rehabilitation of the Paralysed (CRP), P.O. CRP-Chapain, Savar, Dhaka 1343, Bangladesh. Tel: +88 02 7710464-5.
Fax; +88 02 7710069
E-mail: crp@bangla.net Website: www.crp-bangladesh.com

in the UK – **Friends of the Centre for the Rehabilitation of the Paralysed (FCRP)**, Monksmead, 27 East Street, Ilminster, Somerset TA19 0AN.
Tel: +44-1460-52347. Fax: +44-1460-52436
E-mail: wbestfcrp@aol.com Website: www.fcrp.org.uk

IMPACT Foundation Bangladesh 4/5 Iqbal Road (2nd Floor), Mohammadpur, Dhaka 1207, Bangladesh. Tel: +88 02 912 9018.
Fax: +88 02 811 7988
E-mail: impact@bangla.net

in the UK – **IMPACT Foundation UK**, 151 Western Road, Haywards Heath, West Sussex RH16 3LH. Tel: +44 1444 457080.
Fax: +44 1444 457877
E-mail: impact@impact.org.uk Website: www.impact.org.uk

The Leprosy Mission England, Wales, The Channel Islands & The Isle of Man Goldhay Way, Orton Goldhay, Peterborough PE2 5GZ. Tel: +44 1733 370505.
Fax: +44 1733 404880
E-mail: post@tlmew.org.uk Website: www.leprosymission.org.uk

GLOSSARY

Baby Taxi	An auto-rickshaw: covered three-wheeled scooter employed as a taxi
Bapa Pitta	Rice flour cake with a sweet filling
Bari	House
Betel	Nut chewed as a mild stimulant, tends to leave a red stain on lips and teeth
Bideshi	Foreigner
Boro Din	Christmas (lit. 'Big Day')
Burkha	Tent-like dress worn by orthodox muslim women to preserve their modesty. Generally black, and always of sufficient length to cover wrists and ankles, it may be extended further by use of a veil
Busti	Slum
Cha	Tea
Chanachur	Tasty snack made from flour, dal (qv), nut and spices
Chola	Small round pulse baked or fried with spices and most usually eaten at Iftar (qv)
Dal	Split pulses or a dish made from such
Ghat	Landing place

221

Iftar	Meal eaten at sunset during Ramadan in order to break each day of fasting
Kirtan	Song style dance of Hindu origin
Kohl	Small drum held horizontally across the body
Lakh	100,000
Lungi	Full length cotton loin cloth worn by men
Madrasa	Muslim school with an emphasis on religious studies
Moksha	(Hinduism and Jainism) Release from the cycle of rebirth
Mishti	Very sweet desert
Mukti Bahini	Bangladesh Freedom Fighters in the Liberation War
Muri	Fried rice
Orna	Shawl worn with the salwar kameez (qv) and placed over the shoulders so that the ends hang down the back while the main part of the cloth conceals the curves of the bosom
Pan	A delicacy and digestive which consists of a folded leaf containing betel nut (qv) lime and other goodies
Puja	Hindu rite of worship
Punjabi	Long shirt with full sleeves and round neck

Sati	Banned custom whereby Hindu widows used to burn themselves on their husbands' funeral pyre
Rooti	Bread
Tabij	Amulet provided by a holy man, usually worn round the arm or neck to ward off evil influences or to fulfil wishes
Taka	Currency unit of Bangladesh
Thana	Administrative area under each police station
Topi	Small round hat, generally white, worn by men - particularly on religious occasions
Vangari	Uncovered flat-bed rickshaw used for transporting goods

SELECT BIBLIOGRAPHY

David Bornstein, *The Price of a Dream – the story of the Grameen Bank and the idea that it is helping the poor to change their lives* (New York, Simon & Schuster 1996)

Robbins Burling, *The Strong Women of Modhupur* (Dhaka, The University Press Ltd 1997)

Betsy Hartmann and James K.Boyce, *A Quiet Violence – View from a Bangladesh Village* (Dhaka, The University Press Ltd 1983)

Rafiqul Islam, B.U., *A Tale of Millions – Bangladesh Liberation War 1971* (Dhaka, Ananya 1997)

Manderangni Jagring, Johannes Sandgren (commentary) *Images of the Garos of Bangladesh* (Dhaka, The University Press Ltd.1999)

Jeannie Lockerbie, *On Duty in Bangladesh* (New Jersey, Association of Baptists for World Evangelism, Inc.1985)

Alex Newton, Betsy Wagenhauser, Jon Murray, *Bangladesh: a Lonely Planet travel survival kit* (Victoria, Australia, Lonely Planet Publications 1996)

Nafeesur Rahman (Editor) *A Directory of Organisations Working in the Field of Disability in Bangladesh* (Dhaka, ActionAid Bangladesh & The National Forum of Organisations Working with the Disabled 1999)

Sultana S. Zaman, *Research on Mental Retardation in Bangladesh* (Dhaka, 1990)